NATIONAL
INCOME AND OUTLAY

MACMILLAN AND CO., Limited
LONDON · BOMBAY · CALCUTTA · MADRAS
MELBOURNE

THE MACMILLAN COMPANY
NEW YORK · BOSTON · CHICAGO
DALLAS · ATLANTA · SAN FRANCISCO

THE MACMILLAN COMPANY
OF CANADA, LIMITED
TORONTO

NATIONAL INCOME AND OUTLAY

BY

COLIN CLARK, M.A.

UNIVERSITY LECTURER IN STATISTICS, CAMBRIDGE
FORMERLY ON THE STAFF OF THE ECONOMIC ADVISORY COUNCIL

MACMILLAN AND CO., LIMITED
ST. MARTIN'S STREET, LONDON
1937

PRINTED IN GREAT BRITAIN
BY R. & R. CLARK, LIMITED, EDINBURGH

INTRODUCTION

In 1932 I published *The National Income, 1924–1931*. This book seemed to fill a need, as the only other publications related to the national income in the year 1924, and, for a book of this nature, the demand was considerable. During the last four years no other writers have made any contributions to the subject of the determination of the national income, and this new work on the subject is therefore published. It was originally intended to prepare subsequent editions of the previous book incorporating up-to-date figures. But so many new sources of information have become available that it was decided that the book should be enlarged and completely rewritten. This volume represents the results of four years' continuous work on the subject. On the question of the amount of expenditure on certain commodities, it incorporates some published and unpublished work by Mr. A. E. Feavearyear. Otherwise it consists entirely of original work.

The principal new sources of information on the National Income since 1932 have been the Occupation and Industry volumes of the 1931 Census of Population (published in 1934) and the various volumes of the Reports on the 1930 Census of Production, published between 1932 and 1935. This information has necessitated some small adjustments of figures hitherto published. Figures up to the year 1931 may now be taken as final, but for years subsequent to that date remain liable to small amendment as the results of later Censuses of Population and of Production become available.

In the introduction to the previous book I made strong complaint about the condition of British official statistics, and drew attention again to the positive proposals for improvement made by the Macmillan Report in 1931. During the last few years the Board of Trade have made tremendous improvements in the statistics which they issue, and have put statisticians very much in their debt. They obtained powers under the Import Duties Act of 1932 to take what is in effect an annual Census of Production of the principal manufacturing industries. The index number of wholesale prices has been extended and recast so as to show separately the prices of manufactured and of semi-finished goods. In conjunction with the Bank of England and the Incorporated Association of Retail Distributors they have increased and widened the scope of retail trade statistics.

This improvement in one department unfortunately only serves to heighten the darkness elsewhere. The construction of the new Cost of Living index number has been quite unnecessarily postponed for five years. No steps appear to have been taken with regard to one of the most important of the Macmillan Committee's recommendations, namely, that the Bank of England should secure current returns of all projects and new orders placed in the capital-goods industries, particularly building and engineering. No steps have been taken to extend wage statistics to cover the numbers or earnings of salaried workers. The Census of Distribution seems as far away as ever. The Federation of British Industries have successfully maintained their obscurantist attitude against the publication of true figures of industrial profits as shown by the income-tax assessments. Their object is to conceal the high profits which are being made in certain trades, but owing to the publication of annual figures under the Import Duties Acts this will not be possible for much longer.

It may be noted that in the United States the assessed profits of each industry, analysed in a number of ways, are published by the Federal Income-tax Authorities. It is the democratic rule in Norway, and in certain States of the U.S.A., that the assessed income of each wealthy individual should be published and should be open to comment in the local papers. Without wishing to suggest any procedure so alien to British traditions, I would hold that figures relating to the profitability of different industries as a whole are a matter of public concern which no vested interests have any possible right to conceal.

Work of the nature involved in the preparation of this book, like experimental work in the natural sciences, cannot properly be done by single individuals, but requires considerable expenditure in the provision of both academic and clerical assistance. Such limited funds as are available for the provision of research assistance in economics are at present fully occupied in other types of work, many of a theoretical nature. As a result I have had to do the entire work of investigation and calculation for this book with the exception of such clerical assistance as I paid for out of my own pocket. The more detailed investigations, which are needed to bring our knowledge of this subject to the extent and precision to which it has been brought in America and Germany, cannot be made by individual investigators. If the saying is true, that economics is eventually capable of benefiting the human race as much as the other sciences put together, it must be equipped not only with the scientific spirit, but also with the financial resources, of the older sciences.

I had originally intended to include a section relating to international comparisons of national incomes, on which question I have made certain investigations, but have decided to include these in a separate publication.

C. G. C.

CAMBRIDGE, *June* 1936

CONTENTS

CHAPTER X

CHAPTER XI

CHAPTER XII

CHAPTER XIII

APPENDICES

SUMMARY

CHAPTER I

The case is submitted that accurate factual knowledge of the national income, its growth and distribution, are essential if economic science is ever to give concrete results. The purpose of economic science, following Pigou, is taken to be to study the possibilities of increasing the amount of the national income, diminishing the inequality of its distribution, and regularising its fluctuations through time, and these provide the three principal heads of statistical study. The definition of the national income is discussed in detail, and the principal change suggested is the inclusion in the gross total of Government revenue from indirect taxes. The reason for this is that, in comparing one year with another, national income figures have to be divided by price-index numbers, which incorporate the effects of changes in indirect taxation.

CHAPTER II

During the last thirty years the proportion of children in the population has been decreasing and of adults has been increasing. In the next two generations the proportion of children will almost certainly continue to decrease, and the proportion of aged will rapidly increase. The economic effects of these changes are examined, but it is shown that they will be less than might have been supposed. The most remarkable effect, which will show itself from now on, is a relative shortage of female labour and a rise in women's wages.

The reconciliation of the Census with Health and

CHAPTER XI

CHAPTER XII

Some results of great importance in economic theory can be established as empirically valid at any rate over the period studied :

(i) There is a numerical relationship between changes in the value of output of investment goods, and changes in the national income as a whole, corresponding to a multiplier of about 2, subject to a fairly rapid secular increase in the propensity to consume.

(ii) In view of the above, and in view of the fact that the principal source of savings is companies' undistributed profits, it is interesting to find that the " propensity to pay dividends " on the part of companies is 0·46 of each increment of profits, the remainder being saved.

(iii) Outlay by the working classes, subject to a fairly constant rate of saving, closely follows their income. But expenditure by the more prosperous classes shows a delay of nearly two years in following movements of income, and does not fall so violently as income during a period of slump, owing to the maintenance of their customary standard of living by spending capital.

(iv) It is generally held that during a period of recovery the price of investment goods rises relative to that of consumption goods, and that it falls during a period of slump. The exact opposite is the case.

(v) The average real labour costs of production per unit of output in industry fall strongly with increasing output, the proportion of overhead labour being high. Marginal labour costs, however, also show a tendency to fall with increasing output. About 1930 the whole curve of labour costs per unit of output was shifted to a lower level, which has since been maintained.

(vi) In non-manufacturing industry constant and not increasing returns prevail.

CHAPTER I

PURPOSE AND DEFINITION OF NATIONAL INCOME MEASUREMENTS

NEARLY all the propositions of economic science are concerned with statements about the national income. "Generally speaking," writes Professor Pigou in the *Economics of Welfare*, "economic causes act upon the economic welfare of any country, not directly, but through the making and using of that objective counterpart of economic welfare which economists call the national dividend or national income. Just as economic welfare is that part of total welfare which can be brought directly or indirectly into relation with the money measure, so the national dividend is that part of the objective income of the community which can be measured in money." The propositions of economic science are largely concerned with questions of whether particular measures will have a beneficial or adverse effect upon the national dividend. The measurement of the national dividend, unfortunately, has hitherto been regarded as one of the most difficult and uncertain branches of statistical science. As a result, economic theories are rarely put to the test of fact, and modern economics has shown a lop-sided development in an over-theoretical direction, of which outside critics justly complain.

Professor Pigou's *Economics of Welfare* gives the clearest and most concise statement known to me of the whole purpose of economic study. The framework around which the book is written is that the economist must discover methods which will advance, and counsel the rejection of proposals which will hinder, the following three objects :

(1) To increase the average national dividend.
(2) To regularise its flow through time.
(3) To equalise its distribution between persons.

The student of economics soon becomes aware that proposals which may advance one of these objects will injure another, and it is the duty of the economists to attempt to find methods for balancing the gains and losses of human welfare caused thereby.

Professor Pigou's point of view has won wide acceptance throughout the English-speaking world. Some opponents deny in effect that economics has a "purpose". They say that it is a "science" concerned with discovering how the economic mechanism works, without any preconceived ideas of the use to which this knowledge can be put. Such writers are generally sceptical about the existence, or at any rate the measurability, of Economic Welfare, the central subject of Professor Pigou's work. Those who feel so strongly that economics is a pure science should be those who are most anxious to apply the scientific canon of bringing each hypothesis to the test of fact, but this is by no means always the case.

Others, while willing to accept Professor Pigou's statement of the purposes of economic science, think it important that its propositions should be stated in an ethically neutral form. Professor Sargant Florence, in a recent pamphlet,[1] proposes to rewrite the *Economics of Welfare*, substituting for the words "good" and "bad", whenever they or similar adjectives occur, the words "irrend" and "non-irrend". This new adjective is coined as a concise way of defining any measure calculated to increase, regularise the flow, and equalise the distribution of the national dividend. He points out that the study of economics has fallen into much discredit and confusion owing to our failure to keep clear the distinction between Knowledge, Purpose and Application. If our grammar were as perfect as that of the ancient Greeks, we would make the three sorts of statements in the Indicative, Optative and Imperative moods, and who knows if a better grammar might not even promote clarity in our thought? At any rate, Professor Florence would have all treatises on economics

[1] *Uplift in Economics*, Kegan Paul, 1929.

written in the Indicative Mood, with the introduction of one or two new adjectives. Economists will not be free of their "superstitions, dogmas and prejudices" until they confine themselves to statements of facts and causes, and eschew all mention of the purposes to which their knowledge can be put, or of the methods and agencies by which it can be applied. "Science is open," he writes, "to be used by all comers."

Many of us (particularly those who, like myself, began life as physical scientists) hope that within a measurable time economics will have acquired the same degree of completeness of information, of unanimity between its professors, and prestige with the general public, as the older sciences enjoy today. But it is doubtful whether these ends will be achieved by a renunciation of statements of the purpose to which this knowledge must be put. Economic science is at the same time difficult and incomplete, abstract and yet touching closely the prejudices and convictions of everyday life. Professor Florence concedes that economists, provided they "sum up their findings in the indicative mood, may, in their other capacities, express their wishes and recommendations". Professor Pigou, after having been careful to describe in a measurable and objective manner the purposes to which he would like to see economic science applied, throws the whole weight of conviction behind them, and in a memorable passage addressed to the student beginning the study of the subject, tells him that "the complicated analyses which economists endeavour to carry through are not mere gymnastic, but are instruments for the bettering of human life". He might perhaps have added, that the economist must be content sometimes to see the knowledge which he has created used for purposes of which he may heartily disapprove.

My own position on this question, so far as national income studies are concerned, follows (as I understand it) that of Professor Pigou. There is some purpose in discovering and in saying that the national income has increased from £4000 millions to £4400 millions during a certain period, though nobody supposes that this means a 10 per cent improvement in economic welfare. There is some purpose in stating that the average income produced per worker is £250 per year, and that nearly half of the product is taken by 10 per cent of the population, although no presumption is involved as to whether the national income, if redistributed equally, would not work out to a lower, or higher, figure per head.

The national dividend must always be conceived in real, but measured in money, terms. The measurement of differences through time or between different countries always involves therefore the difficult practical and theoretical problems concerned with index numbers, which will be dealt with in a later chapter. In any case, however, a dividend consisting of an infinite variety of goods and services can only be reduced to a common measure by means of a money unit. We may as a standard take the dividend of any place or time we wish, and by the use of price index numbers express other real dividends in terms of this standard. This process can never claim complete logical watertightness, but we can be satisfied that it works well enough in practice for comparisons over periods up to, say, twenty years, or for comparisons between communities whose ways of living are not too widely different. Comparisons over a wider range of time or space must become less reliable, while comparisons between the average real dividend per head in, say, Britain and India, or between the twentieth century and the Middle Ages, can only be accepted subject to very big qualifications. This does not imply, however, that they are not worth making.

The money dividend of a community is thus a clearer concept than the real dividend, and although for most purposes we want to translate money dividends into real terms, there is a certain utility in the measurement of money dividend alone, as is the case, for instance, in the study of industrial fluctuations.

The national dividend may be defined for any period as

those goods and services which flow into being during that period which are customarily exchanged for money, avoiding, of course, double reckoning of those goods and services which are produced at one stage but then used up again in another stage of the productive process. We require a net total of the value of goods and services available for consumption or investment.

We may next draw a distinction between what is described as gross and net income. Net income corresponds to the above definition subject to a deduction equal to the cost of repairing and (in the course of years) replacing all the capital instruments used up in the production of the dividend ; gross income is before the provision of such allowances. In commercial terminology, the deduction for any one year will cover all repairs and maintenance, as well as depreciation and obsolescence properly attributable to that year (the actual payments under these heads during the year may have been greater or less than this). It will be seen that these allowances must be to a considerable extent a matter of conjecture. For this reason gross income is a more precise concept than net income, and for certain purposes at any rate is equally useful.

In our original definition, by the use of the phrase *customarily exchanged for money*, we have drawn a line excluding certain services, enumerated by Marshall as " the services which a person renders to himself and those which he renders gratuitously to members of his family or friends ; the benefits which he derives from the use of his own personal goods, such as furniture and clothes ". Marshall also seeks to exclude the services supplied by public enterprise (roads, water-supply, education, defence and the like), but modern economists in every case now include the value of such services in the national dividend. It is clearly absurd that the services provided by a school or a water-system should be reckoned as part of the national dividend if they are run as commercial concerns, but should cease to be so reckoned if they are taken over by the State or municipality.

The money measurement of the national income will comprise therefore all goods and services provided by capitalist enterprise, reckoned at the prices at which they are actually sold. Of the services provided by public enterprise, those which are sold in the market (e.g. postal services, municipal trading services) will similarly be reckoned in at the prices at which they are actually sold; others, such as public health services or free education, must be reckoned in at cost price. This will represent the value of materials used, the wages and salaries paid to public servants, and the interest on capital borrowed by the State or municipality for the purpose of these services.

These distinctions are not a mere pedantic necessity, for in many communities a substantial proportion of the national dividend is provided by communal enterprise.

Returning to our criterion of "customary exchangeability", we may reasonably regard services rendered by public authorities as exchangeable for money, either in the form of rates and taxes, or directly. The utility which a private individual derives from his own stock of goods, clothes, furniture, crockery, motor-car and the like, is not customarily exchangeable for money. On the other hand, the leasing of houses is certainly a customary form of exchange, and if a man occupies a house which he himself owns, we should regard the annual value of the house, as indeed do the British income-tax authorities, as part of his income. By the same token we must define dwelling-houses as capital in that they will produce real income or dividend in the future, while denying the appellation of capital to private motor-cars, furniture and the like.

Will the national income be equal to the sum of all individual incomes, and if not, by what items will they differ? Before we can go any more deeply into the question of how far the national income, as we have defined it, differs from the aggregate of private incomes, as the ordinary man understands his income, we must examine more closely the customary concept of income. We may take as our standard the definition of income used for the purposes of British income-tax assessment.

The forms of return sent out every year to British income-taxpayers give a full statement of those expenses which may, and which may not, be deducted for the purpose of computing income. Income saved or devoted to capital purposes is still income, and is subjected to tax (in some countries, however, is taxed at a lower rate); but apart from income devoted to capital expenditure, all "expenses incurred for the purpose of the trade" are deductible. In the British income-tax system the taxpayer is also allowed to deduct under the following heads:

Expenditure actually incurred on the repair and maintenance of plant, machinery and (in effect) of buildings.

An allowance for depreciation and obsolescence ("wear and tear") of plant, machinery, etc., and an allowance for buildings.

Costs of replacement of plant, machinery, etc., so far as the cost of replacement exceeds the total of allowances which have been made in previous years under wear-and-tear provisions.

Bad debts.

Writing down of inventories to current price-level, if that is below the cost price of the goods.

Trading losses incurred at any time within the past six years.

Incomes derived from agriculture are assessed on a nominal basis which in the majority of cases understates the true income.

No deductions are allowed for:

Expenses of maintenance of the persons assessable or their households.

Sums paid in direct taxation.

Amortisation of natural wasting assets (e.g. coal seams).

Depreciation of the value of securities, land or other assets held by the taxpayer: in the same way appreciation of such assets is not reckoned as a positive contribution to income.

The principal difference between the British system and those of the United States of America and Germany is in the last item. Under certain circumstances in these two countries appreciation of capital values is reckoned as part of taxable income, and depreciation of values is reckoned as a deduction. In some countries income from agriculture is not subject to taxation: in Britain, as we have seen, it is only partially so subject.

Does the official definition of income do violence in any respect to the ordinary man's concept of income? Certain British industrialists complain about the inadequacy of the wear and tear allowances, but it is not always realised that if the cost of replacing the machinery turns out to be greater than the allowances which have been made, an additional allowance can be claimed. In fact, such allowances are very rarely claimed, and it therefore appears that the official scales of allowance are adequate.

The railway companies, however, and a very small number of industrial concerns, make no claim for wear and tear allowances, electing to be assessed to tax by the alternative method, under which *replacements* are treated as a deductible expense.

In the Finance Act, 1932, all scales of wear and tear allowances were increased by 10 per cent. It is difficult to say whether this should be regarded as a form of tax concession to particular types of industry, or as giving official recognition to the contention that the rate of obsolescence of machinery has become more rapid during recent years. It is more convenient to regard it as the latter, and to accept the total of wear-and-tear allowances as it stands.

This method of calculating income, however, does probably do violence to the ordinary concept of income in respect of amortisation allowances on natural wasting assets. The value of a mine, for instance, may be being gradually exhausted with the using up of the accessible seams in order to earn its current income ; on the other hand, it is always possible that new technical or mechanical discoveries may have the opposite effect, and add value to seams hitherto considered worthless. It is probably the administrative impossibility of assessing a fair amortisation allowance in such cases that has caused its exclusion from the British tax system. In the United States income-tax administration, however, allowance is made for the amortisation of wasting assets such as oil-wells. A similar question might arise when agricultural land is made to yield a certain net income by methods which exhaust the fertility of the soil. On the whole, therefore, we must interpret our concept of the national dividend, as we have hitherto been building it up, as the dividend available subject to deduction for any demonstrable exhaustion of natural resources.

We can now answer, in as general a manner as possible, the question briefly posed, as to what extent, if any, the national income should be expected to differ from the sum of individual money incomes, and we can then compare this ideal standard with the practice adopted hitherto in the principal countries of the world.

In the first place, we must allow for the fact that certain individual incomes do not correspond to the creation of any tangible service and do not therefore by our definition represent any contribution towards the national income. Such are incomes derived from public relief and private charity, allowances made to relatives and friends, and Old Age and Widows' Pensions paid by the State. Income received as interest on War Loan must be excluded. Professor Pigou points out that this rule applies even if we assume that the money spent on the War was " productive " in the sense that it prevented invasion and the destruction of material capital that is now producing goods sold for money, for whatever product War expenditure may have been responsible for in this way is already counted in the income earned by the material capital. In the same way, War Pensions should not be counted as part of the national income. However, interest on a national debt incurred for productive purposes, or on municipal debt, should be reckoned as part of the national income, as contributing to the value of useful services rendered by these public authorities. And pensions paid to retired employees of the State, or of particular firms, should be regarded economically as a form of delayed payment for services performed, or part of the cost of supplying those services, and should be included in the national income.

It is clear that the incomes of public officials, even if they are derived from taxation and not directly from the sale of goods and services, should be included. Also the incomes and remuneration in kind of domestic servants and of personal assistants. Some authors fall into confusion on this point, and say that income reckoned in this way is counted twice; a rich man has a considerable income, out of which he pays a large number of personal servants, or provides for their maintenance, and some people think that from an economic point of view this should only be regarded as the earning of one income and not of two. What they overlook, however, is the fact that certain services have been rendered, or have been supposed to be rendered, in return for this pay and maintenance, and moreover that the rate at which these services have been remunerated must have corresponded approximately to the rate at which these same workers could have sold their services on the market, if they had engaged in other work.

Incomes obtained by force and fraud, against which no real service has been rendered, clearly ought not to be counted. The reader may be interested to know, however, that the British Inland Revenue collects income-tax on the illegal earnings of street bookmakers, and the fact that these earnings were taxable was recently upheld in a High Court case brought against such a firm.[1] In the same way,

[1] See 76th Report of the Commissioners of Inland Revenue, p. 52, *H.M. Inspector of Taxes* v. *A.B.*, also p. 49.

income-tax was sometimes collected on the earnings of bootleggers and racketeers in the United States. The illegal earnings of these enterprises have therefore been included in the national incomes of the two countries.

A factor of considerable importance in the national income of certain countries, which does not correspond to any money income of individuals, is the self-supply or income in kind of the small agriculturist. This is a considerable item in the national incomes of Germany and France, but not very great in Britain. It is customary to reckon the value of such produce at wholesale prices.

Another important category is that which is conveniently described as the category of " non-personal incomes ". These are all incomes, from the national income point of view, not accruing to any particular individuals. The first category of such incomes comprises the incomes of public authorities, not derived from taxation, namely, trading profits and receipts from inter-governmental transactions.

For some years after 1923 there was a considerable negative element in the British national income under this head, due to the payment of War Debt interest and sinking fund to the United States Government. In succeeding years this was gradually neutralised, and became positive, due to receipts from the Dominions and India and from inter-allied debt payments.

A more important category of non-personal incomes, however, consists of the undistributed profits of companies. One particular class of these will be the accrued income of insurance companies, which is due for disbursement to individuals at a subsequent date. Under English income-tax law, assessments are made on joint-stock companies rather than upon the individuals who comprise them, and as a result all undistributed profits, including those of banks and insurance companies, are assessed.

There remains one class of payments which must be included in the national income, not being individual money incomes, for an important but paradoxical reason.

This consists of all receipts by the Government from Customs, Excise and other indirect taxes, and also the receipts of local authorities from rates and similar indirect taxes. At first sight it seems absurd that a Government, by increasing indirect taxation, should be able to increase the national income. But we must reflect that the effect of all indirect taxation is calculated to be a corresponding rise in the price of the articles or services taxed. Real national income is calculated by dividing the money national income by an appropriate price index, and this price index is bound to incorporate the effects of changes in national and local indirect taxation. Looking at it another way, the State and local authorities may be regarded as entering into certain trades as a gigantic monopolist, and the price of goods to the consumer is enhanced thereby. If a private company obtain a monopoly of any commodity and make big profits on it, we include those profits in the national income, pointing out, however, the high price of the commodity in question when we come to consider the effect of the monopolist's action on real income. Exactly the same treatment can logically be applied to the revenue drawn by the State and local authorities from indirect taxation.

Professor Bowley and Sir Josiah Stamp added into their estimate of National Income the figure of the amount paid by employers in compulsory contributions to Health and Unemployment Insurance, on the ground that these payments are deductible as expenses of production in assessing taxable income. In my previous book I also placed local rates on business premises in this category. But reflection shows that there is no logical difference between these payments and all other forms of indirect taxation, such as Customs and Excise duties. They are all treated as deductible expenses for the purpose of tax assessment, and " enter into " prices as determined by index numbers—e.g. the Cost of Living index number of food prices is inclusive of Customs duties, and the index number of house-rents is inclusive of local rates.

In making comparison between the figures of National Income given in this book, and those of my previous book, or between mine and the Bowley-Stamp figure, account must be taken of these differences of definition with regard to indirect taxation. There are no other appreciable differences of definition, besides this, between my two and the Bowley-Stamp estimations.

CHAPTER II

POPULATION AND INCOME-EARNERS

THE geographical area covered in this study of National Income consists of Great Britain and Northern Ireland. The reason for this choice is that many of the most important statistics, for instance those of Income-tax Assessments and of imports and exports, refer to the combined area. Certain statistics, however, are lacking for Northern Ireland and have to be estimated. The statistics do not cover the Isle of Man and the Channel Islands.

The population of Great Britain and Northern Ireland at mid-1934 was officially estimated [1] at 46,680,000. The following are the figures for certain principal dates since 1911:

TABLE 1

POPULATION OF UNITED KINGDOM AND RATES OF INCREASE, 1911–34

(Mid-year figures in 000's)

	1911	1914	1921	1929	1934
England and Wales .	36,136	36,967	37,887	39,607	40,467
Scotland	4,751	4,747	4,882	4,832	4,934
Northern Ireland . .	1,249	1,242	1,258	1,246	1,279
United Kingdom . .	42,136	42,956	44,027	45,685	46,680

RATE OF INCREASE PER ANNUM

1911–14 . .	273,000
1914–21 . .	153,000
1921–29 . .	207,000
1929–34 . .	199,000

The year 1929 is shown in the table for the reason that it was a turning-point in migration. In the years 1921–9 emigration, though not at pre-War level, had been active.

[1] *Registrar-General's Statistical Review of England and Wales for the year 1934.* Tables, Part II.

In that year it abruptly ceased, and has been replaced, in each of the years 1930 to 1935, by a net inward movement consisting mainly of returning British migrants and of Dominion citizens.

The population was increasing at its maximum absolute rate in the decade 1901–11, when the population of the United Kingdom (including Southern Ireland) showed a net increase at the rate of 376,000 per annum. The excess of births over deaths was 484,000 per annum during this decade, net emigration being 108,000 per annum. By 1911–14 increasing emigration and a declining birth-rate had reduced this rate of increase. Throughout the period since 1921 the birth-rate has been falling steadily, but declining emigration, becoming a net immigration after 1929, has made the population continue to increase by approximately 200,000 persons a year.

Population figures include men and women, adults and children, active and retired persons. From the economic point of view, it is more important to reckon that portion of the population which is occupied in production. If we define production in the narrower of two possible senses, this will cover persons earning incomes from all gainful occupations, as they are described by the Census ; in the broader definition of the word we may also include women engaged in unpaid domestic work in their own homes.

TABLE 2

NUMBERS AND PROPORTIONS OF OCCUPIED PERSONS IN GREAT BRITAIN, 1901–31

(Figures in 000's)

	Male Population	Occupied Males	% of Male Population	Female Population	Occupied Females	% of Female Population	Females aged 15–70	Occupied Females as % of Female Population aged 15–70
1901	17,903	11,548	64·5	19,097	4763	25·0	12,491	38·1
1911	19,755	12,930	65·5	21,077	5424	25·7	14,071	38·6
1921	20,423	13,656	66·8	22,346	5701	25·5	15,541	36·7
1931	21,459	14,790	68·8	23,336	6265	26·8	16,858	37·2

The proportion of the population engaged in gainful

occupations, both male and female, has been steadily rising. This is mainly due to the changing age-composition of the population, the principal factor being the smaller proportion of young children. This is partly offset by the increasing proportion of old persons, the lower average age of retirement, and the later average age of starting work. Contrary to the general impression, it is seen that the increasing number of women in paid work has not been at the expense of the numbers of women working in their own homes. The relative number of women of working age working outside their own homes was at its highest, for this period, in 1911. After a further rise during the War, it had fallen considerably by 1921, and has only shown a slight rise since.

These various tendencies are more fully illustrated in the following table:

TABLE 3

NUMBERS AND PROPORTIONS OCCUPIED IN PRINCIPAL AGE-GROUPS, GREAT BRITAIN, 1911–31

(Figures in 000's)

Age	Males								
	1911			1921			1931		
	Population	Occupied	Percentage	Population	Occupied	Percentage	Population	Occupied	Percentage
Under 14	5,913	98	1·5	5,597	44	0·8	5,117	..	..
14 and 15	772	565	73·1	822	532	64·6	713	451	63·3
16–64	12,154	11,744	96·7	12,901	12,450	96·5	14,204	13,656	96·1
65 and over	915	520	56·8	1,103	630	57·0	1,425	683	47·9
Total	19,754	12,927	65·5	20,423	13,656	66·8	21,459	14,790	68·8

Age	Females								
	1911			1921			1931		
	Population	Occupied	Percentage	Population	Occupied	Percentage	Population	Occupied	Percentage
Under 14	5,892	50	0·8	5,519	29	0·5	5,016	..	..
14 and 15	773	370	47·9	819	366	44·7	703	356	50·6
16–64	13,191	4864	36·9	19,528	5158	35·5	15,726	5754	36·5
65 and over	1,221	140	11·5	1,480	148	10·0	1,892	155	8·2
Total	21,077	5424	25·7	22,346	5701	25·7	23,337	6265	26·8

This table has several interesting features. Firstly, with regard to the higher average age of commencing work, we see that up till 1921 an appreciable number of children under 14 were at work as half-timers. The proportion working between the ages of 14 and 16 fell between 1911 and 1921, but there has been no further fall since. In fact, in the case of girls, the average age of starting work was lower in 1931 than it had been either in 1921 or 1911. In both sexes a heavy drop since 1921 is noticeable in the proportion of old persons over 65 engaged in occupations, largely due to the operation of the Contributory Pensions Acts.

During the last generation, therefore, the community has been considerably enriched, without effort on the part of its members, simply due to its changing age-composition and the increasing proportion of persons of productive age. A part, but only a comparatively small part, of this increased potential productivity has been taken out in the form of an increase in the numbers of the leisured section of the community, i.e. earlier retiral and later age of starting work. The remainder was available for increasing the output of goods and services relative to our total numbers, for reducing the hours of those in work, and for making possible to us the luxury of keeping a considerable proportion of our numbers unemployed. These results will be dealt with in due course, but at this stage it is interesting to isolate the effects of the age-composition factor and the increased-number-of-leisured factor. In the following table a comparison is made between (i) the working population of 1931 and what its size would have been (ii) if average ages of retiral, entry into industry, etc., had been the same as in 1911, and (iii) if, further, the sex- and age-composition of the population had been the same as in 1911. Comparison between (iii) and (ii) shows how much we have gained through the changing age-composition; comparison between (ii) and (i) then shows how much of this gain we have used in creating a larger relative number of leisured persons. In order to compare the different classes of workers, it is assumed that adult female workers can do three-quarters of a man's work, juveniles under 16 can do one-half.

TABLE 4

EFFECTS OF CHANGING AGE-COMPOSITION AND INCREASE IN NUMBERS OF LEISURED, 1911–31, GREAT BRITAIN

(Figures in 000's)

	(i) Occupied, 1931	(ii) Numbers with 1911 Ages of Entry and Retiral	(iii) Numbers with 1911 Sex and Age Composition
Males, 16–24 . .	13,656	13,741	12,905
,, 65 and over .	683	810	571
,, under 16 . .	451	606	720
Females, 16–64 . .	5,754	5,817	5,355
,, 65 and over .	155	217	154
,, under 16 .	356	380	459
Total in man-equivalents	19,174	19,570	18,192

Thus the more favourable age-composition of the population in 1931 as compared with 1911 increased the potential number of units of productive labour from 18,192,000 to 19,570,000, out of a population of 44,796,000. This represents a gain of 7·6 per cent. By releasing certain juveniles and old people from work this gain was in fact reduced to 5·4 per cent.

We cannot, strictly speaking, take as given the numbers of the working and dependent populations. The proportions of men and women in particular age-groups who seek paid work are not fixed, and may indeed show short-period variations in response to changing economic conditions. But neglecting this factor, assuming, in other words, that the proportion of occupied persons in each male and female age-group remains constant, the more purely biological factor of changing age- and sex-composition of the population may have an enormous effect upon economic welfare.

This is likely to be the case in the future. Careful estimates of the future population of England and Wales have been made by Dr. Enid Charles [1] on three separate assumptions :

(i) That mortality and fertility rates remain at the 1933 level.

(ii) That both continue to decline in accordance with recent trends.

(iii) That fertility rates recover by some 10 per cent (i.e. to the 1931 level), while mortality continues to decline.

Method (ii) represents the most logical extrapolation of recent tendencies, but the tremendous future fall in fertility which it postulates may be considered unlikely by some. Method (iii) clearly gives an upper limit to population figures during the next generation. It is improbable that a rise in fertility greater than this will occur within, at any rate, a generation. From the immediate viewpoint, Method (i) appears to be based on a fairly reasonable assumption, though it is likely to forecast population a little too high. The data for 1934 and 1935 (for what they are worth, over so short a period) indicate that since 1933 the heavy fall in birth-rate has been checked, though fertility rates are still falling slowly.

According to Method (iii) the population is likely to go on rising slowly from its present (1935) level of 40·56 millions, till it reaches a maximum of 43·82 millions in 1960. It should then fall slowly and steadily, falling (if we care to extrapolate tendencies so far ahead) to 33·58 millions a century hence in 2035.

Method (i) also indicates a rise for a period, but it is with a far slower rate of rise and an earlier maximum, at 40·88 millions (virtually the present level) to be reached in 1943–4. Thereafter population will fall. By 1970 it is estimated at 37·43 millions, and shortly after that date it should reach its maximum rate of fall, at 3 millions per decade, reaching 19·97 millions in 2035.

[1] London and Cambridge Economic Service, Special Memorandum, No. 40.

On Method (ii), giving the " minimum " result, there is still anticipated a short period of slightly rising population, up to a maximum of 40·66 millions in 1940. From that date onwards a fall is anticipated which is both strong and cumulative. By 1970 the population is estimated at 33·79 millions, by 2000 at 17·68, and after that a still more violent fall to 4·43 millions by 2035. The hypothesis of declining fertility is perhaps here pressed a little too far. But one can summarise the results by saying that a century hence the population of England and Wales will probably be below 20 millions, and may very well be in the neighbourhood of 10 millions.

Without looking so far ahead, we may examine the proportion which the number of occupied males is likely to bear to the whole population at certain future dates. For 1950 at any rate we are working on a fairly certain basis of estimation.

In the table below, the following proportions of males in the age-groups shown are assumed to be at work :

Age-group	*% at Work*
15–19	89
20–59	97
60–64	86
65–69	65
70 and over	33

These figures are based on the 1931 Census results for Great Britain. Similar calculations could be made for females, but it will be appreciated that, if a great fall in the number of children is to be anticipated, a larger proportion of married women will probably engage in gainful occupations in place of child-rearing. They will thus create for the community an economic product only at the expense of a biological product. In any case, prediction of the number of women likely to be occupied is a very speculative calculation, but the average ages for males of entry into and retiral from occupation can more reasonably be taken as given. And a calculation of the proportion of occupied males to the total population will also provide an indication of the relative numbers of females at the active ages of life, whether regarded as mothers or as occupied in industry.

To recapitulate Dr. Charles' assumptions—Method (iii), which is placed first in the following table, gives a maximum figure for future population. Method (ii) gives a minimum. Method (i) gives what might be called a "safe estimate", but is probably on the high side. The present writer's own opinion is that the future course of population will lie between the results given by Method (i) and Method (ii).

TABLE 5

ESTIMATES OF POPULATION OF ENGLAND AND WALES, AND RELATIVE PROPORTION OF OCCUPIED MALES, AT CERTAIN FUTURE DATES

	1935		1950		1975		2015	
	Population. Millions	% of Occupied Males to Population	Population. Millions	% of Occupied Males to Population	Population. Millions	% of Occupied Males to Population	Population. Millions	% of Occupied Males to Population
Method (iii), "Maximum"	40·56	32·9	43·16	33·7	43·02	34·6	36·65	35·1
Method (i), "Safe"	40·56	32·9	40·68	34·6	36·04	35·3	24·47	35·1
Method (ii), "Minimum"	40·56	32·9	39·77	36·1	31·45	38·4	10·46	34·5

It is clear from this table that, owing to changing age-composition, the economic productivity of the population is going to rise during the next generation. On the more extreme assumptions of Method (ii), this factor, *ceteris paribus*, will raise productivity per head of population by 10 per cent between 1935 and 1950, and a further 7 per cent between 1950 and 1975. These results, though appreciable, are not of great order of magnitude compared with the gains to be expected from normal technical and economic progress over similar lengths of time.

On the assumptions of Methods (iii) and (i), no considerable rise in the productivity of the population is to be expected under this head. By Method (i) the maximum rise is only 7 per cent.

All these figures may perhaps be augmented if an increasing proportion of women of given age-groups engage in gainful occupations.

In each case the rise is likely to be followed by a fall during the generation after, between 1975 and 2015. Of the 17 per cent rise to be expected on the assumptions of Method (ii), all but 5 units are likely to have disappeared again by 2015. On the assumption of Method (i), only a small loss is to be expected. Such gain in productivity as we are likely to enjoy under this head during the next forty years, which will presumably be somewhere between 7 per cent and 17 per cent, should rightly be regarded as a form of biological capital, and long-term economic policy should attempt to convert part of this additional productivity into capital goods, in view of the anticipated adversity of the age-composition of the population in later generations.

What is perhaps more interesting is that the decline in the proportion of occupied males after 1975 is comparatively small. It had been anticipated by some that the economic welfare of the community was likely ultimately to be seriously depressed owing to an excessive proportion of unproductive old persons. Within eighty years, at any rate, this does not appear to be the case. Indeed the most interesting feature of Table 5 is that, whichever assumption we adopt, the proportion of occupied males to the whole population in each case comes out at about 35 per cent for 2015, a proportion slightly less adverse than that of 1935.

The exact numbers of occupied persons are only recorded at Census dates, and, as indicated above, knowledge of the age-composition of the population only enables us approximately to calculate the numbers of occupied persons, particularly in the case of females. In Britain, however, there are now important alternative sources of information giving the numbers of a large part of the occupied population, which are available annually. These are the three schemes of social insurance—Health Insurance which was started in 1912, Unemployment Insurance which was made general in 1920, and the Widows, Orphans and Contributory Pensions Insurance which was added to Health Insurance in 1926. The third scheme is the most comprehensive of the three. It does not cover employers or independent workers, or non-manual workers earning over £250 per annum. Otherwise it is compulsory upon the whole working population between the ages of 16 and 64 inclusive, with the few exceptions of those whose conditions of employment are certified by the Ministry to be such as to provide in any case all the benefits obtainable from the scheme. The number of workers thus excepted by certificate is about 60,000, of whom the great majority are policemen. Established staffs in the Civil Service (but only teachers in Local Authority service) are statutorily excepted without certificate, as also are persons employed by members of their own family.

Exception from Health Insurance is granted on the same principles. In this case a larger number of employers give conditions of employment which can be certified as providing benefits at least equivalent to those provided by the National Health Insurance. In Great Britain, 323,000 workers are covered by these certificates, in addition to those excepted from the Contributory Pensions contributions. These are mainly Local Government employees and certain of the clerical grades on the railways.

Persons outside the scope or excepted may, under certain circumstances, become voluntary contributors to the combined scheme of Health and Pensions Insurance, but not to Unemployment Insurance.

From the Unemployment Insurance Scheme are statutorily excepted all persons engaged in two particular industries—agriculture (prior to 1936) and domestic work. Statutory exception is also given to all men in the Forces, to all established workers in the service of the Crown (including postal staffs), to teachers and a large number of other established Local Government servants. Exception by certificate is given to workers whose employment is deemed to be secure against any risk of unemployment. These certificates in 1931 covered 529,000 workers, mainly permanent staffs on the railways, tram and bus service, and gas, water and electricity supply. In 1934 the age of entry to the scheme was lowered from 16 to 14.

After this lucid opening, it must now be confessed that the problem of reconciling Census data with figures collected under these Social Insurance schemes is quite the most tedious and difficult statistical problem which the writer has ever encountered. The working and results are given in Appendix I. A reconciliation between Health Insurance statistics and Census returns was made in 1927 by the Government Actuary,[1] but no more recent reconciliation has been made, nor has there been any attempt on the part of those administering them to reconcile Health Insurance and Unemployment Insurance statistics, which show considerable discrepancies.

These discrepancies became apparent in the calculation of the National Income for 1924, for which Professor Bowley and Sir Josiah Stamp used the figures of occupied population as shown by the Census, and the present writer used Social Insurance statistics. It was found that there was a very wide discrepancy between the numbers of wage-earners and the estimates of the total paid in wages, obtained by the two methods. In fact there was a difference of over a million. This mysterious million, mostly male workers, were recorded as occupied by the Census, but were, in Professor Bowley's words,[2] somehow lost in the Insurance statistics. Professor Bowley continued: "Decision on these problems must be deferred till we can match the Census of Population of 1931 with the Insurance figures".

The results of the Census of 1931 eventually became available, but they do not clear up the situation. As will be seen in the text which follows, the discrepancies appear to have widened, and the Mysterious Million has if any-

[1] Sir Alfred Watson, *Journal of the Royal Statistical Society*, 1927.
[2] *Economica*, May 1933.

thing become greater. Part is explained by the existence of large numbers of chronically unemployed men who are only nominally occupied. Part is also due to evasion, and part to a number of workers in State and municipal employment who are neither insured nor specifically excepted.

My original estimate for the number of wage-earners at work in 1924 was, as Professor Bowley pointed out, somewhat too low in respect of the allowance made for workers under 16 and over 65,[1] but the total appears to have been fairly near the truth. A revised estimate, taking into account the results of the 1931 Census, is given in Table 28.

It appears that a number of statistical difficulties would be solved, and probably a certain amount of evasion of insurance brought to light, if questions were included in the Census schedule asking whether each person was a contributor to (or entitled to benefit from) Health and Unemployment Insurance. This has not so far been done in England, but in the Scottish Census of 1931 each person was required to state whether he or she was entitled to medical benefit under National Health Insurance. The results are analysed in the Appendix. It appears that a number of people who are entitled to benefit are ignorant of that fact, while on the other hand I have been supplied [2] with an example of a particular class of voluntary contributors none of whom in fact were entitled to medical benefit, but most of whom stated that they were so entitled on their Census forms.

Making some allowance for these aberrations, we can use the Scottish data to solve two very important statistical problems, the results of which are useful in considering the English data. The first is the problem of how many insured persons are not "occupied" by Census definition. The second is the estimation of the proportion of persons earning above the exemption limit in certain

[1] My figure was 720,000 for the two classes taken together. Professor Bowley quotes 1,310,000, but this includes agricultural, domestic and salaried workers.

[2] By the courtesy of Mr. W. Grossart, of the Scottish Department of Health.

types of occupation. The results obtained under these heads are used in the analysis of the English data.

The final results of the analysis show considerable discrepancies. Taking male workers first, comparing the numbers of manual workers shown as occupied in the Census (at all ages over 16, including unemployed, excluding the Forces and independent workers) with the estimated number of manual workers insured (omitting voluntarily insured, unoccupied insured and the Forces, including men over 65 who are not definitely retired), we find a deficiency of 486,000 in England and Wales and of 33,000 in Scotland.

This can be accounted for under five different heads:

(i) Statutory exception to certain persons in the service of the Crown, and under one or two other heads, all of which will be inappreciable in the case of manual workers.

(ii) Employment of members of the family.

(iii) Evasion of Health Insurance.

(iv) Lapsing of insurance rights due to long unemployment, among men who still, however, consider themselves " occupied ".

(v) Misstatement on the Census form, by unoccupied men describing themselves as occupied.

It will be seen that (iv) and (v) merge into each other. Special legislation passed in recent years preserves the Contributory Pension rights of men who have been unemployed for considerable periods, but not indefinitely. After a long spell of unemployment they lose their insurance rights, and at the time of the Census it is a more or less arbitrary decision whether they enter themselves as " unoccupied " or as " unemployed ".

There is also a certain amount of overlapping between (iii) and (v), in the case of old men engaged intermittently in paid work. They will probably be recorded as " occupied " in the Census, but do not pay contributions when they are in work. The incentive to pay contributions is of course much less in their case than in the case of younger men. It is estimated in the Appendix that 57,000 of the discrepancy is accounted for in this way.

With regard to evasion by men under 65, I have been informed by those engaged in admininstering the Health Insurance Acts, that during recent years it has been negligible. In fact, since the pension benefits were instituted in 1926, payment of Health Insurance contributions has become a form of taxation which is actually popular. Evasion of contributions by men (under the age of 65) actually in work can probably be put at below ½ per cent of the insurable population, or 50,000.

With regard to statutory exception granted to persons employed by their own families, the exception is, strictly speaking, only granted to persons employed by their own husbands or wives, though in effect probably no contributions are paid in the case of employment by fathers, brothers, etc. We can get some idea of the importance of this exception from statistics of the farming population. There were in Great Britain at the date of the Census 184,000 farmers, excluding those employing no labour, and they employed 84,000 sons, daughters and other relatives (of whom 10,000 were females).

Farming is one of the most familial of occupations, and also one employing a high proportion of males, but unfortunately we do not have statistics of family labour in any other occupation. In the other group of occupations in which family labour is important—namely, retail trade—female labour is as important as male.

In the German Census the numbers of workers employed by members of their own families is recorded, this type of employment being of course frequent in peasant agriculture. Outside agriculture, however, there were in Germany in 1933 only 117,000 males recorded as thus employed; and it must be borne in mind that small trading and manufacturing concerns are relatively as numerous, or more so, in Germany as in Britain. For all occupations taken together, a maximum estimate of the amount of family labour would be 250,000, of which 150,000 would be male.

We have so far the following results :

Evasion of contributions :	*Males, Great Britain*
men over 65	57,000
,, under 65	50,000
Family employment	150,000
Balance, consisting of men " occupied " in the Census but not paying H.I. contributions through long unemployment or other causes .	262,000
Total	519,000

If comparison is now made between Health Insurance and Unemployment Insurance, it is found (see Appendix, p. 287) that there is a further discrepancy of 91,000 in the occupied male population. The Unemployment Insurance Scheme is more carefully administered, and also there is far less incentive for a man who has been long unemployed to maintain registration. Some of the 91,000 should therefore be included with the last category in the above table, but we must not lose sight of the possibility that evasion of Unemployment Insurance is more widespread than evasion of Health Insurance, and an extra 50,000 may be allowed under this head.

In the case of female workers the reconciliation is not so difficult. In this case we may reckon, on the basis of figures given in the Appendix, that all the operatives and 30 per cent of the managerial workers aged 16–64 should be insured unless excepted from insurance statutorily or by certificate.

TABLE 6

OCCUPIED FEMALES IN GREAT BRITAIN AT 1931 CENSUS

(Figures in 000's)

	16–65	65 and over
Operative . .	5316	91
Managerial .	133	19
Numbers insurable	5356	97

The number of females over the age of 65 contributing

is only 61,000, and thus there are among these 36,000 evasions or misstatements on Census forms.

With regard to women below the age of 65, it will be seen from the Appendix that the delimitation of insurability for women under the Health Insurance Acts is very vague, and several different classes of unoccupied women are included. It is therefore better to make comparisons direct between the numbers recorded in the Census and insured for Unemployment Insurance. Assuming evasion as shown, we find by deduction 38,000 women in the last category, namely, returned as " occupied " in the Census but not paying contributions through long unemployment.

Table 7 is based on the conclusions reached above and in the Appendix. It refers to employees only and excludes employers, independent workers and salary-earners receiving over £250 a year.

TABLE 7

Occupied Employees in Great Britain, April 1931
(Figures in 000's)

	Males	Females
Ages, 16–64:		
Insured for unemployment	8,969	3456
Agricultural and domestic workers	970	1253
Forces	313	..
Statutorily excepted from U.I.	560*	360*
Excepted by certificate from U.I.	410	119
Family workers	150	100
Evasion	100	30
Balance of persons not genuinely occupied though shown as such in Census	318	38
	11,790*	5356*
Aged 65 and over:		
Unemployed	136	10
In work contributing to H.I.	293	61
In work not contributing	57	39
	486	110
Aged 14 and 15	451	356
Total of employees not earning above £250	12,727*	5822*

* It is estimated that 100,000 males and 30,000 females with salaries over £250 are included in these figures.

The Census returns give the whole occupied population of Great Britain in 1931 as 14,801,000 males and 6,273,000 females. The former must be raised by 200,000 to allow for seamen and men in the Forces absent from Britain on the day of the Census.

We can now rearrange the data of Table 7 so as to show by difference the numbers of employers and of salaried persons with incomes above £250. Of the "occupied" workers over 65 not paying contributions, it is assumed that half are evading payment and that the other half are not in fact in work.

TABLE 8

ALL OCCUPIED PERSONS IN GREAT BRITAIN, 1931

(Figures in 000's)

	Males	Females
Insured for unemployment	8,969	3456
Agricultural and domestic workers (aged 16–64)	970	1253
Excepted workers and Forces (incomes below £250)	1,183	449
Family workers and evasion	278	150
Workers, 14–15	451	356
Workers over 65 : Employed and contributing	293	61
Unemployed	165	29
Balance not occupied or insured	318	38
Independent workers	921	351
Employers and salary earners above £250	1,453	130
Total	15,001	6273

The Census returns of unemployment are defective. In April 1931 the Ministry of Labour recorded 1,918,000 *insured* male workers unemployed in Great Britain. The Census recorded 1,968,000, but the following deductions must be made from the latter before comparability is established :

Men over 65	134,000
Boys under 16	23,000
Agricultural and domestic workers	84,000
Managers, professional men and other uninsured workers	80,000

—leaving only 1,647,000.[1] Probably a considerable amount of short-time and temporary unemployment escaped record in the Census, and there is little doubt that the Ministry of Labour records are more accurate. They will therefore be used for that part of the working population which they cover, and Census records for the remainder.

Table 9 gives an analysis of all unemployment in Great Britain, insured and uninsured, in 1931, on the same lines as Table 8. We should include with the unemployed the large class of persons who have been unemployed for so long, or whose work is so intermittent, that they have fallen outside the scope of social insurance.

TABLE 9

UNEMPLOYMENT IN GREAT BRITAIN, 1931
(Figures in 000's)

	Males	Females
Persons insured against unemployment	1918	598
Domestic workers, 16–64	22	95
Agricultural workers, 16–64	62	3
Persons over 65	165	29
Persons under 16	23	18
Persons now outside scope of insurance	318	38
Total	2508	781

The true amount of unemployment at that date was therefore 3,289,000, a much more serious figure than had generally been estimated.

Omitting the unemployed, the next table gives the occupied population of Great Britain actually in work at the date of the Census.

Using these Census data as a basis, we can carry backward and forward our estimates of the occupied population. The next step is an analysis of the statistics of the

[1] Possibly further deductions would have to be made, before comparability is reached, to allow for men in trades normally insurable, who are uninsured as a result of prolonged unemployment, not included in the Ministry of Labour statistics.

TABLE 10

Occupied Population in Work, 1931

(Figures in 000's)

	Males	Females
Managerial	1,028	152
Working on own account	921	351
Clerical, commercial and professional workers .	2,207	1491
Agricultural and fishing operatives	892	44
Other manual workers	7,445	3454
Unemployed	2,508	781
Total	15,001	6273

number of incomes assessed to income-tax, which is made in Appendix II.

These figures must be modified in order to take into account the fact that a considerable number of farmers, and of married women, are not assessed as such, although earning incomes above the exemption limit. Also in comparing statistics of assessments with those of the number of occupied persons, we must allow for the fact that a considerable number of assessments are on unoccupied persons.

Data relating to this latter problem have been previously given[1] by the author. It is estimated there that the number of unoccupied persons with assessable incomes was 530,000. On further examination it appeared that this figure should be lowered to about 400,000.

An examination is also made[2] of the numbers and income-distribution of salaried and independent workers earning below £125. All incomes above this level are included in the income-tax assessments, and we therefore require to know not only the average income, but also the frequency distribution of incomes, of these classes of workers, in order to estimate the numbers and average amount of incomes not covered by income-tax assessments. Data for income-distribution are obtained, in the

[1] *Economic Journal*, September 1934, pp. 382-4.

[2] *Loc. cit.* pp. 385-7.

case of salary-earners, from data collected by Professor Bowley and Sir Josiah Stamp [1]; in the case of independent workers, from the results obtained in the sample inquiries in *Social Survey of Merseyside*. It has been objected by Dr. Snow that this latter sample is too small. When Professor Bowley and Sir Josiah Stamp come up against this problem of the frequency distribution of earnings of independent workers, they write :

> "In commerce and finance the majority will be small traders helped by their families, and hawkers of all kinds will be included. We suggest that about one-third of this group make less than £150 per annum." [2]

This conclusion is frankly guess-work. Any sample, however small, would give better results ; and a $\frac{1}{30}$ sample covering the whole of a large industrial area gives considerably better results.

Dr. Snow himself says that he has "knowledge of the character of the frequency distribution of incomes in general" [3] from which he can determine that £120 is the average earnings of independent workers below the pre-1931 income-tax exemption limit (£159 p.a.). I am not aware of the existence of any such source of information.

We may now bring together figures relating to the year 1931. For tax assessments on persons other than wage-earners, we must take the assessments made in 1932–3. These number 5,005,000. We must add 250,000 for married women engaged in salaried and business occupations earning over £125. We must then deduct 530,000 (or perhaps less) unoccupied persons, and 195,000 persons (see Appendix II) who for various reasons are assessed [4] although they earn less than £125.

We thus have a figure of 4,530,000 as the total number

[1] *The National Income*, p. 23.
[2] *Loc. cit.* p. 26.
[3] *J.R.S.S.*, 1933, p. 112.
[4] The numbers of the married women involved are not deducted, as their numbers have not been included by the Inland Revenue in their total number of assessments.

of occupied persons other than wage-earners earning incomes above £125 a year. We also have data [1] for the number of non-wage-earners earning incomes below £125; the numbers are 440,000 independent workers and 1,200,000 salary-earners. There were also approximately 100,000 small farmers not assessed to income-tax: for convenience we will assume that their incomes were below £125, though Schedule B assessment does not necessarily equal income.

We are now in a position to check the whole chain of previous calculations, by comparing these results with the Census data for the number of occupied non-wage-earners. The two sets of data are completely independent.

TABLE 11

INCOME OF OCCUPIED PERSONS (OTHER THAN WAGE-EARNERS) IN 1931 (U.K.)

Income Data		Census Data (Table 10) for Great Britain	
Numbers assessed to tax (corrected figure)	4,530,000	Managerial workers . .	1,180,000
Incomes below £125:			
Salaries . . .	1,200,000	Independent workers . .	1,272,000
Independent workers .	540,000	Clerical, commercial and professional workers	3,698,000
	6,270,000		6,150,000
		Estimate for Great Britain and Northern Ireland	6,320,000

Considering the approximate nature of some of the data, the agreement is good. If the revised estimate of the number of unoccupied persons assessed be accepted, the left-hand total becomes 6,400,000—also a good agreement.

We therefore estimate finally that the income-tax assessments cover 4,580,000 occupied non-wage-earners with incomes above £125 (i.e. 6,320,000 − 1,740,000).

The number of independent workers in Great Britain was 1,272,000 in 1931, or 1,310,000 in the United Kingdom, of whom 540,000 had incomes below £125.[2] The above

[1] *Economic Journal*, September 1934, pp. 386-7.

[2] Assuming for the sake of convenience that all farmers not assessed to Schedule B had incomes below £125.

total of 4,580,000 therefore includes 770,000 independent workers and 1,625,000 salary-earners over £250 and employers.[1] We deduce, therefore, that there were 2,185,000 salary-earners with incomes between £125 and £250. It is important that we should know their numbers, because over this range of income there is an overlap between persons assessed to tax and contributing to social insurance.

Estimates may now be made for years other than 1931. Allowance must be made for the effects of the higher exemption limit in the earlier years. The same number of married women must be added back in either case, while the additional number of farmers remaining unassessed at the time of the higher exemption limit was only about 10,000 (the amount exempted from Schedule B fell by £1·4 million between 1930–31 and 1931–2). In the case of independent workers, we make use of the data of the frequency distribution of their incomes in order to estimate the additional numbers escaping assessment under the higher exemption limit. We must also take into account a small upward trend in their numbers between 1921 and 1931.

It is more difficult to estimate the number of unoccupied persons assessed before 1931. In view of the rapid increase in the number of retired people during the last decade, it is assumed that their numbers have been rising fairly rapidly. The 1931 figure is estimated at 480,000, which will cause the results to balance in Table 11. The precision of the data in the following table declines as their distance from the Censal year 1931 increases.

The number of salaried persons over £250 and of employers is assumed to remain constant at 1,625,000.

The numbers of assessments on non-wage-earners are taken from the table in Appendix II. Assessments made in 1927–8 and in subsequent years refer in general to the income earned in the previous calendar year (or some accounting period close to that), e.g. 1934–5 assessments

[1] Data from Table 8, with allowance for Northern Ireland.

generally refer to income earned in the calendar year 1933. Before 1927–8 the average of the three previous years was taken as the basis of assessment for a considerable number of incomes, and there were certain disturbances to the statistics during the period of transfer. The exemption limit for earned incomes was also changed in 1925. No account is therefore taken of the assessments in 1925–6 and 1926–7. The assessments made in 1924–5 show the numbers of incomes above the £150 exemption limit at a somewhat earlier date in respect of Schedule D assessments, but in respect of other assessments they show the number of incomes in the current year. The assessments of 1927–8 and onwards show the number of incomes in years from 1926 onwards.

TABLE 12

Number of Non-wage-earners assessed, 1924–34, U.K.

(Figures in 000's)

	No. of Assessments (cf. Table in Appendix II)	Including Married Women	Less Salaries over £250 and Employers	Unoccupied Persons assessed	Incomes below Exemption Limit assessed	Independent Workers assessed	Salaries above Exemption Limit and below £250
1924–25	3295	3545	1920	280	250	660	730
1927–28	3441	3691	2066	236	275	640	915
1928–29	3497	3747	2122	244	275	645	958
1929–30	3616	3866	2241	252	275	650	1064
1930–31	3696	3946	2321	260	275	655	1131
1931–32	5010	5260	3635	464	195	765	2211
1932–33	5005	5255	3630	480	195	770	2185
1933–34	4850	5100	3475	496	195	775	2009
1934–35	4905	5155	3530	512	195	780	2043

The figures in the last column form a vital connecting link. We have for each of the years shown above, figures of tax assessments and also of the number of workers covered by social insurance, but we can only make use of them when we know the extent of their overlap, which is here determined.

The number of *employers* (not including independent workers) in Great Britain in 1921 was 735,000. Strictly speaking, a man employing members of his own family should be in this category. In 1931, however, this number was not redetermined. The Registrar-General states: "With the growth of Joint-stock Companies, the old distinction beween 'Employer' and 'Employed' has lost much of its significance; in place of these somewhat ambiguous classes, the categories 'Managerial' and 'Operative' have been substituted".[1] In 1931 the Census recorded 1,180,000 "managerial" persons, which total was meant to include both free employers and salaried managers and managing directors.

A scrutiny of the individual headings in the Census volume in which certain of these persons are concentrated, namely, under various "employers and managers" headings in industry, shows that there was no appreciable change in their aggregate numbers between 1921 and 1931.[2] In retail and other commercial businesses there was an increase of nearly quarter of a million among "proprietors and managers" during the decade, of which about 75,000, however, was accounted for by a rise in the number of independent workers. Of the remainder, it is not possible to tell how many were independent employers and how many were salaried managers employed by chain stores, etc.—but it is known that the latter type of employment has considerably increased. The only conclusion we can reach is that the number of independent employers in 1931 was somewhere of the same order of magnitude as, or perhaps rather less than, the 735,000 recorded in 1921.

Apart from any transference of employers into salaried managers, we can estimate the growth of the salaried class as a whole from the numbers recorded in certain occupations. There was a change in Census classification between 1921 and 1931, certain workers being transferred from "Public Administration" to "Clerical"; but as both these classes are included in the following table it does not affect the result.

[1] Census of Occupations, 1931, Introduction.
[2] *Economic Journal,* September 1934, p. 394.

TABLE 13

INCREASE IN SALARIED WORKERS, 1921–31

	Great Britain (000's)
Commercial and financial occupations .	+ 547
Public administration (less police) . .	– 203
Professional occupations	+ 135
Entertainment (less occupations 837-8) .	+ 30
Clerical occupations	+ 374
Total . . .	+ 883

We must deduct approximately 100,000 for the increase in independent workers under these heads, leaving an increase of 783,000, which may be higher if among " proprietors and managers " there has been a net transfer from the category of employers to salaried workers.

In *The National Income, 1924–1931*, I made a preliminary estimate of the increase in the number of salary-earners between 1921 and 1928 of 705,000, or at the rate of 100,000 per annum. Dr. Snow criticised such an estimate of the rate of increase in the number of salary-earners as impossibly high. The Census results, however, show that it has averaged 80,000 a year between 1921 and 1931.

In the same book I estimated the number of employers and independent workers in Great Britain in 1928 at 1,670,000, a decrease of 14 per cent since 1921 (for males alone the decrease was 17 per cent). This figure was estimated by extrapolation and from a study of Ministry of Labour figures of the rate of transfer of " workers on own account " into insurance, no other information being available. The conclusion was that there was a strong tendency for independent employers to be replaced by salaried managers.

It is possible that I considerably overstated the rate of decrease. Dr. Snow claimed that this was the case :[1] and shortly afterwards, before the publication of the Industry

[1] *J.R.S.S.*, 1933, p. 111.

and Occupation volumes of the 1931 Census, obtained advance copies of the figures from the Registrar-General, purporting to show an increase of 14 per cent in the numbers in this category between 1921 and 1931.[1] Sir Josiah Stamp quoted these results as an illustration of the dangers of extrapolation.[2] Dr. Snow's figure excludes females, and also Scotland, both of which exclusions have the effect of somewhat strengthening his conclusion.

The Census of 1931, however, gives no figures of the number of employers and independent workers. The category " employers " has been dropped, and no comparisons can be made with 1921. I had to study the returns rather carefully to make out how Dr. Snow had reached his conclusions, but as he obligingly gives the figure of the number of " employers and independent workers " in 1931 to the last digit, it is possible to discover how he obtained it. He apparently obtained a figure for the number of " Employers " in 1931 by taking the recorded total of " Employers, Directors and Managers " and deducting from it the total of " Branch and Departmental Managers ". But the result thus obtained is not in the least comparable with the number of employers as recorded in 1921. Dr. Snow's result includes large numbers of salaried managers, and thus his method masks the very tendency which we are trying to examine—the tendency for independent employers to be replaced by salaried managers. Proof that Dr. Snow's result cannot possibly be compared with 1921 can be easily obtained by working out, on his method, the number of " employers " in the first few industries covered by the Census, as in the following table.

The 1931 figures are clearly inflated by the inclusion of all principal salaried managers. No doubt a certain number of these returned themselves as employers incorrectly in the 1921 Census, but the above figures make

[1] *J.R.S.S.*, 1933, p. 659.

[2] *J.R.S.S.*, 1934, p. 439. Though Sir Josiah has stated " decrease " where he meant " increase", and *vice versa.*

TABLE 14

Number of Employers, 1921 and 1931

Industrial Order	Number of Employers	
	1921 (as recorded)	1931 (calculated by Dr. Snow's method)
III, 1. Mining and quarrying . .	1181	2353
III, 2. Treatment of mineral products	298	628
IV. Brick, pottery, glass, etc. .	1774	2099
V. Chemicals	2172	3861

it clear that Dr. Snow's method of calculation gives no basis of comparison.

Granted that the number of independent employers in 1921 was probably not accurately stated, and that the Census authorities were right in abolishing this form of classification in 1931, it is impossible to establish Dr. Snow's contention that the number of employers and independent workers, taken together, increased between 1921 and 1931. The number of employers in 1931 must remain unknown, in spite of Dr. Snow's claim that his figure is officially established and " should be placed on record to avoid further controversy ".

Arising out of this, the question may reasonably be asked whether it is desirable that advance copies of official statistical volumes should be made available to certain parties for controversial purposes.

Finally, this study of the number of income-earners must be brought up to date by comparing the more recent figures of the numbers insured with estimates of the numbers of the occupied population aged 16–64. These latter can only be calculated on the assumption that the proportions of males and females occupied in each age-group will remain the same as in 1931. This of course will not necessarily be the case; and particularly in the case of female workers the proportions of any given age-group who will seek paid work will change very much from time to time with the condition of the labour market. Nevertheless, we can calculate a sort of datum-line for the occupied population in any one year, on the basis of the known age-composition of the population and assuming the 1931 "employability" of each age-group. For males, where there are comparatively few unoccupied persons between 21 and 64, the scope for fluctuation will not be great. In the case of females, if the occupied population does in fact move differently from the population calculated by the above method, we may assume that this represents increasing or decreasing willingness on the part of women at any given age to seek paid work.

We have the age-composition of the population of Great Britain for 1931, and the number of persons in each age-group occupied. Estimates by the Registrar-General give us the age-composition for the middle of the year 1933, and it is not difficult to carry the estimate forward for another five years. The adult population will change fairly smoothly from year to year. The biggest discontinuities will of course occur as a result of the entry into manhood of those born after 1914. Between 1914 and 1922 the movements of the birth-rate were very discontinuous. If we carry our estimate forward to 1938, this will mean that all the age-groups, including those up to 24 years of age in 1938, will be subject to discontinuous changes.

The method used therefore is to estimate the population in the age-groups 25 and upwards for the quinquennial intervals only. The numbers in the lower age-groups are estimated separately year by year.

The material for this latter estimate is obtained from some figures published in the *Ministry of Labour Gazette* in October 1934, which show the estimated numbers of boys and girls, of ages 14, 15, 16 and 17, in each year for the next fifteen years, and also the numbers estimated to be seeking employment. It is possible to carry these figures forward so as to estimate the numbers in the age-groups 18–20 and 21–24 in each year up to 1938. The proportions of each age-group occupied in 1931 can be taken as follows :

TABLE 15

PROPORTIONS OF POPULATION AVAILABLE FOR EMPLOYMENT, GREAT BRITAIN, 1931

Age	Males	Females
14	55	43·2
15	75	61·5
16	84	71·7
17	94	80·2
18–20	95·3	78·2
21–24	97·3	65·4
25–29	98·5	42·7
30–34	98·6	28·7
35–44	98·2	24·4
45–54	96·7	20·9
55–59	94·1	18·8
60–64	85·6	16·3
65–69	65·4	12·2
70 and over	33·4	5·9

On the basis of these calculations the estimated number of occupied persons in 1933, 1938 and (as a matter of interest) 1943 is given in Table 16. This table estimates by quinquennial age-groups only and will therefore, for the reasons stated, have to be supplemented by more detailed estimates in the first two age-groups for 1933 and 1938.

TABLE 16

ESTIMATED NUMBER OF OCCUPIED PERSONS IN CERTAIN AGE-GROUPS, GREAT BRITAIN

(Figures in 000's)

Age	1931		1933		1938		1943	
	Males	Females	Males	Females	Males	Females	Males	Females
16–20	3,282	2587	..	..	..	..	1,311	1093
20–24							1,892	1300
25–29	1,787	827	1833	843	1850	837	1,700	737
30–34	1,572	537	1720	551	1803	575	1,819	552
35–44	2,740	807	2785	819	3056	858	3,380	874
45–54	2,476	613	2474	622	2484	639	2,526	658
55–59	1,799	387	1050	237	1073	254	1,068	260
60–64			799	169	847	188	861	200
Total	13,656	5758					14,557	5674

The corresponding numbers in April 1931 were 13,656,000 males and 5,754,000 females. Looking ahead first of all to 1943, we see that between 1931 and 1943 the number of occupied males in the age-groups covered by social insurance is likely to rise by 900,000. The number of occupied females is likely to fall, if the present " occupability coefficients " of the different age-groups are maintained. This curious result follows from the fact that occupied females are mostly in the lower age-groups, and therefore their numbers will be affected sooner as a result of the decline in the number of births after 1914. Among men the tendency to decline in the lower age-groups is more than neutralised by a rising tendency in the middle age-groups, particularly the groups 30–34 and 35–44. These age-groups in 1931 covered the generation which had suffered most from the war of 1914–18.

In Table 5, estimates have already been made of the probable changes in population between 1935 and 1950. It was estimated that by that date the total population of England and Wales might conceivably be about 2½ millions above the 1935 level, but would be much more likely to be just about at the 1935 level—depending of course on the hypothesis adopted about the future of the birth-rate. The persons who will form the occupied population in 1950 are, however, all born by now, and estimates of the *occupied* population at that date are therefore on a surer basis than estimates of the *total* population. These figures refer only to England and Wales, and cover a different age-grouping from that of Table 15, but their changes will be similar. Table 5 shows 13·35 million occupied men in 1931, and between 14·1 and 14·6 million (according to various hypotheses about mortality rates) in 1950.

It may be estimated therefore that the absolute number of occupied men may continue to rise even after 1943, though at a diminishing rate. In the years [1] prior to 1931, the number of insured male workers in Great Britain was

[1] 1923–7 and 1928–31. There was a change in classification in 1927–8.

rising at an average of 137,000 yearly, while for the twelve years 1931–43 an aggregate rise of 900,000, or an average of 75,000 per year, is forecast.

TABLE 17

NUMBERS OF OCCUPIED PERSONS IN GREAT BRITAIN BETWEEN THE AGES OF 16 AND 64, FINAL ESTIMATE, 1931–37

(Figures in 000's)

	April 1931	Dec. 1932	Dec. 1933	Dec. 1934	Dec. 1935	Dec. 1936	Dec. 1937
Males, Aged:							
16–17	695	654	606	560	581	716	795
18–20	1,103	1,113	1,097	1,057	998	947	960
21–24	1,483	1,480	1,493	1,522	1,525	1,499	1,444
25–64	10,375	10,596	10,706	10,796	10,887	10,977	11,068
Total .	13,656	13,843	13,902	13,935	13,991	14,139	14,267
Females, Aged:							
16–17	600	552	508	471	486	597	665
18–20	934	908	894	855	801	756	765
21–24	1052	1036	1030	1025	1018	1003	968
25–64	3168	3215	3252	3274	3296	3318	3340
Total .	5754	5711	5684	5625	5601	5674	5738

Table 17 gives more detailed estimates year by year between 1931 and 1937. The lower age-groups have been filled in by year-to-year estimates. It will be seen that of the 900,000 rise in male working population between 1931 and 1943, two-thirds is estimated to take place between 1931 and 1937, at an average rate of 100,000 increase per year, and that after that date the increase will average about 50,000 per year. The female working population is estimated to decline throughout, except for rises in 1936 and 1937, due to the coming of age of the exceptionally high numbers of children born in 1920 and 1921.

These figures will only provide very moderate comfort to those who are hoping that a slowing-down in the rate of increase of population will help to mitigate unemployment. Unemployment is at present most seriously concentrated on males, and their numbers are due to increase, while the numbers of females will diminish. This latter phenomenon will probably cause a number of important economic changes, among which may be expected a remarkable rise in women's wages during the next few years.

The increasing number of older men must also be taken into account. Modern industrial conditions and the psychology and training of older men do not seem too well adjusted to each other, judging from the incidence of unemployment on men of various ages, shown in the following table.[1]

TABLE 18

PERCENTAGE OF UNEMPLOYMENT AMONG MEN OF VARIOUS AGES

		Per cent
All men aged	21–64	15·2
Men aged	21–24	15·2
" "	25–29	13·5
" "	30–34	12·6
" "	35–44	13·0
" "	45–54	15·9
" "	55–59	20·2
" "	60–64	26·0

While considering the future general level of unemployment, we may examine the results of another interesting analysis which was made possible for the first time by the results of the Census of 1931. This is an analysis of unemployment by *occupations*. For many years the Ministry of Labour published the figures of unemployment by *industry*, and we have a good knowledge of the industries in which unemployment is the most concentrated. But we have no information of the incidence of unemployment of the various types of occupations, skilled, unskilled, office workers and the like. The data given in the 1931 Census Report make this possible for the first time, and the results were very remarkable. The table which follows gives an analysis of the male unemployed in England and Wales. The occupations are classified into social grades, corresponding roughly to work requiring various degrees of training. As has been pointed out above, the Census

[1] Census of England and Wales, Occupation Tables, p. 63.

return understates the amount of unemployment, probably mainly by the omission of short-time unemployment, and therefore the disparities of unemployment experienced between different classes are probably still greater than those shown in the table.

TABLE 19

UNEMPLOYMENT AMONG DIFFERENT OCCUPATIONAL CLASSES, 1931

	Population (000's)	Unemployed (000's)	% Unemployment
Unskilled manual workers	1334	407	30·5
Skilled and semi-skilled manual workers	7118	1027	14·4
Agricultural workers	838	64	7·6
Forces	166	..	..
Personal service workers, barbers, waiters, etc.	359	35·6	9·9
Salesmen and shop-assistants	624	49·3	7·9
Clerks and typists	694	38·0	5·5
Higher office workers	304	15·4	5·1
Professions	519	28·4	5·5
Retail traders, innkeepers, bookmakers, etc.	538	12·2	2·3
Farmers	303	1·5	0·5
Proprietors and managers of other businesses	462	6·0	1·3

The variations in this table are most remarkable. A very large proportion of unemployment is concentrated on the unskilled workers, and a more detailed analysis of the second figure would probably reveal a high proportion of unemployed among some of the lower semi-skilled occupations. In spite of frequent statements to the contrary, unemployment in the "clean collar" occupations is found to be much lower than among manual workers, and in the professional and managerial occupations lower still. Of the unemployment among professional men, 11,500 is accounted for by actors and musicians, put out of work by cinemas, and in other professions the percentage rate of recorded unemployment is only a little over 2 per cent.

It appears that a large, and perhaps increasing, proportion of unemployment is accounted for by a relative over-supply of the more untrained types of labour. Modern mechanical and technical developments are dispensing with the need for a considerable proportion of this labour, apparently creating requirements for the more highly remunerative types of labour which are at present only just being filled. Vocational training which equipped more young people to undertake the better-paid types of work would probably benefit not only them but the community as a whole.

The changes between 1931 and 1935 may now be examined in more detail. The estimates for the numbers of occupied males between the ages of 16 and 64 had risen by 187,000 between April 1931 and December 1932, by 244,000 between April 1931 and December 1933, and by a further 33,000 only to December 1934. The corresponding increases in the numbers insured for Health Insurance (excluding voluntary contributors) were only 87,000 and 49,000 to December 1932 and December 1933 respectively. The latter figure takes into account some 95,000 unemployed who had been put out of benefit through prolonged unemployment but who still retain pension rights. A corresponding figure is not recorded for December 1934 and calculations cannot be made for that date, but the numbers otherwise insured (omitting voluntary contributors) fell by 80,000 between December 1933 and December 1934. There must be many others who have fallen out of benefit through prolonged unemployment who are not included in the 95,000 given above.

On page 28 above it was estimated that the discrepancy between the number of occupied men recorded in the Census and the numbers covered by Health Insurance was 519,000. Of this, 257,000 was explained by evasion and family employment, leaving 262,000 men who were occupied by the Census definition but were not covered by Health Insurance owing to long unemployment, intermittency of work, or other causes.

It appears that by December 1933 this figure, already alarmingly high, had risen by a further 195,000 to the huge total of 457,000, while a further 95,000 are in benefit for pensions only. By December 1934 the number of "occupied" persons out of benefit for Health Insurance had risen again from 552,000 to 665,000.[1]

It was pointed out above, and in Tables 7 and 8, that the scope of Unemployment Insurance in 1931 was not so wide as that of Health Insurance, and a further 91,000 men who were covered by the latter were not covered by the former. Table 8 can now be made to serve as a basis of comparisons for subsequent years. The following calculations refer only to workers between 16 and 64.

TABLE 20

NUMBERS OCCUPIED AND INSURED IN GREAT BRITAIN, 1931–5

(Figures in 000's)

	Males				Females			
	July 1932	July 1933	July 1934	July 1935	July 1932	July 1933	July 1934	July 1935
Increases over April 1931:								
Persons insured for unemployment	+170	+212	+298	+387	−52	−17	−33	−32
Agricultural workers .	−14	+4	−18	−29	−6	−5	−10	−16
Others . . .	−26	+1	−18	−51	+28	−35	−57	−93
Total, occupied population aged 16–64	+130	+217	+262	+307	−30	−57	−100	−141

The figures in the third line are obtained by difference. If we allow for the effects of migration the figures for males will probably become positive. The figures for females will not be considerably changed, and will not show such high negative values. The forms of employment covered

[1] In comparing changes in the number of insured males with changes in the number of occupied persons as calculated from age-composition of the population, no allowance has yet been made for emigration or immigration. In the four years 1931–4 inclusive there was a net inward movement of migrants into this country of 270,000. There are stringent restrictions on the entry of aliens into this country to take paid work here. However, 92 per cent of this net immigration represented British (or Irish) subjects. Many of these will undoubtedly be persons with incomes over £250 a year, or outside the scope of insurance for other reasons. But it is quite possible that about one-third of these migrants will be insurable males. If we make such an allowance, the number of occupied men outside the scope of insurance must be even greater than was indicated in the above paragraph.

are (i) domestics, (ii) excepted workers and the Forces, (iii) family workers and persons evading insurance, (iv) "occupied" persons by Census definition who have fallen outside the scope of insurance, (v) independent workers, (vi) employers and higher salaried workers.

In both sexes it is clear that (ii), (iii) and (vi) are unlikely to change considerably during four years (among males also (i)). Changes, if they have occurred, must therefore be looked for in the other categories; or we may conclude that the aggregate numbers of the occupied population have in fact moved differently from the estimates based on age-composition. The latter explanation is more likely in the case of the female population.

In the case of men, therefore, it is only in categories (iv) and (v) that any considerable changes are likely to have taken place. The number of male independent workers increased during the previous decennium, very largely owing to expansion in the retail trades, and it is unlikely that this process has been reversed. The figures for males given in the third line of Table 20, allowing for migration, are probably to a small extent positive. Allowing for the growth in the number of independent workers, it is probably the case that the numbers in category (iv) did not change appreciably in the years 1931–5.

The numbers of the occupied population aged 16–64 in Table 20 have been estimated from statistics of age-composition, and the estimates must be modified if there has been any change in the average age of entry into or retiral from work (which has probably been the case with female workers). In the case of males, however, there is some evidence that there has been no change in the average age of entry into work. Information can be obtained thanks to the fact that boys of 16 and 17 are separately distinguished in the Unemployment Insurance statistics. The estimated numbers occupied in this age-group (Table 17) fell between April 1931 and July 1935 from 695,000 to 570,000: the numbers insured from 582,000 to 462,000, or by almost exactly the same amount. We also now have information about the number of boys of 14 and 15 in insured work. The article in the October 1934 *Ministry of Labour Gazette* (previously referred to) gives estimates year by year of the number of occupied juveniles, and interpolated to March 1935 their estimate is 534,000 boys. In 1931 the Census showed that 11·1 per cent of the occupied boys aged 14 and 15 were in uninsurable work (agriculture and domestic service). The number of insured boys [1] in March 1935 was 427,000, and raising this figure by the above proportion we obtain a figure of 532,000.

From these two calculations it can safely be said that, for males, the average age of entry into industry has remained unaltered. It is also very doubtful if the average age of retiral has increased. What appears to have happened is that the scope of Unemployment Insurance has remained unchanged, and about the same number of the chronically unemployed now maintain registration under the Unemployment Insurance Acts, though an increasing number of them are losing their rights to Health Insurance. Turning again to Table 8, we may deduce that there were in 1935 some 267,000 men between the ages of 16 and 65 normally occupied as manual workers who were unemployed and outside the scope of Unemployment Insurance, as against 318,000 in 1931. An increase might have been expected in view of the fact that administrative changes between October 1931 and March 1932 were estimated [2] to have put 150,000 workers (of whom a considerable proportion were men) outside the scope of insurance. We must conclude that improving employment during the last few years has brought a considerable number of them back within the scope of insurance.

In the case of female workers the interpretation of the results is very different. The third line in Table 20 first shows a positive figure in 1932. This is the result of a number of women being put outside the scope of insurance

[1] *Ministry of Labour Gazette*, April 1935.
[2] *Loc. cit.*, April 1932.

as a result of the Anomalies and Means Test regulations of 1931–2, mentioned above. But in each succeeding year the increasing shortage of the natural flow of female working population, as indicated in the fourth line, caused a negative figure. This may partly be explained by a withdrawal of labour from domestic service (or from independent work). Otherwise by earlier entry and later retiral.

On the first point we have definite evidence. Taking first figures for girls of 14 and 15, who are not included in Table 20, and calculating in the same way as is done above for boys, we find that there were 376,000 girls insured in March 1935, and the Census proportion of girls working in uninsurable trades was 20·4 per cent. Using this ratio, we find 473,000 girls occupied at that date, as against only 419,000 estimated from the 1931 average age of entry into work. It is not of course possible to say how far this difference of 54,000 represents a transfer of young girls away from domestic service, and how far the entry into work of girls who would normally have been unoccupied.

For girls aged 16 and 17, the estimates given in Table 17 are 600,000 occupied girls in 1931 and 480,000 in July 1935, a fall of 20 per cent. The numbers insured were 440,000 and 359,000. In 1931 at these ages 26·6 per cent of the girls were in uninsured occupations, and assuming this ratio continued to 1935, we should have expected 352,000 girls insured, as against an actual figure of 359,000.

Only among girls under 16 therefore can we say that there was been any advancement of the normal age of entry into occupations. As a matter of fact, Table 15 shows that 70–80 per cent of girls of 16 and 17 are normally occupied, and there is here little scope for an increase.

A partial explanation of the data shown in Table 8 may, however, well be in a later average age of retiral of women from industry, and in the continuance of work by married women.

Changes in the numbers of women covered by Health Insurance have not been very different from changes in the estimated occupied population.

TABLE 21

CHANGES IN FEMALE OCCUPIED AND INSURED POPULATION, 1931–5
(Figures in 000's)

	Dec. 1932	Dec. 1933	Dec. 1934
Change since April 1931 :			
Estimated number of females occupied, 16–64	-43	-70	-129
Insured for H.I. (excl. voluntary) and excepted	-40	-96	-103

The fact that Health Insurance covers domestic workers, while Unemployment Insurance does not, implies that a considerable part of the gain in the numbers of industrial occupations may be at the expense of the numbers in domestic work. This factor, an increase in women's average age of retiral from work, and also the absorption of the unemployed women outside the scope of insurance (estimated in Table 8 at 38,000 for 1931) must between them account for the discrepancy of 93,000[1] indicated for 1935 in Table 20.

[1] Or less, if we assume that an appreciable number of immigrants are women who will take paid work.

CHAPTER III

INCOMES ASSESSABLE TO INCOME-TAX, 1924–33

THE scope of the Inland Revenue statistics enables us to obtain comprehensive and accurate totals of the incomes of all classes except wage-earners. For the incomes of wage-earners, the Inland Revenue assessments cover only about a third of their numbers, and also, as the majority of those assessed are not, in fact, liable to tax, the statistics are perhaps not so carefully and comprehensively prepared as they are in the case of the incomes of salary-earners and business men. As good statistics about wages can be obtained from other sources, the assessments on wage-earners have been omitted from the Inland Revenue totals.

It should be noted that for statistical purposes the Inland Revenue regard shop-assistants, clerks and workers of similar status as salary-earners. This point had, I think, escaped the notice of both Dr. Bowley and myself in previous work, and was responsible for considerable ambiguities in the wage totals.

Statistics of income-tax assessments are now far more comprehensive than they have ever been before. The Finance Act (No. 2) of 1931, passed during the week of crisis which preceded Britain's departure from the gold standard, enacted among other provisions the lowering of the exemption limit for earned income to £125. This provision, though it must have been the despair of Inspectors of Taxes, has been of enormous advantage statistically. It has meant that the incomes of practically all salary-earners and entrepreneurs have been brought within the net of assessment, even though the great majority of the small incomes are entirely exempted from tax by the operation of rebates and allowances.

The Inland Revenue statistics are therefore considered

our source of information for the incomes of all salary-earners and entrepreneurs down to £125 per annum, and from knowledge of the frequency distribution of the incomes of small independent workers and of the lower-paid salary-earners we shall be able to make a fairly good estimate for the earnings of those receiving below £125 per annum in these classes.

The 1931 Census of Population, as mentioned above, has introduced one considerable change in classification of industrial status. Hitherto the classification has been into employers, employees and workers on own account. Reflection will show that this leaves ambiguous the position of a large and increasing number of managing directors, managers of shops, factory departments, etc., who are technically employed by a company but whose status is almost exactly the same as that of an independent employer. The Census authorities, therefore, are no longer attempting to separate employers from managers, but have created the two new grades of Managerial and Operative persons. These terms are considered to be self-explanatory.

One other innovation in methods of calculation will be made here, namely, with regard to incomes from agriculture. The farmer alone of all classes is exempted from making a full return of his income, and is assessed on a conventional assessment which in fact often seriously understates his net earnings. As we can get full information from direct sources about the value of the net output of agriculture, figures of wages, rents, and profits earned in agriculture will not be included in the calculation of the national income as such.

The 78th Report of the Commissioners of His Majesty's Inland Revenue for the year ended 31st March 1935 was made available to the public in March 1936. This enables us now to obtain accurate figures of assessments made on the incomes of the year 1932, and provisional figures for 1933. But no more recent data can be obtained from this source.

The taxpayer himself does not have to submit his return

until some time after the conclusion of the year in which the income was earned, and for various administrative reasons the publication of the information has to be delayed for a very long period after that. The result is that the final estimates of the national income can only be made some years after the conclusion of the period to which they refer, but methods are available for bringing these estimates up to date to a fairly close degree of approximation.

The British income-tax is assessed under five schedules, dating back to the time of Pitt. Schedule A covers the rents received from land, buildings and certain minor forms of real property. Schedule B represents assessments made on farmers' incomes. Schedule C covers assessments on incomes from British Government securities and certain foreign and colonial securities. Schedules D and E are the most important. The former covers incomes from any trade, business, profession, property or securities not specified above : the latter all remuneration by way of salary or wage.

Under Schedules A, B and C the income is now assessed in the same year as it is earned : under Schedules D and E a year later.

As pointed out above, the assessments on farmers do not necessarily represent their real incomes, and it is more expedient to make a direct estimation of the income derived from agriculture by the net output method. At this stage, therefore, we must exclude from our reckoning all incomes derived from agriculture. These will be Schedule B assessments and part of Schedule A assessments. We have an independent source of information on the amount of agricultural rents included under Schedule A. The Ministry of Agriculture in their 1930–31 Census estimated gross (i.e. before deducting cost of repairs and management) agricultural rents at £37 millions for England and Wales. There were also £3 millions of tithe in that year. The gross Schedule A assessment on " Lands " in 1930–31 was £41·7 millions in England and Wales, and £49·8 millions in the United Kingdom. This includes some small assessments on lands used for sport, forestry, etc. We may put gross agricultural rentals (including tithe) for the United Kingdom at £48 millions and net at £39 millions, or £38 millions excluding property held by persons with incomes below the exemption limit. This figure shows little change from year to year.

As pointed out in the previous chapter, the effect of the change from the three-year average system in 1927–8 was that figures for the actual income earned in any particular year can only be carried back to 1926. The published figures for the first two years after this require a small correction to allow for the effects of administrative change.[1] During the régime of the three-year average it was clearly impossible to deduce the income earned in any one year from the published data. The only year for which a figure is available is 1924, for which year Professor Bowley and Sir Josiah Stamp made use of the results of a very large sample inquiry in order to disentangle the figures of the one-year from the three-year average. Their result requires correction in view of the fact that the final published figures of assessments made in 1924–5 differed from the provisional figures which they had been using ; and also, as the Inland Revenue have pointed out to me, the Schedule D assessments for that year included a special non-recurring assessment of £35 millions on the railway companies in respect of a large payment received by them from the Treasury as compensation for Government war-time control.

For calculation of the net national income, an estimate of the sums lost in trading must of course be deducted from the aggregate of recorded profits. On the other hand, under the income-tax regulations, a trader is allowed to regard a previous loss as an offset against any profits which may be earned within six years of the loss being incurred. The result is that in each year certain losses are being incurred which for our purpose we wish to deduct from the total of assessments ; but, on the other hand, certain

[1] See *The National Income, 1924–1931*, p. 67. The source of these figures is a communication from the Board of Inland Revenue.

profits are not being brought into assessment, as a result of an offsetting of losses incurred in previous years. Appendix 11 to the Report of the Colwyn Committee on National Debt and Taxation enables us to form some idea of the amount of trade which is carried on at a loss. This document, prepared by Dr. W. H. Coates, at that time Director of Intelligence and Statistics at the Inland Revenue, shows the amount of turnover in various industries on which losses were made. These figures refer to no year later than 1922, and refer only to joint-stock companies (i.e. exclude individual businesses). It is unfortunate that no figures are available for any later year ; all that can be said is that 1922 was a year not very different in trading results from the other years of the period up to 1929. The exclusion of individual businesses probably has the effect of overstating the proportion of trade which was carried on at a loss. Dr. Coates' figures show, among manufacturing industries, a proportion varying from 10 per cent in the food and woollen trades, to 30 per cent in the cotton trade, of turnover carried on at a loss ; the average loss on this portion of the turnover being anything from 2 to 10 per cent in the different industries. In wholesale distribution 10 per cent of the turnover was carried on at an average loss of 2 per cent, and in retail distribution 5 per cent of the turnover at an average loss of 3 per cent. The orders of magnitude of the annual turnover of industry, wholesale and retail distribution respectively, are £4000 millions, £3000 millions and £2500 millions. An estimate of £30 millions for the annual aggregate of trading losses, for the years up to 1929, seems to be justified.

A sample examination was made by the present writer of the trading results of a number of companies having in an aggregate £350 millions of capital. The results of all companies showing a loss at any period during the last ten years were segregated to provide a sample in order to determine as far as possible the extent to which trading losses had increased since 1929, and also to estimate the amount of offsets which were likely to be expected in each trading year. The following table is based on the results obtained from this sample, assuming aggregate losses in 1929 to have been £30 millions :

TABLE 22

TRADING LOSSES, 1929–33

(£s million)

	Aggregate of Trading Losses	Aggregate of Offsets	Net Amount to be deducted from Recorded Assessments
1929	30	5	25
1930	100	5	95
1931	165	10	155
1932	140	25	115
1933	120	30	90

It was pointed out in the previous chapter that the incomes of a number of persons *earning* less than £125 will be included in the assessments. The numbers of persons and the aggregate income involved (excluding wage-earners) are calculated in Appendix II.

Income belonging to charities, educational institutions, etc., which is exempt from tax, must be added back at this stage. About half of these are under Schedule D, and half under Schedules A and C. The data are therefore lagged by half a year on the average in adding them.

Estimates of the amount of evasion are exceedingly difficult. Sir Josiah Stamp and Dr. Bowley estimated £75 millions for 1924, and although the amount of evasion may have changed widely, there is not sufficient evidence to justify any new figure, and this estimate is retained throughout.

In my previous work on this subject, I have pointed out that local rates and employers' contributions to social insurance are allowed as deductions before computing assessable profits ; these represent part of the cost of production of output, but do not as such become income to any earner. In this respect, I have contended, the national income reckoned as the sum of the incomes of individual earners is likely to be deficient.

It appears to be more logical and expedient, however, to put these payments with all other payments of indirect taxes, whose place in the national income is discussed in Chapter I. They will not therefore be included at this stage. This will account for a difference of £100–130 millions between the results given below and my previous estimates of income covering the same field.

We must next make allowance for the writing down of inventories in years of falling prices, in accordance with present-day accounting practice. As is pointed out in Chapter I, the national income will be understated if we make these deductions from profits. The necessary discussions and calculations are made in Appendix III.

We can now summarise the available information. The income under the various schedules is placed against the year in which it was earned.

[Table 23

TABLE 23

Actual Income above Exemption Limit (excluding Agricultural Incomes and all Wage-earners), 1924 and 1926–33

(£s million)

	1924	1926*	1927	1928	1929	1930†	1931	1932	1933
Actual Income :									
Schedule A ‡ .	224·6	246·5	258·4	267·1	274·3	284·1	290·5	298·8	303·0
„ C . .	135·5	135·6	142·6	153·4	155·0	160·8	160·7	157·8	151·9
„ D . .	1116	1013·2	1064·9	1077·7	1032·5	922·1	801·7	756·4	800·0
„ E . .	651·4	700·0	710·0	721·9	743·7	804·5	783·2	766·4	780·0
Total of above .	2127	2095	2176	2220	2205	2171	2036	1979	2035
Agricultural incomes included above	−39	−39	−39	−39	−38	−38	−38	−38	−38
Change from 3-year average	..	+30	+12	..	..	..	..	..	..
Trading losses . .	−25	−25	−25	−25	−25	−95	−155	−115	−90
Incomes below exemption limit	−60	−69	−69	−69	−69	−39	−39	−39	−39
Incomes of charities, etc.	+30	+37	+38	+39	+41	+43	+42	+43	+45
Evasion . . .	+75	+75	+75	+75	+75	+75	+75	+75	+75
Writing down of inventories	..	+74	+88	+23	+81	+251	+102	+51	..
	2108	2178	2256	2224	2270	2368	2023	1956	1983

* The following estimate may be made for the year 1925 :

The most difficult series to interpolate is Schedule D assessments. Sir Josiah Stamp's index number of profits (*J.R.S.S.*, 1932, p. 663) stands at 199 for 1924, 183·2 for 1926, and 199·6 for 1927. Using these as a basis for interpolation, we may estimate £1070 million from the index figure of 196·3 for 1925.

Schedule E was affected by the change in the exemption limit. In 1925 the new exemption limit was in force, and £690 millions may be estimated under this head.

The income of charities was £35 millions, and the amount written off inventories £221 millions. Other series present no difficulty in interpolation. We thus obtain £2329 millions.

† The new exemption limit (£125 earned, £100 unearned) applied to all assessments made in 1931–2 and later years—i.e. it first applied to 1930 incomes under Schedules D and E, and to 1931 incomes under Schedules A and C. So that the new exemption limit may be applicable uniformly to data for 1930 and all subsequent years in the above table, the Schedule A figures for 1930 have been raised by £2 millions, the additional amount brought into assessment by the change in exemption limit. The effect on Schedule C was inappreciable.

‡ Properties liable to Schedule A are re-assessed at fairly long intervals. Between re-assessments, new properties built are valued and assessed, but the rising letting value of old properties is not taken into account. The effect of re-assessments in 1922 and 1930 can be clearly seen in the following statistics of Actual Income under Schedule A :

	£s million
1922–3	189·1
1923–4	222·4
1924–5	224·6
1925–6	224·0
1926–7	238·7
1927–8	248·0
1928–9	254·1
1929–30	258·7
1930–31	263·8
1931–2	290·5
1932–3	296·2
1933–4	297·8
1934–5	300·5

It may be estimated that the accumulated increases in value of the past eight years, brought into assessment in 1931–2, were £21 millions. The figures for other years are therefore raised cumulatively by £2·6 millions per annum.

CHAPTER IV

THE WHOLE NATIONAL INCOME

TABLE 23 covers the whole of that part of the national income which is or might be assessed to income-tax. We may now enumerate the other elements which remain to be calculated:

(i) Earnings of wage-workers, i.e. manual workers.
(ii) Net income of agriculture.
(iii) Earnings of salary-earners and entrepreneurs with incomes below the earned-income exemption limit.
(iv) Income from property held by persons not included in the income-tax assessments.
(v) Government income [1] from trading services and international transactions.
(vi) Payments of indirect taxation and local rates.
(vii) If gross income is required, expenditure on maintenance and depreciation must be added back to the total.

(i) *The earnings of wage-workers*

The number of persons so covered can be determined from Table 10 as 8,337,000 males and 3,498,000 females in Great Britain. These figures are exclusive of unemployed.

The largest part of these represent workers employed in industry—manufacture, mining and construction. The next most important group are agricultural workers, whose incomes will be included in the reckoning of the net output of agriculture, but a separate reckoning of their numbers and income is desirable. In the case of females, there will be a very considerable number of domestic

[1] The income from trading services of local authorities, the B.B.C., etc., is assessed to tax and has already been included.

servants. We must then include all the manual workers outside the scope of ordinary "productive" industry, i.e. the manual working staffs of distribution, transport, government and the service industries, covering such occupations as lorry-drivers, warehousemen, police, soldiers, postmen, etc.

The first and largest category represents workers covered by the Census of Production. In 1930 a voluntary wage inquiry was held in conjunction with the Census and a substantial proportion of the firms circularised in each industry returned figures of their aggregate wage-bill in 1930. The General Report on the 1930 Census of Production (pp. 105-6) gives £723 millions as the aggregate of wages paid to manual working operatives in Great Britain in 1930 (£734 millions for the United Kingdom). This estimate includes wages paid in firms employing under ten workers, which did not make returns in the Census of Production. It does not, however, cover the following trades :

Oil shale mining.
Salt mines, brine pits and salt works.
Government departments.
Public utility services (including industrial work done by local authorities).

Under the two former headings, only some 6000 operatives are employed, and it is assumed that their average earnings are the same as those of other workers in non-metalliferous mines and quarries. Under the latter headings, although returns are not available showing the aggregate earnings during the year, they are available for the average earnings in a particular week, and an estimate can be made for the annual total. Excluding artisan staffs on the railways, whose wages are included in the railway totals, there is £77 millions in 1930 and £70 millions in 1924 to be added under these heads.

Including the numbers estimated to have been employed by small firms and by firms from which no information was received, the total number of persons engaged (including working proprietors) in the industries covered by the Census was 7,899,000 in the United Kingdom in 1930, of whom 6,964,000 were operatives. From these must be deducted 219,000 operatives in railway workshops, leaving 6,745,000. The total of operatives is not subdivided by sex, owing to lack of knowledge of the sex of the operatives employed by small firms. Examining these latter industry by industry, it may be estimated that they totalled 395,000 males and 152,000 females. The whole total may therefore be analysed into 5,006,000 males and 1,739,000 females, with an aggregate income of £811 millions, of whom 75,000 males and 61,000 females were in Northern Ireland.

These relate to the earnings and numbers of the year 1930. The years 1930 and 1931 were a period of rapid decline in employment and earnings, and therefore we must be careful to give precision to our dates. In order to correspond with Census data, we must express numbers and rate of aggregate earnings for a date as close as possible to April 1931. At that date the number of *insured* workers in employment in industries within the scope of the Census of Production was 6·31 per cent below the average level of the year 1930, and wage-rates were 1·4 per cent below.[1] Just at that month, or in the second quarter of the year 1931, we can say that earnings were at the rate of £749·2 millions per annum, and that the numbers of operatives earning in Great Britain[2] were 4,620,000 males and 1,572,000 females. Before comparing this with the Census of Population results, however, we must make allowance for sickness. Sick persons were not generally described as " out of work " in the Census of Population; but they were excluded from the returns of employment in the Census of Production. The Ministry of Labour estimate that at any one time 3½ per cent of the insured population are not working through illness. For com-

[1] *Economic Journal*, September 1934, pp. 388 and 393.

[2] The analysis at this stage is made to refer to Great Britain only, as no Census of Population was taken in Northern Ireland in 1931.

parison with Census of Population results the numbers therefore become 4,788,000 and 1,629,000.

In March 1931 the railways recorded 616,000 persons as employed by them in Great Britain. Omitting office and clerical staffs, and workers in ancillary undertakings (hotels, etc.), this figure becomes 500,000, of whom all but 30,000 were males. Their aggregate earnings at that date were at the rate of £83 millions a year in Great Britain, or £85 millions for the United Kingdom. In June 1931 there were 829,000 agricultural employees in work in Great Britain, of whom 120,000 were females. In this particular industry the difference between April and June may have been considerable. The Census records for agriculture (including poultry farming, market gardening and fruit farming, but not nursery culture or " undefined " gardening) show for April 1931 only 690,000 in work and 57,000 unemployed. Even if we assume that all the unemployed of April were in work by June (which is not very far from the truth) there still remains a deficiency of 82,000 workers.

The Census figures of employed and unemployed added together, however, only show 43,000 female workers as against the 120,000 of the agricultural returns. We must conclude that the two-thirds of these 120,000 female workers returned in the Agricultural Returns as " regular workers " did not in fact work through the year, and that most of them were working for a short summer spell only. We may take the Census figures as they stand, and when we estimate the aggregate paid in wages must discount a considerable part of the female labour recorded in the agricultural statistics.

We are thus left with a little over 4 million wage-earners. Their aggregate earnings will be estimated from a weighted average comprising the information available about the wages of the more important occupations included in this range.

Very conveniently, the Ministry of Labour inquiry in connection with the Census of Production, referred to

TABLE 24

NUMBER OF WAGE-EARNERS IN GREAT BRITAIN, APRIL 1931 (EXCLUDING UNEMPLOYED BUT NOT SICK)

(Figures in 000's)

	Males	Females
Industries covered by Census of Production	4788	1629
Railways	517	31
Agriculture	650	40
Rest	2382	1798
Total	8337	3498

above, strayed a little beyond the scope of the Census of Production itself, and gave us figures of average earnings for two important groups—Tram and Bus Service and Carting and Warehousing. These averages are based on large samples. Average earnings in laundries were obtained for 1929, and special inquiries into average earnings in the catering trade, including the estimated value of tips and allowances in kind, were made in 1925 and 1929.

The average weekly earnings for male workers calculated by the Ministry of Labour under the two heads given above are 66s. 10d. for tram, bus and coach drivers and conductors, and 54s. 5d. for carters and warehousemen. The latter trade employs a considerable number of females at an average wage of 25s. a week.

In the catering trade, 16 per cent of the male and 27 per cent of the female workers are under 21. The average earnings for adults, as given in the two inquiries, come to 63s. and 40s. respectively (all inclusive). Taking 25s. and 20s. as the inclusive earnings of boys and girls, we obtain an average of 56s. 11d. for males and 34s. 7d. for females.

For postmen, where very few juveniles are employed, the average earnings may be put at 57s. 6d. The same applies to seamen and dockers, where the averages may be taken at 62s. and 60s. a week (seamen's wages inclusive of keep). The average pay (including allowances and the value of keep) of men in the Forces is some 47s. per week.

For male and female domestic workers the average value of earnings (inclusive of keep) is taken at 60s. and 30s. per week. For charwomen, office-cleaners and domestic workers not in regular work, the average earnings will probably only be £1 a week. The average earnings of female laundry workers are approximately 25s. a week.

The weights used in the calculation below are obtained from the Census, including sailors, etc., absent on the Census day.

TABLE 25

AVERAGE EARNINGS OF NON-INDUSTRIAL WORKERS, 1931

Males			Females		
	Weight	Average Earnings		Weight	Average Earnings
		s. d.			s. d.
Tram and bus .	3	66 10	Warehousing .	2	25 0
Carting and warehousing	4	54 5	Catering .	3	34 5
Catering . .	1	56 11	Domestics (regular)	12	30 0
Postmen . .	1	57 6	Charwomen, etc.	6	20 0
Dockers . .	2	60 0	Laundries .	3	25 0
Forces . .	4	47 0			
Seamen . .	2	62 0			
Domestics .	1	60 0			
Weighted average	..	57 0	Weighted average	..	27 3

The numbers to whom these averages are applicable are 2,382,000 and 1,798,000 respectively for Great Britain, to which some 2 per cent may be added for Northern Ireland. In converting these weekly figures into annual, an allowance must be made for sickness as well as holidays, and a multiplier of 48·7 is used.

This gives annual averages of £138·9 and £61·4 respectively, and total earnings at the rate of £450 millions per year.

In agriculture the aggregate paid in wages can be obtained, though, as explained above, this total is not at present required for the calculation of the national income. For the period 1930–31 the Ministry of Agriculture calculated that average weekly earnings, including the value of all allowances in kind, overtime and harvest payments, were 37s. 5d. for horsemen, 39s. 1d. for stockmen and 33s. 8d. for other agricultural workers. The relative numbers of these classes of workers are stated in the Census to be 1 : 1 : 5, but Dr. Carslaw (*J.R.S.S.*, 1935, p. 606) suggests that this ratio is too low, and suggests a ratio of 2 horsemen and stockmen to 3 ordinary workers. For lads under 21 we may assume an average wage of £1. For female workers, in view of the intermittency of their work, we should reckon only £25 per annum for regular and casual workers taken together. We may assume further that casual male workers obtain on the average 20 weeks' work per year,[1] and that regular workers (other than horsemen and stockmen) lose on the average one week's work per year in unemployment, holidays, etc. These assumptions give us an average annual income of £91·2 for the regular adult male worker (£99·4 for stockmen and horsemen and £85·8 for others), £33·7 for casual men, £50 for regular and £20 for casual male workers under 21.

Applying these to the average of the numbers recorded as employed in England and Wales in the different categories in June 1930 and June 1931, we obtain a total of £50·8 millions for England and Wales.

In Scotland precise figures of agricultural wages are not available, but they are said to be distinctly higher than in England. The living-in system is more prevalent and unemployment is probably less. Moreover, the proportions of horsemen and stockmen are very much higher than in England. It will be assumed that on the average Scottish wages are 15 per cent higher than for the corresponding categories in England. This gives us a total of £8·6 millions, or £59·4 millions for Great Britain. For the United Kingdom the total may be taken at £62 millions.

The total of wage earnings in Great Britain and

[1] Carslaw, *loc. cit.* p. 607.

Northern Ireland, at a date near to April 1931 but expressed at an annual rate, was :

	£s million
Industry	811
Agriculture . . .	62
Railways	85
Others	450
	1408

This result will now be used as a basis for a calculation of wage totals in separate years.

The problem remaining to be solved is the determination of an annual series of wage-data from the results for a single date in 1931. For this we require knowledge of the changes of the numbers of wage-earners in work, which can be obtained primarily from Unemployment Insurance returns. (Health Insurance statistics are too uncertain for any very definite calculations to be made from them.) From the Insurance returns must be deducted the numbers of insurable salary-earners, and additions must be made for workers in excepted employments, agriculture and domestic service, or aged over 64 or under 16.

From Tables 12 and 32 can be determined the number of salary-earners receiving below £250. Uninsured salary-earners in excepted occupations will be included with these, and therefore we add back all workers in excepted occupations, manual and salaried, with the exception of salary-earners receiving over £250. The number of agricultural workers is known in each year, and the number of domestic workers is assumed to be increasing at the same rate as its average over the decade 1921–31.

We can obtain an independent set of data of the amounts paid in wages for 1924. As stated above, the General Report on the 1930 Census of Production gives an estimate of the aggregate paid in wages in 1924 in the industries within its scope. Wages paid on the railways (including the wages of the shop and artisan staff) are estimated as before from the Ministry of Transport returns. In agriculture, Mr. Ramsbottom's index number shows that wages on the average were 10 per cent lower in Great Britain in 1924 than in 1930–31. It is assumed that annual earnings of all categories of agricultural workers were lower in this proportion, and the estimates of 1924 earnings thus obtained are applied to the numbers of workers in different categories in that year, giving a total of £54·8 millions in Great Britain, or £57 millions for the United Kingdom.

In the residue of wage-workers not employed by industry, agriculture or rail transport, it is assumed that the weighted average wage-rates for 1931 previously calculated, adjusted in proportion to the general fall in wage-rates between 1924 and 1931, can be used. The 1931 proportions between the sexes (2·4 million males to 1·8 million females) give us a weighted average wage of 44·2 shillings per week. Allowing for holidays, this gives an annual average of £111·8, or £116 at 1924 wage-rates. The numbers to whom this wage is applicable are determined by difference, from the total given in Table 28 (after deduction for sickness).

TABLE 26

WAGES IN 1924, UNITED KINGDOM

	Numbers (000's), excluding sick	Wages (£s million)
Census of Production industries, excluding railway workshops	6,908	857
Railways, including railway workshops	600	87
Agriculture	950	57
Others	3,437	398
Total . .	11,895	1399

The total of 11,895,000 wage-earners shown above for 1924 is after deducting 3½ per cent for sickness, and the original figure was 12,325,000. Dividing the wage total by this latter figure, we find overall average earnings to be as follows :

	£ *per annum*
1924 . . .	113·5
1931 . . .	114·9

The Ministry of Labour wage index (1924 = 100) stood at 97 for April 1931,[1] and in the absence of " bias " in the wage-earning population an average wage of £110·1 for 1931 might have been anticipated as against the £114·9 actually found. In fact, of course, the bias is considerable, due to the movement of men out of worse-paid into better-paid employment. For instance, miners and agricultural workers numbered 16·0 per cent of the wage-earning population in work in 1924, 11·6 per cent in 1931 and only 9·7 per cent in 1935. The following table gives the principal categories of low-paid workers at those three dates—referring only to persons in work.

TABLE 27

NUMBERS OF CERTAIN CLASSES OF WAGE-EARNERS IN WORK IN 1924, 1931 AND 1935

(Figures in 000's)

	Middle of Year		
	1924	1931	1935
Coal miners	1186	691	586
Agricultural workers	820	733	694
Domestics*	1485	1674	1782
Women and girls covered by unemployment insurance	2845	2944	3201
Juveniles under 16 (male and female)	900	820	1100
Juveniles, 16–18 (insured males)	564	589	462
Total of above	7800	7451	7825
As % of all wage-earners	63·3	61·5	58·7

* Estimate only—from the results of the Censuses of 1921 and 1931.

This table shows that since 1931 the decline in the proportion of lower-paid workers has continued and indeed been accelerated. The proportion of miners [2] is declining

[1] Mr. Ramsbottom's index (*J.R.S.S.*, 1935, p. 655), which is on a more comprehensive basis, stood at 96·8 in June 1931 (1924 = 100).

[2] Miners only belong to the " low-paid " category when they work a short week, as they have since 1927. If working full time, they earn above the average wage of all wage-earners, but below the average wage of adult men.

at a somewhat slower rate, but the proportion of women workers is now declining, while before 1931 it was increasing. In the seven years 1924 to 1931 the " bias " affected the figures of average annual earnings to the extent of £4·8. It will be assumed that this movement has continued at the rate of £0·7 yearly since 1931, and was linear between 1924 and 1931.

During the period since 1924, three successive index numbers of wage-rates have been calculated. Professor Bowley has published an index monthly since 1920 in the *London and Cambridge Economic Service.* In 1933 the Ministry of Labour began publication of an index number, which agreed very closely with Professor Bowley's, but was based on somewhat wider data. In 1935 Mr. E. C. Ramsbottom, Director of Statistics in the Ministry of Labour, published in the *Journal of the Royal Statistical Society* an index number on a much more comprehensive basis still, giving results half-yearly. For the years since 1926 it has agreed very closely with the Ministry of Labour's index.

In certain later calculations the Ministry of Labour's index is used, as being the most comprehensive available for short periods. For the annual figures in Table 28 adjustment is made by use of Mr. Ramsbottom's index.

The data are in such a form that it is possible, if we wish, to work out quarterly as well as annual figures of the total of wages paid. For comparison with other quarterly data, quarterly wage totals are calculated since 1929. The Ministry of Labour employment figures are corrected for seasonal variation. Other figures, being obtained by interpolation from annual data, do not need this correction.

Data for the numbers of occupied juveniles are obtained from the October 1934 issue of the *Ministry of Labour Gazette,* and of old persons from the Annual Reports of the Ministry of Health.

TABLE 28

WAGES—ANNUAL TOTALS, 1924–28 : QUARTERLY FIGURES (FREE FROM SEASONAL VARIATION), 1929–36
(Figures in 000's)

	Insured Persons in Work in Great Britain (deducting for Trade Disputes but not for Sickness)	Insured Persons in Work in N. Ireland (deducting for Trade Disputes but not for Sickness)	Occupied Juveniles under 16 (U.K.)	Occupied Workers over 65 (U.K.)	Agricultural Workers aged 16–64 (U.K.)	Domestic Workers aged 16–64 (U.K.)	Excepted Workers and Forces	Family Employment and Evasion	*Deduct*—Salary-earners below £250	Wage-earners in Work	Average Annual Earnings at 1924 Wage-rates, allowing for Bias £	Average Annual Earnings at Current Wage-rates, allowing for Bias £	Total Wages (£s million)			
1924	9,914	212	900	365	845	1183	1270	475	2839	12,325	113·5	113·5	1399			
1925	10,004	200	900	365	846	1210	1326	475	2917	12,409	114·2	115·8	1437			
1926	9,462	201	900	365	842	1237	1382	475	2995	11,869	114·9	116·4	1382			
1927	10,419	216	900	365	816	1264	1438	475	3073	12,820	115·6	116·4	1492			
1928	10,427	209	900	365	814	1291	1494	475	3151	12,824	116·3	115·3	1479			
													(i)	(ii)	(iii)	(iv)
1929	10,634	221	891	365	806	1321	1557	475	3229	13,042	115·4	113·9	368·0	372·2	373·5	372·7
1930	10,222	204	853	365	781	1349	1613	475	3307	12,553	116·1	114·2	367·0	359·5	356·4	350·7
1931	9,858	193	817	361	756	1376	1669	475	3385	12,120	116·8	112·7	342·8	343·1	337·8	342·2
1932	9,787	194	766	343	744	1405	1725	475	3434	12,126	117·2	111·4	337·7	332·8	327·8	334·6
1933	10,123	195	722	335	752	1430	1766	475	3541	12,256	118·2	111·1	331·5	334·9	344·3	350·9
1934	10,588	208	840	335	732	1432	1837	475	3619	12,853	118·9	112·2	352·7	359·4	363·1	366·9
1935	10,824	209	1066	335	715	1484	1893	475	3697	13,303	119·6	114·2	369·7	376·3	385·0	388·6
1936(i)	10,972	216	1035	335	705	1501	1928	475	3745	13,422	120·0	. .	392·6	400·8	. .	. .

(ii) *The net income of agriculture*

We may next reckon the net income of the agricultural community, including landlords, farmers and labourers, but deducting the payments made by agriculturists for the goods or services (e.g. fertilisers, transport) supplied by other industries and used up by them in the course of production.

Censuses of agricultural production were taken in England and Scotland for the year ended June 1931, and a gross output of agricultural produce of £240·4 millions was recorded ; an estimate of £250 millions may be made for the whole of the United Kingdom. This represents the produce "sold off farms" or consumed by the farmers themselves, and is net after the deduction of seeds, fodder and all other produce of home agriculture used up in the course of production, whether on the grower's farm or on another.

A figure of the true net output can be calculated in the following manner.[1] It is convenient first to add back the cereal products estimated to have been used as fodder on the farms, and then to deduct them later. From statistics of retained imports and of home production (Census of Production), figures can be obtained showing the quantities of fertilisers, cake, milling offals and other manufactured feeding-stuffs available for use in agriculture. In the case of cereals and potatoes the home output is also added in. Wheat, barley and oats, however, unlike the other products, are used partly as animals' fodder and partly for our own bread, beer and porridge. The Census of Production and the Report of the Commissioners of Excise give data from which can be estimated the quantities used for these purposes (or added net to stocks in the case of wheat) in the Censal year, and the remainder is assumed to be used as fodder. Finally, a deduction has to be made for the estimated consumption of town horses and of poultry kept by non-agriculturists. Prices are

[1] From an unpublished thesis by Miss O. S. Wells, Newnham College, Cambridge.

reckoned from the tables published by the Ministry of Agriculture, showing the price of two-ton or similar lots of fertilisers and feeding-stuffs at the principal centres, with a 15 per cent addition for the estimated costs of transport and merchanting.

The total thus obtained is £110 millions for 1930–31, including feeding-stuffs (by far the largest item), fertilisers, seeds and Irish store cattle. The estimate for feeding-stuffs checks up closely with a quite independent estimate of the average values of purchased foodstuffs consumed by each head of stock, at the prices prevailing in that year, multiplied by the numbers of each type of stock.

In order to obtain the true net output, we must allow for all other payments made to non-agriculturists. A satisfactory source of information is to be found in the detailed analysis of the accounts of over 1000 East Anglian farms made by Dr. Carslaw of the Cambridge University Farm Economics Department.[1] Table 4 in this survey shows the "miscellaneous expenses" on farms in this sample. For our purpose we should exclude rates, motor-car and petrol, and coal, which are largely, though not entirely, for household use, and expenditure recorded as capital outlay. There remain the costs of machinery, implements, tools, harness, tackle hire, fencing and draining materials, huts and sheds, transport, twine, insurance, telephone, horse-shoeing, veterinary services and certain minor expenses. These altogether add up to 11 per cent of the gross output of the farms,[2] and this proportion is nearly independent of the size of the farm. It probably gives a fair basis for a general estimate.[3]

[1] *An Economic Survey of Agriculture in the Eastern Counties of England, 1933,* published by the Department.

[2] "Expenditure in England and Wales on these sundry items (which do not appear in the official estimates of farmers' requirements) must amount to a figure in the neighbourhood of £20–30 m. annually."—Graves and Carson, *Journal of the Ministry of Agriculture,* November 1935.

[3] The estimate of net output given here differs considerably from a previous estimate made by the present writer (*Economic Journal,* September 1934). It was pointed out to me that I had not made

We thus have :

TABLE 29

Net Output of Agriculture

(£s million)

		1930–31
Agricultural output sold off farms, U.K.		250
Add back cereals		26
Gross output		276
Fertilisers, feeding-stuffs, seeds and store cattle	110	
Other purchases	30	
Landlords' repairs to buildings and cost of management	10	150
Net output		126

This figure of £126 millions represents the net income of agriculture in the United Kingdom in 1930–31 available for distribution to landlords (cost of repairs and management having already been met), tithe-owners, farmers and labourers. It is a net income computed closely in accordance with income-tax definition, but it must be noted that under the definition of " net output " used in the Census of Industrial Production the figure would have been slightly higher, as no deduction would have been made for repairs of buildings or for certain other payments—payments for services (other than transport) and not for material goods. This figure covers agriculture, poultry farming and fruit and flower farming, but not other horticulture or forestry.

adequate allowance for miscellaneous expenses ; and fodder consumption has also been much greater than was anticipated. The only official estimate of the net output of agriculture was for 1924–5, and in this no deduction was made for miscellaneous expenses, landlords' maintenance charges, or difference between wholesale and farm prices of the goods purchased by farmers.

If these net output figures are to be compared with results from *Economic Survey of Agriculture in the Eastern Counties* or similar surveys, account must be taken of the fact that such surveys generally omit small specialist farms producing poultry, fruit, etc., on which net output per man and per acre is generally highest.

For other years these figures can be only approximately calculated. The Ministry of Agriculture make annual estimates of the value of agricultural output in England and Wales for " agricultural years " (September to August for crops and June to May for livestock products), but there are no estimates from year to year of the consumption of fodder and other requirements.

In the total of £110 millions given in Table 23 for the cost of these purchases, £93 millions is represented by purchases of fodder (including cereals and potatoes grown for fodder on British farms). Annual data of fodder consumption are estimated by the following method (Table 24). The quantities of home-produced and imported fodder supplies are calculated at 1924 prices, the whole supply of wheat and other cereals being included at this stage. The home-produced supplies of cake are known for the Censal years and are estimated for the intervening years from changes in the volume of imports of oil-seeds. The total is diminished by the value of the flour and malt used for human consumption, and raised by the amount of the net value added by milling. We thus obtain a figure comprising the offals and other milled fodder products plus the unmilled grain used for stock-feeding. The figures are reduced to current prices by the Ministry of Agriculture's index of Feeding Stuffs Prices, and an addition is then made for the cost of fertilisers, seeds and imported store cattle.

The procedure is to add in (at a later stage) the net value produced by the milling industry (including the value added to the grain by transport, etc., before it reaches the mills) and to deduct the value of the flour produced, and also of the barley used for malting. The remainder will therefore consist of the value of wheat offals and other cereal products sold for fodder by the mills, and of the grain consumed raw. The amount of wheat, both home-produced and imported, used for livestock feeding, appears to be greater than has hitherto been estimated.

TABLE 30

IMPORTS OR ESTIMATED OUTPUT OF CERTAIN PRODUCTS REVALUED AT 1924 PRICES

(£s million)

	1924	1925	1926	1927	1928	1929	1930	1931	1932	1933	1934
Wheat imports	69·0	56·9	56·5	64·9	60·8	65·6	61·5	70·2	62·0	66·1	60·2
Wheat, home production	16·8	16·8	16·2	17·7	15·8	15·8	13·4	12·0	12·7	19·8	22·1
Barley imports	12·1	8·8	6·5	9·2	7·2	6·7	8·5	8·6	5·7	8·9	8·7
Barley, home production	16·2	16·4	14·6	13·6	15·9	15·6	11·8	12·0	11·8	9·8	11·6
Oats imports	4·3	3·5	3·2	2·5	3·1	2·9	4·0	3·7	2·7	2·3	1·3
Oats, home production	21·0	20·2	21·6	19·1	20·7	21·9	19·3	17·8	19·5	18·6	17·3
Maize imports	17·0	12·4	14·3	18·9	14·9	15·7	15·4	24·0	23·8	23·1	27·7
Cake imports	3·5	4·3	4·7	4·6	3·5	4·6	4·2	4·3	3·9	3·6	4·4
Cake, home production	13·7	13·3	10·9	10·2	12·0	11·8	9·5	10·6	10·6	9·9	10·0
Total	173·6	152·6	148·5	160·7	153·9	160·6	147·6	163·2	152·7	162·1	163·3
Deduct											
Flour for human consumption	70·5	72·1	67·6	67·0	68·5	67·3	65·0	65·5	67·4	65·5	65·5
Barley for malting	13·5	13·5	12·8	12·5	12·4	12·2	11·9	10·7	8·3	8·5	9·4
At current prices	89·6	67·3	61·2	75·2	74·9	75·1	45·3	48·2	48·7	49·9	53·7
Net value added by milling	18	18	18	18	18	18	18	17	17	17	17
Total	108	85	79	93	93	93	63	65	66	67	71
Estimated value at current wholesale prices of all feeding-stuffs, fertilisers, seeds and stores	154	122	113	130	131	131	95	96	96	95	99
Estimated price on farm	177	140	130	149	151	151	109	110	110	109	114

Expenditure by farmers on fertilisers and seeds was the same in 1924 as in 1930–31. Expenditure on imported store cattle is roughly estimated from changes in the numbers imported from Ireland (almost the sole source) shown in the agricultural statistics.

TABLE 31

NET OUTPUT OF AGRICULTURE, 1924–33

(£s million)

	1924	1925	1926	1927	1928	1929	1930	1931	1932	1933
England and Wales: output for calendar year	237	233·5	217	219	224	223	212	196	190	199
Estimated for U.K.	300	295	273	274	279	277	262	241	233	244
Including corn and potato crops used for fodder	327	332	300	301	306	304	288	269	259	270
Fodder, fertilisers, seeds and stores	177	140	130	149	151	151	109	110	110	109
Other purchases	36	36	33	33	34	33	32	30	29	30
Landlords' repairs, etc., to buildings	10	10	10	10	10	10	10	10	10	10
Net output	104	146	127	109	111	110	137	119	110	121

Having in view the methods of calculation, these results should not be taken as a precise measure of year-to-year fluctuations. Nevertheless, the curious maxima in 1925 and 1930 are in accordance with other experience. They represent the effect of a sudden fall in the price of cereals, not immediately accompanied by a fall in the price of the livestock products which form the larger proportion of British agricultural output.

(iii) *Earnings of salary-earners and of entrepreneurs with incomes below earned-income exemption limit*

For the year 1931, when the exemption limit was £125, the necessary calculations are made in the *Economic Journal*, September 1934, pp. 386–7.

From Table 13 and subsequent data it appears that the number of employers and of salary-earners taken together was increasing on the average at a rate of 78,000 a year between 1921 and 1931. During the same period the number of independent workers, excluding farmers, was increasing by 7000 per annum. We will assume that these rates of change were applicable to the period 1924–33. With the data of Table 12 we obtain the following results :

TABLE 32

NUMBER OF INCOMES BELOW TAX EXEMPTION LIMIT, 1924–33
(Figures in 000's)

Year in which Income was earned	Employers and Salary-earners			Independent Workers		
	Above Exemption Limit	Below	Total	Above Exemption Limit	Below	Total
1924	2355	2109*	4464*	660	601	1261
1926	2540	2080	4620	640	635	1275
1927	2583	2115	4698	645	637	1282
1928	2689	2087	4776	650	639	1289
1929	2756	2098	4854	655	641	1296
1930	3836	1096	4932	765	538	1303
1931	3810	1200	5010	770	540	1310
1932	3634	1454	5088	775	542	1317
1933	3668	1498	5166	780	544	1324

* The difference between these figures and those given by Bowley and Stamp (pp. 12 and 26) is due to the inclusion of a large number of shop-assistants.

The deduced numbers below exemption limit, in the case of independent workers at any rate, need not be regarded as well substantiated figures. The main purpose of this table is to ensure that the whole working population is covered, and for categories of persons near the borderline it does not make much difference whether they are reckoned above or below it.

For independent workers (other than farmers, whose incomes will not be reckoned here, as they are included in the net output of agriculture) it was calculated previously that the average earnings of those below the present exemption limit (£125) were £72. With exemption limits of £150 and £162 they become £86 and £92 respectively, using the same frequency distribution.

The corresponding figure obtained for the average of salaries below £125 was £85. From data given in Bowley and Stamp, the average earnings of salary-earners receiving below £150 were £90. It appears that the average salary below the limit of £162 will not be much higher. Extrapolation of the frequency distributions given by Bowley and Stamp for individual industries gives the result that there were in the aggregate at that time 106,000 salary-earners between £150 and £162, as against 1,125,000 salaries below £150. We thus deduce that the average salary below the £162 limit was £95·5.

TABLE 33

EARNED INCOME BELOW EXEMPTION LIMITS, 1924–33

(£s million)

	1924	1926	1927	1928	1929	1930	1931	1932	1933
Salaries	190	199	202	200	200	93	102	124	127
Independent workers	43	49	49	50	50	32	32	32	32
	233	248	251	250	250	125	134	156	159

(iv) *Income from property held by persons not included in the income-tax assessments*

Income from property, as defined above, is meant to refer to income from securities and land only, and not to the incomes of small entrepreneurs.

For 1924, Bowley and Stamp estimated £77 millions as the income from property due to those *whose total incomes were below £150 in 1924.* A considerable amount of this was in fact included in the assessments, in the case of persons who had earned incomes in addition to their property incomes, and also in the case of pure property incomes lying between £135 (the then exemption limit for unearned incomes) and £150—this latter class, however, being probably very small. In Chapter III, however, the incomes—property and earned—of these persons have been excluded from the totals.

The definition required here differs slightly from that adopted by Bowley and Stamp. We require to know the unearned income derived from property by persons who had an *earned* income below £125 (or whatever was the current exemption limit for earned income), or with incomes totally unearned below the current exemption limit for unearned incomes. From examination of the changes in the amount of exempted income recorded in Schedules A and C at the time of changes in the exemption limit, the following estimates are made :

	£s million
1924–5	77
1925–6 to 1930–31 . .	80
1931–2 to 1934–5 . .	70

(v) *Government income from trading services and international transactions*

The Government's income from international transactions is estimated each year by the Board of Trade as an item in the Balance of Payments. These represent mainly, but not entirely, the balance of inter-governmental debt and Reparations transactions, including certain payments which were nominally capital transactions. There are also small items representing the balance of overseas payments for the Forces, etc.

For the sake of convenience we may include the whole net balance of inter-governmental transactions, treating capital as income—with the single exception of the debt payment of £29 millions made to the United States Government in December 1932. This sum was paid in gold and was specifically treated by the British Government as a capital transaction, i.e. it was not provided for in the Budget, while other capital payments and receipts were treated as part of the ordinary Budget.

The other items to be included are Government profits from specifically trading services, i.e. those receipts which form part of the selling value of goods and services definitely " sold " to the consumer rather than being supplied out of the proceeds of taxation. For this purpose we must include profits on the Post Office, the Crown Lands, Post Office Savings Bank (the last Finance Accounts show £4,332,000 paid into the Exchequer as surplus of interest from securities held by the Post Office Savings Bank above sums paid to depositors) and the profit on the Note Issue. It has already been pointed out that local authorities' net receipts from trading services, estates, housing schemes, etc., are assessed to income-tax. Other fees and recoupments received by local authorities are all in aid of services which represent a net charge on the rates.

TABLE 34

GOVERNMENT INCOME, 1924–35

(£s million)

	1924	1925	1926	1927	1928	1929	1930	1931	1932	1933	1934	193[illegible]
International transactions	−24	−11	4	1	15	24	19	14	5	−2	7	−[illegible]
Other income . .	12	10	11	13	15	16	17	18	18	21	21	2[illegible]
Total .	−12	−1	15	14	30	40	36	32	23	19	28	1[illegible]

(vi) *Payments of rates, indirect taxes and social insurance contributions*

There are three principal forms of payment under this head. First are rates levied by local authorities, almost entirely assessed on the occupation value of buildings. Rates on commercial premises are deducted as an expense before reckoning profits for income-tax. Rates on private houses are, in the majority of cases, paid by the owner and then recovered from the occupier by increasing his rent. The index number of rents included in the Cost of Living index number is inclusive of rates.

In the case of State taxation, the principal forms of indirect taxation are included in Customs and Excise. Two other forms of taxation should also be included, namely, the tax on commercial motor vehicles (which is clearly a business expense) and Stamp Duties. The latter are obscure in their incidence but largely take the form of "expenses of production" in industry and commerce. Tax on private cars is best regarded as a direct tax. It is not of course an allowable deduction in the reckoning of taxable income (if we include cars run by doctors, etc., as commercial). Excess Profits Duty and Corporation Profits

Tax were allowable as deductions in computing income-tax, and the small sums recorded as paid under these heads in the years round 1924 must be added back.

Employers' contributions to social insurance are reckoned by them as an expense in computing taxable income. Workers' contributions, however, must be treated as direct taxes. It is convenient at this stage to include employers' payments under the Workmen's Compensation Acts. These resemble indirect taxation in the sense that they are obligatory, though in fact the payments are nearly always organised through insurance companies. The incomes of the recipients of these payments (except for that part of the employers' payments which goes in administrative expenses) have not already been included in the national income as previously reckoned.

The figures in the following table are mainly for the financial year, which differs from the calendar year by three months, but this does not appreciably affect the validity of the figures.

TABLE 35

INDIRECT TAXATION AND SOCIAL INSURANCE PAYMENTS, 1924–34

(£s million)

	1924	1925	1926	1927	1928	1929	1930	1931	1932	1933	1934	1935
)cal rates .	162·1	169·4	181·7	190·7	190·7	177·4	170·1	166·8	165·3	167·8	173·5	184·4
ıstoms and Excise	234·5	238·0	240·5	250·8	253·0	247·4	245·4	256·1	288·1	286·2	289·7	303·3
amp Duties .	22·8	24·7	24·8	27·0	30·1	25·7	20·7	17·1	19·2	22·7	24·1	25·8
.x on commercial vehicles	8	9	10	11	12	13	14	14	15	16	17	17
xcess Profits Duty and Corporation Profits Tax	18·8	13·7	8·5	1·8	1·7	2·2	3·0	2·5	2·2	1·8	2·3	1·3
nployers' contributions to social insurance and workmen's compensation	40	40	46	49	49	49	48	49	51	51	53	54
Total .	486	495	511	530	537	515	501	506	541	546	560	586

The size of the sums of money involved is striking ; and perhaps even more striking is the rise of £74 millions between 1924 and 1934. The reasons for the inclusion of these sums in the national income are set out in Chapter I and need not be restated here. Even though the prices of taxed commodities and services have not risen during this period (in the two principal commodities involved, namely, beer and tobacco, the price is now the same as it was in 1924, and in most other cases it has fallen), we must conclude that these increasing Government revenues have been at the expense of slowing down the fall in prices of a number of commodities.

(vii) *Maintenance and depreciation*

The figures hitherto assembled cover the whole of the *net* national income, using the word *net* in the sense that allowances for the maintenance, repair, depreciation and obsolescence of capital goods have been deducted from gross incomes. For many purposes we require to know gross income.

Allowances for the maintenance and depreciation of buildings were made under Schedule A amounting to £101·4 millions in 1931–2. Including the allowances which would have been made to persons and institutions exempt from tax, this figure becomes £109 millions.

The actual cost of repair and maintenance work to buildings and similar property done in 1930 was £117 millions.[1] This total, however, includes some work done on gas mains, tramways and other properties assessable under Schedule D, and some work on sewers, etc., not assessable at all. Scrutiny of the items [2] suggests that £13 millions are in the former category and £7 millions in the latter. This leaves £97 millions as the cost of repairs to properties assessed to Schedule A, while £109 millions were allowed by the Inland Revenue to cover depreciation and maintenance.

The gross annual rental of all buildings, exclusive of land and sites, is of the order of magnitude of £350 millions per annum. Death Duty returns show that their average

[1] See p. 172 below.

[2] Fourth Census of Production, Part IV, p. 188.

capitalisation may be taken at 11·1 years' purchase, giving a capital value of £3900 millions. To depreciate this value over a period of sixty years (a reasonable estimate of the average life of a building) a sinking fund of ½ per cent is required, assuming 4 per cent compound interest, or £20 millions per annum.

It appears, therefore, that in 1930 the Inland Revenue allowances fell short of providing for depreciation of buildings by about £8 millions.

In 1924 the cost of repairs and maintenance to property was £85 millions only, of which £22 millions appears to have related to properties assessable under Schedule D and £6 millions to untaxed properties. Allowances under Schedule A were £75 millions, or £82 millions including exempted properties. This gives a margin of £25 millions over the cost of repairs. Both rents and the number of years' purchase were somewhat lower in 1924 than in 1930, and so the figure for annual depreciation requirements might theoretically be reckoned a little lower in 1924 than in 1930. However, owing to the high cost of repair work in 1924, there was some tendency to postpone repairs in that year, while possibly arrears were being met in 1930.

Taking one year with another, it is permissible to say that the scale of Inland Revenue allowances under Schedule A provides for the cost of both repairs and depreciation. Under Schedule D, wear-and-tear allowances of £87·6 millions were made in 1931, and of £88·8 millions (under the new scale) in 1932. Taking into account firms making losses, and assuming that the new scale better represents modern conditions, we can take a figure of £95 millions as giving the value of wear and tear in 1931. To this must be added the cost of repairs and maintenance, of renewals on the railways,[1] and of "maintenance and minor improvement" on the roads and depreciation of Post Office equipment, which as publicly owned services are not covered by tax assessments. The cost of repair and maintenance work other than on railways, roads or buildings,

[1] See p. 177.

can be determined from the Census of Production, and is given on p. 178 below as £87·6 millions for 1924 and £72·5 millions for 1930. The Annual Report on the Administration of the Road Fund gives £36 millions as the cost of maintenance (including minor repairs) of roads and bridges in 1931, nearly half of which was on unclassified roads. For years prior to 1931 the full costs are not shown, but from the figures published it appears that the total was about £39 millions in the period 1924–9.

Construction and maintenance work done on the railways, excluding work done on private wagons, was £70·7 millions in 1924 and £60·9 millions in 1930; deducting capital outlay included in the above, we obtain figures of £61·6 millions and £54·6 millions in the two years. Maintenance of other untaxable properties, including the telegraph and telephone system, can be estimated at £8 millions in 1924 and £9 millions in 1930.

The total is compiled in the following table. Wear-and-tear allowances are given approximately, and the 10 per

TABLE 36

Maintenance and Depreciation, 1924–34

(£s million)

	1924	1925	1926	1927	1928	1929	1930	1931	1932	1933	1934
Schedule A allowances	82	82	88	89	93	95	99	109	112	115	118
Wear-and-tear allowances	55	70	75	75	85	95	100	95	92	100	105
Railway renewals and maintenance	62	61	52	59	57	57	55	49	46	45	46
Post Office depreciation	7	7	7	8	8	8	8	8	9	9	9
Roads maintenance	39	39	39	39	39	39	36	36	33	33	34
Maintenance of other untaxed property	8	8	8	8	9	9	9	9	9	9	9
Other repair and maintenance	88	86	84	82	80	78	73	69	65	61	65
Total	341	353	353	360	371	381	380	375	366	372	386

cent increase in 1932 is smoothed out over the preceding years. The railway statistics are interpolated from the maintenance figures shown in their annual accounts. The cost of other repair and maintenance (shown in the last line) in years between 1924 and 1930 is estimated by interpolation.

The Import Duties Act Inquiry of 1933 shows that

there was a considerable fall between 1930 and 1933 in expenditure on engineering and electrical repairs. Some recovery may be estimated in 1934.

The upward trend of this total is noticeable.

We are now in a position to compute the whole national income for each of the years 1924 and 1926–33. The lack of data for 1925 is due to changes in the assessment of income-tax around that period, and the gap can only be bridged indirectly.

The following deductions must be made: (i) income belonging to foreigners, (ii) internal national debt interest included in the assessments, (iii) wages of agricultural workers, which have been counted twice.

By adding back all depreciation and maintenance payments which have previously been deducted as costs of production, we obtain a true measure of *gross national income.* This is a very concrete concept, representing the actual aggregate value of finished goods and services produced. The concept of net national income is not quite so clear. To obtain this we must deduct all costs of maintaining and depreciating existing capital. We have shown above that the Inland Revenue allowances are approximately accurate in the case of depreciation, but in the case of repair work we should, strictly speaking, deduct not the value of repairs actually performed in any one year, but the value *properly attributable* to that year—which may be very different.

Over the period in question it may have been the case that during the years 1931–3 actual expenditure on repairs fell short of expenditure properly attributable. It is, however, very difficult to say in which years, if any, a corresponding excess of expenditure occurred. The whole question is so uncertain that the figures will for the present be left as they stand.

This series differs in definition from previous calculations of the net national income, in the inclusion of all rates and indirect taxation. Sir Alfred Flux (*J.R.S.S.*, 1929, Part I), in his calculation of the national income from

TABLE 37

THE NATIONAL INCOME, 1924–33

(£s million)

	1924	1925	1926	1927	1928	1929	1930	1931	1932	1933
Incomes above exemption limit (Table 21)	2108	2329	2178	2256	2224	2270	2368	2023	1956	1983
Wages (Table 25) .	1399	1437	1382	1492	1479	1486	1434	1366	1333	1362
Agricultural income (Table 28)	104	146	127	109	111	110	137	119	110	121
Earned and unearned income below exemption limit (Table 30 *et seq.*)	310	328	328	331	330	330	195	204	226	229
Government income (Table 31)	−12	−1	15	14	30	40	36	32	23	19
Rates and indirect taxes (Table 32)	486	495	511	530	537	515	501	506	541	546
Maintenance and depreciation (Table 33)	341	353	353	360	371	381	380	375	366	372
Deduct :										
Internal National Debt Interest	278	288	279	284	283	278	265	274	260	212
Income due to foreigners	25	25	25	25	25	25	25	25	25	25
Agricultural wages .	57	64	64	64	64	64	63	62	60	61
NATIONAL INCOME :										
Gross (i.e. including maintenance and depreciation)	4376	4710	4526	4719	4710	4765	4698	4264	4210	4334
Net (i.e. excluding maintenance and depreciation)	4035	4357	4173	4359	4339	4384	4318	3889	3844	3962

Census of Production data, added in Customs and Excise Duties but not local rates or other indirect taxes. Bowley and Stamp included only employers' contributions to social insurance. The present writer in his previous book included only these contributions and rates on commercial premises. Dr. Coates' [1] estimate for 1931 included only employers' contributions ; and no deduction was made for National Debt interest and pensions.

In *Ways and Means : A Series of Broadcast Talks on the National Income*, Mr. Geoffrey Crowther gave £3500 millions as the national income for 1931 and £4000 millions for 1935, but gave neither source nor definition.

Allowing for these differences of definition, and deducting maintenance and depreciation, we have the following comparison with previous estimates :

[1] Manchester Statistical Society, December 1931.

TABLE 38

NATIONAL INCOME COMPARED WITH PREVIOUS ESTIMATES

(£s million)

	1924	1926	1927	1928	1929	1930	1931
Net income as determined above	4035	4173	4359	4339	4384	4318	3889
Bowley and Stamp: as given	3803	..	..	..	..	..	..
Adjusted to new definition	4255	..	..	..	..	..	..
Sir Alfred Flux: as given	3975	..	..	..	..	..	..
Adjusted to new definition	4226	..	..	..	..	..	..
Colin Clark: as given	3586	3684	3887	3849	3996	3938	3499
Adjusted to new definition	3977	4071	4287	4256	4391	4323	3890
Dr. Coates: as given	..	..	..	..	..	..	3842
Adjusted to new definition	..	..	..	..	..	..	3945

For 1924, the new estimate comes out higher than the present writer's previous estimate, but below the Bowley-Stamp and Flux estimates. The present writer's estimates in *The National Income, 1924–1931*, appear to have been too low over the period 1924 to 1928, but are closely confirmed for the later years. The precision of Dr. Coates' total, considering that it was estimated actually during the year 1931 to which it relates, is most remarkable, but the details of his estimate cannot be so closely confirmed.

Although the growth and distribution of incomes will be dealt with in later chapters, one or two comments may be made at this stage. Gross money income jumped sharply between 1924 and 1925, and then did not increase appreciably between 1925 and 1929. There was a sharp drop in 1926. After 1929, the drop in 1930 was slight, but 1931 and 1932 fell very heavily below the 1929 maximum.

For the year 1933 the annual figure is only slightly above that of 1932. Examination of the quarterly data given in Chapter IX shows, however, that 1933 was a year of rapid recovery from the second quarter onwards.

This upward movement continued through 1934 and 1935. Anticipating the results of the short-period analysis of the national income, which can be kept currently up to date, we can give the following figures for national income in 1934 and 1935 :

	£s million	
	Gross	Net
1934 . . .	4624	4238
1935 . . .	4926	4530

The money value of the national income in 1935 thus overpassed the previous peak of 1929, and its real value, after allowing for changes in prices, showed a considerably greater rise.

CHAPTER V

THE DISTRIBUTION OF THE PRODUCT OF INDUSTRY

It is possible to make two separate analyses of the distribution of the national income. The first is an analysis of its distribution between factors of production, distinguishing separately :

(1) Wages.
(2) Salaries (i.e. contractual earnings of all non-manual workers, including clerks and shop-assistants).
(3) Rents of land and buildings.
(4) Profits and Interest—
  (*a*) from overseas ;
  (*b*) home produced.

This analysis is made possible owing to the specification of sources of income in the Inland Revenue assessments. The analysis can be made from the above data for each year from 1924 to 1935, and the results can claim almost as high a degree of precision as the Inland Revenue aggregates.

Most interesting comparisons can also be made with 1911. The data for this year are given in Professor Bowley's *Division of the Product of Industry*. This is a work of remarkable statistical boldness, and its material is very condensed, differing considerably in scope and style from Professor Bowley's later work. The most interesting table, from our present point of view, is one analysing separately the distribution of income in industry, agriculture, transport and other economic sectors. It is possible to make a comparable analysis for 1930.

The second analysis is by personal incomes irrespective of source, i.e. an analysis showing the number of incomes, and the proportion of national income taken, by persons with incomes over £2000, £250 and various other specified figures. This calculation presents considerably greater difficulties and is made for the years 1929 and 1932.

In the analysis of distribution between factors of production we must confine ourselves to the four headings enumerated above, as the Inland Revenue returns do not make possible any finer distinction. It is thus not possible to separate interest from profits. Up to 1924 the Inland Revenue statistics of Actual Income distinguished between " earned " and " unearned " incomes, but this is not a distinction of importance in economic analysis. A man with capital invested in his own business was reckoned as having earned income from it, but if he held ordinary shares in another business the income was held to be unearned.

We may first proceed to the analysis of income-distribution to the factors of production. The figures for wages are included as such in Table 37, and figures for 1934 and 1935 are prepared by the same method. That part of the national income which is intercepted by the State and local authorities in the form of indirect taxation and local rates, and also profits on the Post Office, the Post Office Savings Bank and similar exactions, is shown separately. Figures are available showing the amount of income derived from property held overseas, which are subtracted to leave the figure of home-produced income. For this purpose are used the annual Board of Trade estimates of the income from overseas investments and also the income derived from " short interest, commissions, etc." This latter is of an ambiguous nature, but seems to partake more nearly of the nature of the income from property than from " export of services ".

The income of salary-earners is taken each year from the Schedule E assessments, with an addition for the income of salary-earners below exemption limit (Table 33). The current figures given do not show the assessments for years later than 1933 ; it is assumed that from 1933 to

1935 the total paid in salaries increased by £15 millions per annum, the average rate of increase over the period 1924–9.

The income from rents is taken from the Schedule A assessments, with the addition of an allowance for the net income from rents of charities and of persons below the exemption limit. Figures at present available show the income up to the year 1934. Between 1934 and 1935 a rise of £5 millions is assumed. We thus have the following table. The figure for profits and interest is obtained by difference.[1]

Figures for the year 1911 are taken from Professor Bowley's *Division of the Product of Industry*. Income from National Debt Interest and Old Age Pensions is excluded, making the definition of income the same as that now used. Professor Bowley gives a figure of £194 millions for income from overseas, which is raised to £220 millions to allow for short interest, commissions, etc.

In this work Professor Bowley classed shop-assistants as wage-earners, while now they are classed as salary-earners. 1,060,000 male and 410,000 female wage-earners engaged in " dealing " in 1911 have therefore been transferred to the salary-earning class. It is assumed that their average annual incomes were £57·4 and £32·5 respectively, i.e. the general averages for industrial workers. This transfer explains the difference of the figure of the proportion going to wages from the figure previously given.

The table on page 94 deserves careful examination. It gives the distribution of incomes over the whole trade cycle, and makes possible the observation of both cyclical and secular tendencies.

In the first place, the decline in relative importance of overseas income may be noted. In 1911 income from overseas represented 11·0 per cent of home-produced income. After falling very low after the War, it revived during the period 1926–9 to nearly 8 per cent of home-produced income. There was then a heavy fall to a mini-

[1] In the corresponding table given in my previous book, certain Government income was included with profits.

TABLE 39

DISTRIBUTION IN INCOME BETWEEN FACTORS OF PRODUCTION 1911 AND 1924–35

(£s million)

	1911	1924	1925	1926	1927	1928	1929	1930	1931	1932	1933	1934	1935
Home-produced income	1990	3755	4047	3863	4046	4024	4069	4043	3689	3669	3772	4033	4315
Income from Overseas .	220	280	310	310	313	315	315	275	200	175	190	205	215
Ratio of Overseas to Home-produced income	**11·0**	**7·5**	**7·7**	**8·0**	**7·7**	**7·8**	**7·7**	**6·8**	**5·4**	**4·8**	**5·0**	**5·1**	**5·0**
Net Government income *	148	435	455	487	505	528	516	501	502	531	532	554	570
Per cent of Home-produced income	**7·4**	**10·6**	**11·2**	**12·6**	**12·4**	**13·1**	**12·7**	**12·4**	**13·6**	**14·5**	**14·1**	**13·8**	**13·2**
Home-produced income less Government income	1842	3320	3592	3376	3541	3496	3553	3542	3187	3138	3240	3479	3745
Distribution of above :													
Wages . . .	728	1399	1437	1382	1492	1479	1486	1434	1366	1333	1362	1442	1520
Per cent . . .	**39·5**	**42·1**	**40·0**	**40·9**	**42·1**	**42·3**	**41·8**	**40·5**	**42·8**	**42·5**	**42·0**	**41·5**	**40·5**
Salaries . . .	288	841	890	900	912	922	944	898	885	890	907	922	937
Per cent . . .	**15·6**	**25·4**	**24·8**	**26·7**	**25·8**	**26·4**	**26·6**	**25·3**	**27·8**	**28·3**	**28·0**	**26·5**	**25·0**
Profits and interest .	623	834	1014	823	853	801	821	902	620	590	642	781	949
Per cent . . .	**33·8**	**25·1**	**28·2**	**24·4**	**24·1**	**22·9**	**23·1**	**25·5**	**19·5**	**18·8**	**19·8**	**22·4**	**25·4**
Rents . . .	203	246	251	271	284	294	302	308	316	325	329	334	339
Per cent . . .	**11·1**	**7·4**	**7·0**	**8·0**	**8·0**	**8·4**	**8·5**	**8·7**	**9·9**	**10·4**	**10·2**	**9·6**	**9·1**

* See footnote on p. 102.

mum of 4·8 per cent in 1932, and there has only been a very slight subsequent rise.

The next point which may be noticed is the slowly rising tendency of indirect taxation. In 1911 7·4 per cent and in 1925 11·2 per cent of the current selling value of home-produced goods and services was taken in the form of State and local indirect taxes. Subsequent years saw the addition of silk and petrol to the list of taxed commodities, while in general the system of indirect taxation has been so designed as to fall upon a number of commodities and services whose consumption is increasing. The figure reached its maximum in 1932, when the duties on beer and petrol were raised to new high levels (the former has subsequently been reduced). During the last three years, however, the yield of indirect taxation has not risen so rapidly as the national income, but remains well above the relative level of a decade earlier.

Turning now to the more specific factors of production, we notice first that, in accordance with the generalisation which has been often made previously, wages represent a high share of the national income in times of slump and a low share in times of boom. Wages took their highest share of the national income in 1931 and 1932, their lowest in 1925.

It must be noted, however, that the years 1925 and 1930 were abnormal in an important respect. They were both years of rapidly falling prices of basic commodities, not accompanied by any corresponding fall in the price of finished industrial products. The result was that for a short time profit margins were considerably increased. In ordinary industrial accounting, these profits were more than offset by the necessity for writing down the value of stocks and materials, which caused some firms very heavy losses. As a result, the high aggregate profits shown for these years, and the high proportion which they bore to the whole national income, although representing a genuine surplus of proceeds over costs of production, yet would not have been reckoned as a profit in ordinary accounting.

Omitting these two years, and also 1926 owing to the

big labour disputes of that year, wages relative to the national income stood at their post-War minimum in 1934 and 1935, followed by 1929. Profits and interest stood at their post-War maximum in 1935 at 25·4 per cent of the national income. In 1929 they stood comparatively low at 23·1 per cent and in 1924 at 25·1 per cent.

Between 1911 and the post-War period there seem to have been certain permanent shifts in the distribution of the national income. The first is a slight permanent rise in the proportion of the national income taken by wages. 1911 was a year of active trade and low unemployment, and the share of wages in the national income was probably a little lower than it was in the more depressed pre-War years. It should be compared with years like 1929 or 1935, in which case it appears that the share of wages in the national income now claims an extra 2 per cent of the product as compared with twenty-five years ago. It is interesting to notice that the rise in average wages between 1911 and 1929 was about 90 per cent if we use Professor Bowley's index number, which takes into account the transfer of workers from worse-paid to better-paid occupations. The average income per head of all occupied persons in work rose by approximately 75 per cent during that period; it thus follows that the average rate of remuneration of non-wage-earners must have risen by a considerably smaller proportion. This rise in wage-rates relative to other incomes was associated with some increase in unemployment, but the share of labour in the income of the community was in the aggregate somewhat raised. When 1935 is compared with 1929, however, there has been a decline in wage-rates and an increase in the average incomes of non-wage-earners, but at the same time there has been a rise in unemployment as substantial as that between 1911 and 1929.

Attention may be next drawn to the share of the national income taken by rents. Incomes drawn from rents are more stable than almost all other types of income, and as a result the proportion of the national income going to rent rises most during depressions and falls most heavily during periods of good trade. It will be seen that the proportion of the national income going to rent reached a maximum in 1932 and since then has fallen heavily. In 1932 it just failed to reach the pre-War level. Ever since 1924, however, the trend has been upwards. Rents increased more rapidly than the national income during the period of expansion 1924–9. It appears that, now with a slower rate of increase, the share of rents is gradually rising again to the level which it held in 1911.

The explanation of the low level in 1924 is of course in the operation of the Rent Restriction Acts, by which the rent of the majority of working-class and middle-class houses was fixed at 40 per cent above the 1914 level. New houses were not subject to these Acts, and as the years went by a number of old houses became derestricted for various reasons. Since 1931 certain classes of houses have been derestricted by legislation.

It is not possible to distinguish the rents of land from the rents of buildings in the Inland Revenue statistics. The net incomes received from rents and tithe on agricultural land included in this total amount to £38 millions in recent years. In this figure is included, however, the value of farmhouses and farm buildings, drainage and other improvements not naturally created, and it is probably the case that the pure economic rent of agricultural land is very small.

Still greater difficulties lie in the way of the determination of the pure economic rent of urban land. Proposals for the taxing of land values were included in the Finance Act of 1931, which necessitated making a valuation of all sites. This valuation was to have been made on the assumption that each site in turn was clear of buildings, with all the buildings around assumed to be still standing. The Inland Revenue commenced the determination of the annual value of all land by this procedure, but the valuation has since been suspended, and no figures of site value are available.

An estimate of the pure economic rent of urban land can, however, be prepared by a method for which I am indebted to Dr. H. W. Singer.[1] Broadly speaking, his method is to compare the changes in the annual value of buildings, between the reassessment years, when their current letting values are determined, and in other years, when only the letting value of *new* buildings is added to the assessments. Assuming that the number of new buildings in the reassessment year itself was similar to that in adjacent years, and allowing for demolitions and the value of sites newly built on, he is able to analyse the assessments in each valuation year to show how much is due to the original cost of the buildings and how much to site rents. An adjustment is then made to allow for changes in the cost of building between the time when the buildings were erected and the valuation year in question. He then has figures analysing the valuation of buildings into the *annual income from existing buildings required to provide for their long-period replacement at current building costs, and the remainder which represents pure site rent*. The Inland Revenue valuations began in 1845, and an assumption was made as to the amount of site value included at that date. In the big cities where most of the urban site rents originate, areas built up by 1845 now represent mainly commercial building sites; areas built up since 1845 largely, but by no means entirely, housing sites. In Table 40 are given the figures for 1910 and 1931 for England and Wales.

It appears that the revenue from urban buildings comprised about £50 millions of pure site rents in 1911, but that in 1931, owing to the operation of the Rent Restriction Acts, long leases and other factors, the revenue derived from urban buildings was insufficient to pay for their maintenance and interest and depreciation on their capital (replacement) value.[2] Since 1931, owing to the fall

[1] In a Cambridge doctoral dissertation at present unpublished.

[2] This, of course, does not necessarily imply that urban property-owning has been unprofitable throughout the post-War period. So long

TABLE 40

BUILDING VALUES AND SITE RENTS

(£s million)

	Aggregate Value	Building Value	Site Value
1910 :			
Areas built up before 1845 .	67	32	35
Areas built up after 1845 .	129	115	14
Total . .	196	147	49
1931 :			
Areas built up before 1845 .	94	64	30
Areas built up after 1845 .	300	341	-41
Total . .	394	405	-11

in the rate of interest and in maintenance and replacement costs, and a slight rise in rents, a surplus has reappeared.

It is held by some that most of the rent of agricultural land in this country is required to meet interest and depreciation on the value of improvements, leaving comparatively little for pure rent.

The most striking feature of Table 39 is the increase in the proportion of the national income taken by salaries. Professor Bowley's original figures for 1911 have been altered so as to make them agree as closely as possible with the definition of "salary-earner" now used. The figures of the amount of salaries paid in 1934 and 1935, as explained above, have had to be estimated, and too much importance must not be attached to them. Between 1911 and 1929, however, 11 per cent of the national income was added to the income of salary-earners. Their numbers during the same period have risen from 3,140,000 to 4,342,000,[1] which, though substantial, by no means accounts for their increased share in the national income.

Is it the case that the decline in the share of profits and

as there are a considerable number of pre-1914 buildings in existence, rents received from them probably provide a profitable return on their *actual* cost of building, but not on their *replacement* cost.

[1] The former figure also includes Southern Ireland.

the increase in the share of salaries is merely a reflection of the transfer of functions from independent employers to salaried managers? Some light can be thrown on this question by the analysis in Table 41 of the numbers and the share of the national income taken by profit- and salary-earners. In 1911 the income-tax exemption limit was £160, and the numbers and income of salary-earners above this level can be given. Fortunately, this corresponds fairly closely in purchasing power with an income of £250 today. It must be noted that Professor Bowley's figures referred to the then boundaries of the United Kingdom, including Southern Ireland. Separate figures for the number and income of salary-earners cannot be obtained for this territory, but comparability is not seriously affected. In the case of employers and independent workers the distinction is of more importance, as a very high proportion of the population of Southern Ireland are of this category. The Census of the Irish Free State of 1926 gives the numbers of employers and independent workers in that country, which can be added to those for Great Britain and Northern Ireland. As has been previously pointed out, the number of " employers " in Great Britain is not known (i.e. men managing businesses of which they themselves are the proprietors) and can only be estimated.

The table relates to occupied persons exclusive of unemployed. The Census of 1931 was compiled to show the data in this form. For 1911 it was assumed that unemployment amounted to 500,000 among wage-earners, and was inappreciable among salary-earners.[1] Soldiers and sailors serving abroad were added back to the Census of Population.

This table draws attention to a most striking growth in the " salariat ". The numbers of well-paid salary-earners have increased nearly threefold since 1911, and their share of the national income has risen from 7 per cent to 13–15 per cent. Their incomes appear to fluctuate in the same

[1] The incomes of salary-earners below £250 are derived in Table 46 below, and the incomes above £250 by difference.

TABLE 41

NUMBERS AND SHARE OF INCOME TAKEN BY PROFIT- AND SALARY-EARNERS

	Numbers (000's)	% of Occupied Population in Work	% Share of Home-produced National Income
Salaries above £160 (1911) .	385	1·9	7·0
Salaries above £250 (1931) .	1035	5·6	(1929) 14·7 (1932) 12·6
Employers and independent workers (1911)	2830	14·2	33·8
Gt. Britain and N. Ireland (1931)	2000 (approx.)	12·0 (Gt. Britain and N. Ireland and Irish Free State)	* (1929) 23·1 (1931) 19·5 (1932) 18·8
Irish Free State (1926) .	374		
Salaries below £160 (1911) .	2755	13·8	8·6
Salaries below £250 (1929) .	3229	15·9	11·9

* Great Britain and Northern Ireland.

direction as profits, perhaps consisting to a considerable extent of commissions and similar forms of variable income. It will be noticed that the major part of the increase in the salaried population is in this higher category. The numbers and incomes of the lower-paid salary-earners have not increased nearly so rapidly.

When we examine the other part of the proposition, that salary-earners are displacing independent employers, we find that the number of employers and independent workers has shown a decline relative to the total occupied population somewhat less than the increase in the number of salary-earners. Figures for the incomes of this category in the Irish Free State are not available, but if they had been included it appears that the post-War figures of the share of profits in the national income would have been higher by only about 0·2 per cent.[1] Comparing 1911 and 1929, 10·5 per cent of the national income has been lost to " profits ", of which 7·7 per cent has been taken by " higher

[1] See Kiernan, " National Income of the Irish Free State ", *Economic Journal*, 1933.

salaries ". The remainder has gone to labour and to " lower salaries ".

We can now proceed to examine the distribution of individual incomes. The data for this purpose are not adequate and only a rough classification can be made. The analysis is made for the two years 1929 and 1932. These years are chosen as representing extreme conditions of good and bad trade. It will be seen from Table 39 that the distribution of income was relatively most adverse to labour in 1929, and most adverse to profits in 1932. They are also both close to the Census year 1931.

The first step is the distinction of personal and non-personal incomes. It was pointed out in Chapter I that the national income differs in a number of important respects from the aggregate of individual incomes, and these points are set out in the table which follows.

TABLE 42

PERSONAL AND NON-PERSONAL INCOMES, 1929 AND 1932

(£s million)

	1929	1932
Net national income	4384	3844
Government net income	−516	−531
Income of charities	−41	−43
Writing-down of inventories	−81	−51
Undistributed company profits, etc.	−290	−120
Trading losses not deducted from assessments	+25	+115
National Debt interest	+260	+278
Personal incomes (including £75 millions of incomes evading tax)	3741	3492

The first four headings represent items of national income not accruing to particular individuals. The next two items must be added back[1] if we wish to obtain

[1] For this particular calculation, which is a comparison of *net* incomes, we must use the figure of Government income after deduction of the cost of upkeep of the roads. This has been deducted in estimating the net national income, but is not a deduction which has been allowed for in the calculation of any personal income.

the total of individual incomes rather than social income. The adding back of the figure of losses may require some explanation. The figure of losses not allowed for in tax assessments was deducted in the calculation of the social income. It will be seen that it was the case that a certain number of positive individual incomes were thus offset by certain negative incomes, largely incomes of companies. When an individual or company is carrying on two branches of business, a loss made at one can be offset against the profits in another for purposes of income-tax assessment.

The items given are all taken from previous tables, with the exception of "Undistributed company profits, etc." Undistributed company profits were estimated at £194 millions for 1924 in the Report of the Committee on National Debt and Taxation, and profit statistics compiled by *The Economist* show that the level of undistributed profits was approximately the same in 1929. In addition there were some £90 millions of other non-personal incomes (income accruing in the hands of insurance companies, etc.).[1]

For 1932, we can make use of an answer given to a parliamentary question on the 23rd May 1933, relating to the yield of income-tax and surtax in that year (i.e. assessed on the profits of 1932). From this it appeared that £250 millions of income- and surtax was collected from individual incomes, leaving £29 millions of income-tax from non-personal incomes, representing £120 millions of income.

The only incomes for which a detailed analysis of distribution is given by the Inland Revenue are incomes above £2000 a year assessable to surtax.[2] The principal practical difficulty in using these figures lies in the fact that assess-

[1] Mr. A. L. Beck, in discussion of paper by Mr. L. R. Connor, *J.R.S.S.*, 1928.

[2] The following paragraphs were written before the reading of Sir Josiah Stamp's paper to the Royal Statistical Society on 19th May 1936. The figures and conclusions given below agree in outline with the conclusions reached in that paper.

ments to surtax may be made any time up to nearly six years after the end of the period in which the income was earned. Thus the last completed year for which surtax statistics are given in the 78th Report of the Commissioners of Inland Revenue, issued in 1936, is 1928–9.

The examination of a series of past reports, however, makes possible some generalisations which will enable this difficulty to be overcome. The bulk of the surtax is in fact assessed within a year or two, and the completion of the assessments during the remaining years is linear through time.

The following table can be deduced from a graphical examination of the year-by-year increases in assessments.

TABLE 43

INCREASES IN SURTAX ASSESSMENTS DURING THE SIX-YEAR ASSESSMENT PERIOD

Number of Years before Complete Assessment is due	Percentage Deficiency	
	Numbers of Taxpayers	Aggregate Incomes
1 year . . .	0·8	0·9
2 years . . .	1·6	1·8
3 ,, . . .	2·3	2·6
4 ,, . . .	3·1	3·5

By the use of this table it is possible to give estimates of the completed number and assessments of surtax-payers up to the year 1932–3 (i.e. incomes earned for that year).

TABLE 44

INCOMES LIABLE TO SURTAX, 1928–32

	Numbers (000's)	Aggregate Income (£s million)
1928–9 . .	108·4	599·5
1929–30 . .	109·8	598·5
1930–31 . .	102·1	554·4
1931–2 . . .	95·5	487·9
1932–3 . . .	88·7	436·2

Table 45 gives the detailed results for the years 1929 and 1932.

TABLE 45

CUMULATIVE TOTALS OF NUMBERS OF SURTAX-PAYERS ABOVE CERTAIN INCOME LEVELS

Income	1929		1932	
	Nos.	Income (£s million)	Nos.	Income (£s million)
Over £100,000	142	29·2	88	15·2
£75,000–	264	39·7	133	19·1
£50,000–	545	56·6	313	29·9
£40,000–	826	69·1	475	37·2
£30,000–	1,395	88·6	823	49·2
£25,000–	1,950	103·8	1,164	58·5
£20,000–	2,956	126·3	1,719	70·7
£15,000–	4,888	159·4	2,929	92·0
£10,000–	9,946	220·8	6,411	134·1
£8,000–	14,340	260·1	9,473	161·5
£7,000–	17,766	285·7	11,898	179·7
£6,000–	22,609	317·1	15,612	203·8
£5,000–	30,095	358·0	21,167	234·3
£4,000–	41,977	411·1	30,655	276·8
£3,000–	63,583	485·6	47,377	338·1
£2,500–	82,024	536·1	64,117	381·3
£2,000–	109,762	598·4	88,711	436·6

Information with regard to incomes below this level can only be obtained for the incomes above and below two particular points. The first of these is the income-tax exemption limit, which was £125 in 1932 and £162 in 1929. We also have the number of incomes above and below £250. For independent workers the income distribution previously given is used. In the case of employers, it is assumed that 100,000 small employers make incomes less than £250, aggregating £20 millions. In the case of unoccupied persons with incomes above the tax-exemption limit, it is assumed that the proportions above and below £250 per annum are the same as the proportions of occupied persons above and below that figure. No estimate can possibly be made of the number of unoccupied persons below tax-exemption limit receiving incomes. It may be several millions. The majority of the incomes concerned are very small.

In Table 46 the figures estimated as above are given in italics.

It will be remembered that this table relates to personal incomes as earned, and includes no incomes from Unemployment Benefit, Public Assistance, etc., but includes National Debt Interest. Also a man earning e.g. £120, with £10 income from property, will be classed below £125, as the data refer only to earned incomes.

TABLE 46

NUMBERS (000's) AND AGGREGATE INCOMES (£s million) IN CERTAIN INCOME GROUPS, 1929 AND 1932

	Numbers							
	1929				1932			
	Under £162	£162–£250	Over £250	Total	Under £125	£125–£250	Over £250	Total
Wage-earners .	12,283	759	..	13,042	9608	2365	..	11,973
Salary-earners below £250	2,098	1131	..	3,229	1454	2009	..	3,463
Independent workers	641	275	380	1,296	542	387	387	1,316
Employers and higher salaried workers	..	*100*	1525	1,625	..	*100*	1525	1,625
Unoccupied . .	Not known	*140*	*120*	260*	Not known	*356*	*140*	496*
Total .	15,022	2405	2025	19,452*	11,604	5217	2052	18,873*

	Aggregate Income, 1929				Aggregate Income, 1932			
	Under £162	£162–£250	Over £250	Total	Under £125	£125–£250	Over £250	Total
Wage-earners .	1341	145	..	1486	933	400	..	1333
Salary-earners below £250	200	222	..	422	124	330	..	454
Independent workers	60	54			42	71		
Employers and higher salaried workers	..	*20*	1591	1833	..	*20*	1464	..
Unoccupied . .	80	*28*			70	*38*		1705
Total .	1681	469	1591	3741	1169	859	1464	3492

* Excluding unoccupied persons with incomes below exemption limit. If this limit had been the same in both years, the 1929 totals would have been about 200,000 higher.

The available data may be plotted on a diagram to be examined for a Pareto curve. Pareto's famous generalisation can be most concisely expressed in the form, that the logarithm of the number of persons above a certain income

DIAGRAM I

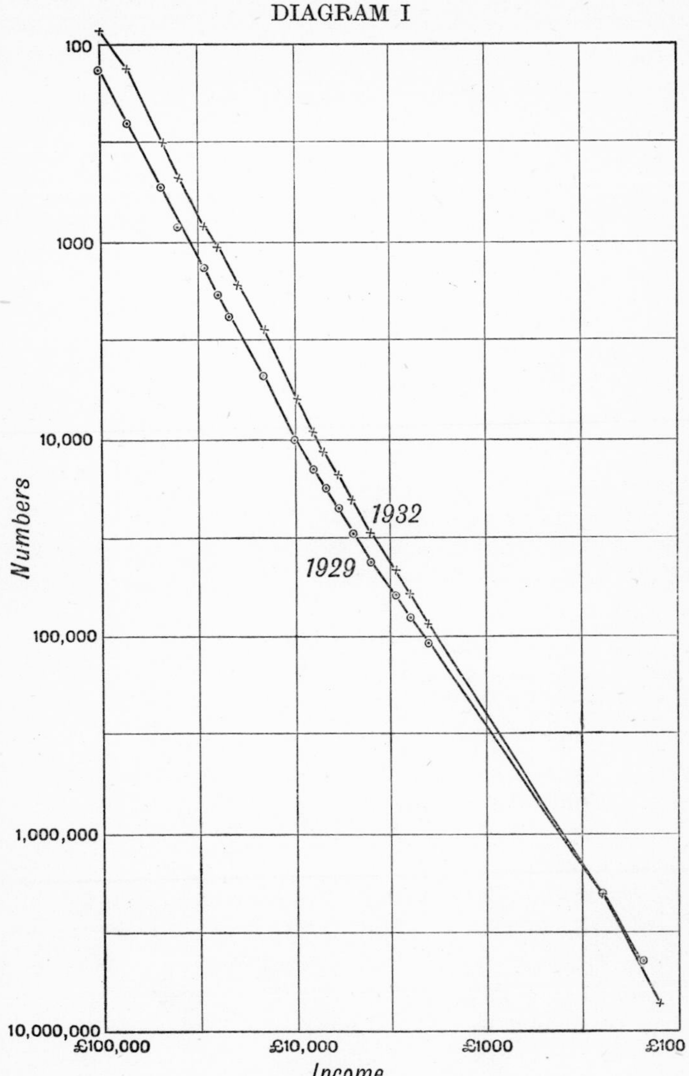

Income Distribution, 1929 and 1932

and the logarithm of the income are in a linear relation. The data are plotted on logarithmic scale in Diagram I.

This generalisation (which is purely empirical) cannot, of course, be true for the whole range. As we reach lower income limits, above which must lie nearly the whole of the earning population (i.e. at the bottom right-hand corner of the diagram), the curve must turn round and become asymptotic to a horizontal line representing the total numbers of the population.

Translated into the logarithmic form, the surtax data are seen to cover more than half of the whole range of the diagram. Our next point shows the number of incomes above £250, which may be regarded as established for the year 1931, but only conjectural for 1929 and 1932. We next have two well-established data of the number of incomes above £162 in 1929 and £125 in 1932.

Careful examination will show that the lines are by no means straight, but are very definitely curved. Both curves can with some confidence be produced to the point for £250, after which they appear to change direction. This interpolation is arbitrary, but can be checked in a way shown below, and appears to be accurate.

The curve for 1932 is much steeper (i.e. more equalitarian). It cuts the 1929 curve at about the £250 point and then appears to cross it. This is the effect of the fall of a number of salaries and profits to a lower income grade than they had occupied in 1929.

The question now arises whether readings from this curve can be used to give the numbers and aggregate incomes of persons in the range £250 to £2000, for which no direct data are available. The validity of such a procedure can be tested by interpolating at close intervals to prepare estimates of the aggregate income of each income class and summing these over the whole range £250–£2000. This total may be checked against the total obtained by deduction from the national income, and we thus have an independent test of the validity of our assumption as to the shape of the curve.

The known total of personal incomes between £250 and £125 is deduced as follows :

	1929 (*£s million*)
All personal incomes	3741
Less incomes evading tax	75
Assessed incomes above £2000	598
Incomes below £250	2150
Incomes between £250 and £2000	918

Interpolation from the curve gives :

	1929 (*£s million*)
Incomes between £2000 and £1000	251
,, ,, £1000 ,, £500	330
,, ,, £500 ,, £250	430
	1011

—showing a difference of 10 per cent from the calculated results. Only approximate accuracy therefore is claimed for the data within this range.

Adjusting these figures proportionately, using data from Tables 45 and 46, and making allowance for evasion, we obtain the distribution given in Table 47.

TABLE 47

INCOME DISTRIBUTION OF PERSONAL INCOMES, 1929

	Numbers (000's)	Income (£s million)
Over £10,000	10	228
£2000–£10,000	100	388
£1000–£2000	195	235
£500–£1000	481	309
£250–£500	1,249	402
£125–£250	5,827	1009
Under £125	11,800	1170
Total	19,652	3741

The numbers include persons in receipt of unearned incomes above £125. Below this level, unearned income is included in the income aggregates, but persons receiving it are not included in the number of income-earners, and the classification of the numbers of income-earners at £125 and £250 is based on the distribution of earned income only. Income from Unemployment Benefit and Old Age Pensions is not included, nor is direct taxation deducted. It is assumed that the income evading tax is distributed between the various classes in the same proportions as is the income paying tax.

It will be seen from Table 39 that the distribution of income between the factors of production in 1935 was similar to that of 1929. The share taken by profits and rents had risen appreciably, the share taken by salaries had slightly declined. The absolute level of income, including incomes from overseas, was almost exactly the same in the two years. It appears, therefore, that the income distribution figures for 1929 are probably fairly closely applicable to 1935 conditions. The deviation will probably be in the direction of a slightly greater inequality of income in 1935.

The inequalities of distribution are very considerable. Speaking of the years 1929 or 1935, we can say that one-tenth of the whole working population, with incomes over £250, took 42 per cent of the whole total of personal incomes, or just under half if we allow for the fact that the greater part of the non-personal incomes, in the form of undistributed company profits and such, accrued for the benefit of the rich. A small class comprising 1½ per cent of the population, with "four-figure incomes" and upwards, took 23 per cent of the whole total of personal incomes.

For many purposes, including market analysis, knowledge of the distribution of individual incomes is less important than knowledge of the distribution of family incomes. The income-tax assessments provide no help in this direction. A survey of the distribution of families according to income per head was made in *Food, Health and Income* by Sir John Orr. He reached the striking conclusion that half of the population had family incomes of less than 20s. per head per week, and spent less than 9s. per head per week on food, which was below the optimum requirements for the maintenance of health. The statistical basis of these estimates was very rough. The present writer's name is mentioned in the note of acknowledgement of *Food, Health and Income*, but in fact his investigation was completed too late for inclusion in the calculations.

The distribution of families according to their average income per head was obtained by the analysis of 23,000 families which had been taken as a random sample of the results of the 1931 Census. The detailed analysis of such a large number of cards presented a very difficult problem. It was done by mechanical tabulation. Mr. John Mandeville, of the British Tabulating Machine Co., was successful, after a number of experiments, in perfecting a technique whereby the aggregate income of the family, and the income per head, could be mechanically calculated and entered on the card.

About half the population live in families comprising two or more earners, and an estimate had to be made of the aggregate income of each family included in the sample. The first step was the rating of the average incomes earned in each of the hundreds of occupations coded in the Census returns. Tables of average incomes for adult men and women in each occupation were compiled from the Ministry of Labour's published volume of wage-rates and from other sources. For professional and similar occupations only an estimated minimum income was given. For occupied males under 21 and females under 18 the average wage was estimated according to age. This made it possible to rate the earnings of each occupied person, except in cases of unemployment. A mechanical process was devised whereby the age, sex and occupation of each earner could be read from the card, the estimated earnings punched in another column, and finally the earnings of all working members of the family totalled.

The rating of unemployed persons was rendered difficult by the fact that approximately half the adult male unemployed at the present time are applicants for U.A.B. allowances and the remainder for ordinary benefits. The great majority of women and juvenile unemployed, however, are applicants for ordinary benefits, and they were therefore rated on the cards with the rate of benefit appropriate to their age and sex. In the case of unemployed men who are the sole earners of their families, it may also be assumed that the amount of the U.A.B. allowance will not differ considerably from what their Unemployment Benefit would have been. We are left, therefore, with the cases of adult male unemployed who are not the sole earners of their families. It is assumed that among these men, as among the general body of adult male unemployed, one-half will be on benefit and one-half on U.A.B. allowances. The cards concerned are therefore sorted according to income (of the employed earners) and to numbers in family, and half the unemployed men in each group are rated with full Unemployment Benefit, while the other half are rated with an approximate estimate of the allowance, on the usual P.A.C. scale, payable in view of the family income and composition.

Finally, the numbers of persons over 65 in each family were counted, and the family was rated with an extra 10s. of income in each case.

It was assumed that retired persons, when retired from occupations rated at incomes of £5 per week and over, had an income of two-thirds of their previous income, but that other retired persons had no income apart from the Old Age Pension.

The cards were sorted into four regions as follows :

TABLE 49

Distribution of Population by Districts, 1931

	Districts	1931 Population (000's)	% of Whole Country
A	Greater London . .	8,202	20·6
B	Towns over 20,000 in North, Midlands and Wales	14,354	35·9
C	Towns over 20,000 in South	3,676	9·2
D	Towns under 20,000 and rural areas	13,721	34·3

Within each region the cards were cross-tabulated according to aggregate family income and numbers in family. The tabulating machine was so arranged that it counted, for any given income per head, the number of children under 14, of adolescents 14 to 21, and the total of persons of all ages. The most novel feature of this procedure was that it made possible the tabulation, from the original family schedules, of the number both of adults and of children living in families where the average weekly income per head was below 10s., 15s. or any other assigned figure. The results obtained are as follows :

TABLE 50

PERCENTAGE DISTRIBUTION OF POPULATION BY INCOME GROUPS AND BY DISTRICTS (ENGLAND AND WALES)

Income per Head per Week	All Persons				Weighted Average of Districts	Children under 14				Weighted Average of Districts
	District					District				
	A	B	C	D		A	B	C	D	
Up to 10s.	9·0	13·9	11·5	17·0	13·7	17·1	25·2	22·3	31·0	25·3
10s. to 15s.	13·1	18·1	14·9	18·6	16·9	23·5	27·2	25·8	28·5	26·7
15s. to 20s.	15·3	17·3	16·9	16·3	16·5	21·8	21·5	25·1	17·2	20·2
20s. to 30s.	26·7	25·4	26·6	24·0	25·3	24·7	18·3	20·1	15·9	19·0
30s. to 45s.	24·7	17·8	20·7	17·4	19·4	11·0	6·6	7·5	5·8	7·3
Over 45s.	11·3	7·4	9·4	6·7	8·1	2·0	1·3	1·2	1·6	1·5

In these estimates no allowance has been made for incomes from property nor for incomes from war pensions, widows' and orphans' pensions, compensation payments or public assistance. The effect of the omission of these various items will be, of course, to magnify the proportion in the lowest group and to minimise that in the top group. On the other hand, as in the earlier calculations, no allowance has been made for sickness and short time.

In the circumstances, the results of this independent investigation may be regarded as supplying satisfactory confirmation of the rough proportions of the population placed in each group for the purpose of the main Report.

But this investigation brings to light a result not

suspected in the previous calculation, namely, that while 13·7 per cent of the whole population live in Group I (the poorest section), no less than 25·3 per cent of all the children in the country are being brought up under these conditions.

We may now return to examination of the distribution of personal incomes.

For comparison with Professor Bowley's figures of 1911, we require to use a total including personal incomes and undistributed company profits, and without deducting National Debt interest.

The income of charities, Government income and the other items of Table 42 are excluded. The total distributable income on the above definition was £2048 millions in 1911 and £4031 millions in 1929, received by 20·2 million persons in 1911 and 19·65 million persons (in a smaller geographical area) in 1929. These figures exclude unemployed, and include soldiers and sailors abroad, and unoccupied persons with incomes above £125 now, and a corresponding number in 1911.

For 1911 we have the numbers and incomes above £160, corresponding almost exactly, if the change in the cost of living is allowed for, to £250 at the present time ; and the numbers and incomes above the then supertax limit of £5000. People at this range of income can hardly be said to have a " cost of living ", but their numbers may be compared with the numbers above £7000 at the present day. The 1911 figures include Southern Ireland, but the results are not appreciably affected. The income figures of the upper class are increased to allow for evasion in the same proportion as in Table 47 : allowance should be made also for the fact that a considerable proportion of the non-personal incomes accrued for their benefit.

Since 1911 we have doubled the relative size of our middle class and have increased by half the number of our plutocrats. The shares of the national income which these two classes have taken have not increased, but have remained almost exactly as they were before. Allowing for

TABLE 51

COMPARISON OF INCOME DISTRIBUTIONS, 1911 AND 1929

	Percentage of Population		Percentage of Aggregate Income	
	1911	1929	1911	1929
Numbers above £5000 (£7000 now)	0·061	0·090	7·7	7·3
Numbers above £160 (£250 now)	4·53	10·31	45·6	46·0

non-personal incomes, we can say that both in 1911 and 1929 the same proportions prevailed—that 10 per cent of the national income was taken by the very rich, 35 per cent by the rich and middle classes, and 55 per cent by the main mass of the population. Within the wealthier classes, the distribution of income has become somewhat more equal. The working and lower-salaried classes do not enjoy a more equal distribution in the sense of their having a greater share of the national income. What they do now enjoy is a doubling of their (still slender) chance of promotion to the ranks of the middle classes : and the middle classes enjoy a greater chance of promotion to the ranks of the very rich.

Many of the most striking features in present-day social and political life probably flow from this economic cause.

As has been previously shown, one of the most important factors in the above situation has been the growth in the number of highly-paid salaried posts, and it is interesting to discover in which sections of the national economy this has been most important. The most important division is between " industry " (i.e. manufacture, mining and building), as covered by the Census of Production, and other economic activities. Industry as thus defined produces at present about 40 per cent of the national income. A detailed analysis can be made of the distribution of the product within this sphere, and later (in Table 55) the distribution of income is analysed separately for :

(1) Industry.
(2) Agriculture.
(3) Railway Transport.
(4) Ownership of dwellings.
(5) Other trades and services.

The distribution of the product of industry was analysed along these lines by Professor Bowley for 1911, and very interesting comparisons can be made with the results of the present day.

The results of the Census of Production of 1930 are analysed in the Final Report, the authors of which have also undertaken the difficult but necessary task of preparing estimates of the net output and wage payments in small firms not covered by the Census. The number of persons occupied, including working proprietors, was given as 7,899,000 (not including a very small number of outworkers). This figure is inclusive of persons occupied in firms not covered by the Census, and in Northern Ireland.

The Report of the Census of Production draws attention to the difficulty of making comparison between these figures and those recorded by the Ministry of Labour. In general, the Census totals include the following categories of workers who are not recorded under the unemployment insurance statistics :

(1) Employers and working proprietors.
(2) Salary-earners over £250.
(3) Workers under 16 and over 65.

On the other hand, the Ministry of Labour's annual figures of " number of insured workers employed " in particular industries are calculated without making a deduction for those absent from work through sickness, whereas the Census of Production returns exclude such persons.

In particular industries also, there are differences of classification besides the above general discrepancies. In the baking trade it is pointed out that a number of persons engaged in delivery are classified as manufacturing staff under the Census of Production, but by the Ministry of Labour as engaged in the distributive trades. In gas, water and electricity supply a number of manual workers are excepted from unemployment insurance. These two industries are the principal source of discrepancy. There may be a few delivery staffs engaged in other manufacturing industries who are regarded as distributive workers by the Ministry of Labour, and there may be a few excepted workers in the railway workshops and among manual workers employed by local authorities, but their numbers are probably small.

If we allow for the above discrepancies, we can make a comparison between the Census of Production statistics and the Ministry of Labour figures in such a manner as to show by difference the number of employers and of salary-earners receiving over £250. We may first examine the discrepancies arising in the two particular industries mentioned, namely, baking, and gas, water and electricity supply. Comparison may be made of four different figures of the numbers employed in these industries :

(1) as given by the Census of Production ;
(2) as given by the Ministry of Labour (insured persons, less unemployed) ;
(3) as given by the Census of Population, of persons in work, for comparison with the Census of Production ;
(4) as given by the Census of Population, of persons in work between the ages of 16 and 65, omitting persons working on own account and half[1] the salary-earners, for comparison with the Ministry of Labour figures.

The Census of Population figures refer to Great Britain only, and should be raised some 2–3 per cent on that account, but no deduction has been made for sickness, and they should be reduced somewhat on that account.

[1] Assumed proportion earning over £250.

TABLE 52

NUMBERS RECORDED AS EMPLOYED IN CERTAIN INDUSTRIES, 1930

(Figures in 000's)

	Gas, Water and Electricity Supply	Baking
Census of Production, U.K.	231·5	194·2
Ministry of Labour, U.K.	154·2	137·4
Census of Population (Gt. Britain only) for comparison with Census of Production	225·0	235·5
Census of Population (Gt. Britain only) for comparison with Ministry of Labour	213·6	188·6

It will be seen that in the case of gas, water and electricity supply, the Census of Population figures confirm the Census of Production figures, and indicate a deficiency of about 60,000 in the Ministry of Labour figures, due to excepted workers. In the case of the bakery trade the conclusions are not so clear, as the Census of Population figures do not support the Census of Production returns. It appears, however, that the Ministry of Labour classification involves a total considerably lower than the Census of Production classification.

Altogether, approximately 100,000 should be added to the Ministry of Labour figures for comparison with the Census of Production on account of the discrepancies in these two particular industries.

To allow for the differences in age classification, the figures of number of operatives in work below 16 and over 65, as recorded in the Census of Population for the industries covered by the Census of Production, can be used. To allow for sickness, a deduction of 3½ per cent is made from the Ministry of Labour figures.

We can now make the comparison given in Table 53.

A reasonable conclusion from the table is that there are 496,000 males and 57,000 females engaged in industry who were not covered by Unemployment Insurance, i.e. employers and independent workers, and salary-earners receiving over £250 a year. There are very few female salary-

TABLE 53

NUMBERS EMPLOYED IN INDUSTRY, 1930
(Figures in 000's)

	M.	F.	Males	Females
Ministry of Labour figures (June 1930):				
For industries covered by Census of Production			5178	1745
With allowances for discrepancies in bakery and public utilities industries			5263	1770
With addition for operatives in work below 16 and over 65			5644	1970
With allowance for sickness			5446	1901
Census of Production and small firms:				
Operatives . . .	5222	1742	5942	1958
Administrative . . .	720	216		

earners receiving over £250 a year, and the 57,000 females were mainly employers. The number of actual employers engaged in these trades is not known for 1931, but in 1921 was approximately 250,000, taking males and females together. We conclude that there were some 300,000 males earning salaries over £250 a year, and 220,000 below £250 a year, employed in industry, while there were 200,000 employers. Among the female administrative workers, there were 57,000 employers and 160,000 salary-earners. The average salary of males earning over £250 per annum can be calculated from figures given in Tables 46 and 39. The number of salary-earners in work in 1931 was 4,500,000. In 1929 the salary-earning population was probably less by 150,000, but the numbers of unemployed were also probably less by the same amount. From the figures of the number of salary-earners under £250 given in Table 46 we deduce that the number of salary-earners over £250 is between a million and a million and a quarter. The aggregate paid in salaries under £250 is also given in Table 46. Deducting these totals from the aggregate of all salaries given in Table 40, we deduce that £400–500 millions were paid in salaries over £250, giving an average of just over £400 a year.

It is convenient to attribute an income of this size to

each male employer.[1] The average income of female employers is probably lower. Half of the 57,000 mentioned above are proprietors of firms employing less than 10 workers, and an average of £300 may be assumed.

It is now required to estimate the average salaries of males and females receiving less than £250. Available data regarding the dispersion of salaries have been previously discussed.[2] For all occupations, the average is a little over £100 for females, and about £150 for males. In the case of industry, the average female salary is distinctly lower than in other occupations.

We now have sufficient material for estimating the aggregate amount paid in salaries under £250, which does not take a very large part of the net output of industry. The aggregate, as given in Table 54, is £169 millions. Between 1924 and 1930 the number of administrative and salaried workers increased by 12 per cent, and it is assumed that the aggregate salary bill changed in this proportion.

It is difficult to estimate an exact figure for depreciation. Wear-and-tear allowances in 1930 are given as £100 millions in Table 36. A considerable part of this, however, is on ships, motor vehicles and for capital instruments not used in manufacturing industry. On the other hand, an addition must be made for the depreciation and repairs to industrial buildings (which are assumed to be the property of the manufacturer) except in so far as these repairs have been done by his own staff. (The main part of the repairs to machinery, etc., is performed by the industrialist's own staff, using spare parts and materials purchased by him, and thus has already been charged for under materials and wages). An allowance of £75 millions is made for 1930, and £55 millions for 1924.

The charge for local rates is now a small item, since the Derating Act of 1928. Professor Bowley quotes a figure

[1] Except in the case of small firms, the majority of employers probably make a considerably larger income than this. But it is convenient to allow some such sum as a minimum return to management before estimating true profits.

[2] *Economic Journal*, September 1934, and p. 79 above.

showing that in 1907 the annual value of land and buildings occupied by industry, as at present defined, was £29 millions. The annual value is probably rather more than double that at the present time. A figure of £20 millions for rates in 1924 may be estimated, and £5 millions in 1930.

An important item of cost is in employers' contributions to social insurance (including as previously Workmen's Compensation Insurance). The charge on the employer for Health, Pensions and Unemployment Insurance in 1930 was 1s. 3d. per week for adult males and 1s. 2d. per week for adult females, and slightly less for juveniles. The annual average works out at over £4 per employee per annum, and the aggregate at £34 millions. In 1924 pensions contributions were not payable and the aggregate was lower.

Finally there remain certain categories of charges which must be deducted from proceeds before profits are reckoned, but which have not been included under wages, salaries, materials or any of the previous charges. The most important single charge of this nature is advertising, which varies considerably as between one section of industry and another. Estimates have been made of the aggregate amount spent by all advertisers in this country, but it is difficult to distinguish advertising by manufacturers from advertising by retailers and others. The figure is probably in the neighbourhood of £15 millions. A similar allowance is made for expenditure on postages, travel, law and other administrative charges not allowed for under previous headings. It is assumed that these miscellaneous charges were the same in 1924 as in 1930.

The results of this analysis are set out in Table 54. Net output, free of Customs and Excise charges, was £1670 millions in 1924 and £1639 millions in 1930. The share going as profits and income to employers, capitalists and landowners was £501 millions in 1924 and £486 millions in 1930, or almost exactly 30 per cent of the net output in both years.

TABLE 54

DISTRIBUTION OF NET OUTPUT OF INDUSTRIES COVERED BY CENSUS OF PRODUCTION, 1924 AND 1930 (INCLUDING RAILWAY WORKSHOPS)

(£s million)

	1930	1924
Wages	840	887
Salaries : 300,000 men over £250	120	
220,000 males below £250	33	150
160,000 females	16	
Depreciation and repairs to buildings	75	55
Local rates	5	20
Employers' State Insurance contributions (including Workmen's Compensation Insurance)	34	27
Advertising	15	30
Postage, travel and other office expenses	15	
200,000 employers @ £400 each	80	95
50,000 employers @ £300 each	15	
Other profit, interest and rent	391	406
	1639	1670

Later a more detailed analysis will be made of the distribution of the product in the principal industries within this total. For this purpose, it is not possible to make so detailed an analysis showing numbers of employers and higher salary-earners. The Census of Production returns of " administrative, technical and clerical staff " include employers and salary-workers together, and an average salary of £270 is attributed to each male in this category, and of £125 to each female.

We are now in a position to assemble data for the distribution of the product of the principal branches of economic activity, making possible a comparison with the similar table prepared by Professor Bowley for 1911. The " product " of industry in this case will not be exactly the same as its net output, as we must deduct depreciation and similar expenses. Our object is to examine the distribution of " income " from each source, income being defined in the same manner as it is defined by the Inland Revenue.

Figures for the net output of agriculture and the amount taken by wages have been previously calculated.

The number and income of salary-earners in this case is inappreciable.

Railway workshops are transferred from the manufacturing to the railway section of the table. The railway returns [1] give the total paid in wages and salaries each year. The amount paid in wages has previously been calculated, and the division of salaries between those above and below £250 is estimated. The figure of railway profits is taken from their published financial accounts, and the income derived from railways as a whole is aggregated from the previous items.

A new classification has been introduced which was not in Professor Bowley's original table, namely, the income derived from the ownership of dwelling-houses. It is considered worth while to show this separately, because it is one of the most important forms of income due solely to capital and not at all to labour. Gross annual rentals of dwelling-houses were estimated by Mr. A. E. Feavearyear [2] from statistics of inhabited house duty for 1913, and he calculated a figure for 1927 from statistics of the annual value of new houses built during the interval, and of increases permitted in the rental of old houses under the Rent Restriction Acts. Deductions have to be made to convert this gross value into a net value, which can only be approximately determined.

There remains a section covering other transport, commerce and services, which produced about 45 per cent of the home-produced national income both in 1911 and in 1930. The amounts of income in this section are determined by difference. It may be noted that this includes the earnings of domestic servants, which may be put at £90 millions in 1911 and £150 millions in 1930. In 1911 Professor Bowley is able to segregate the income earned by those supplying the services of central and local government and the Forces, which in 1911 amounted to £37 millions of salary and £75 millions of wages. Unfortun-

[1] E.g. *Ministry of Labour Gazette*, September 1930.
[2] *Economic Journal*, March 1931 and March 1934.

ately a similar analysis is not possible for the present time.

Professor Bowley's figures as given have been adjusted, as previously mentioned, by the transference of shop-assistants from the wage-earning to the salary-earning category, and by the inclusion of the earnings of soldiers and sailors abroad and certain other elements which he specified separately.

The results of Table 55 may be analysed in several different directions. Looking across at first horizontally, to see the share of the product taken by the different factors of production in each section, there is a most remarkable similarity between the figures of 1911 and 1930. In industry, the share taken by wage-earners and by lower-paid salary-earners is almost identical in the two years. The only change is a slight transference from the incomes of capital and enterprise to those of the higher salary-earners.

In the railways, the balance has very definitely been shifted. The share of capital has fallen from 52 to 25 per cent of the income. The share of wage-earners has increased considerably, but the increase in the share of the salary-earners is more remarkable still. The division of numbers and incomes between the two categories of salary-earners in 1930, as stated above, is only approximate, and too much reliance should not be placed upon it ; but the increase in the incomes of the salaried classes as a whole is indisputable.

In agriculture, the share taken by labour in 1930 is slightly above that of 1911, but it is doubtful if this movement is greater than can be explained by the exclusion of the Irish Free State from the figures of the later year. It is only in this industry that any appreciable difference is made to the results by this change of boundary. Farming in the Irish Free State is largely carried on by small peasant cultivators, who probably contributed £15–20 millions of "rent, interest and profit" in 1911, while the income of wage-earners in Southern Ireland contributed a comparatively small total.

TABLE 55

Distribution of the Product of Industry, 1911 and 1930

		1911					1930				
		Wages	Salaries below £160	Salaries above £160	Rent, Interest and Profit	Total	Wages	Salaries below £250	Salaries above £250	Rent, Interest and Profit	Total
Manufacture, mining and building†	(Nos., 000's)	7170	350	120	705	8595	6407	636	300	525*	7868
	(Inc., £m.)	389	23	38	238	688	811	44	115	526	1496
	(% of product)	56·6	3·3	5·5	34·6	..	55·7	3·0	7·9	33·4	..
Railways and railway workshops	(000's)	530	80	10	..	620	548	65	35	..	648
	(£m.)	35	6	2	47	90	85	14	16	38	153
	(% product)	38·9	6·7	2·2	52·2	..	55·5	9·2	10·5	24·8	..
Agriculture . .	(000's)	1675	5	..	640	2320	690	10	..	320	1020
	(£m.)	63	1	..	75	139	62	1	..	63	126
	(% product)	45·4	0·7	..	53·9	..	49·2	0·7	..	50·1	..
Ownership of dwelling-houses	(000's)	..	..	..	..	..	..	..	..	..	..
	(£m.)	..	..	..	100	100	..	..	..	217	217
	(% product)	..	..	..	..	..	..	..	..	..	..
Other transport, commerce and services	(000's)	4555	2320	255	1485	8365	4468	2596	700	1155	8919
	(£m.)	241	128	90	371	830	476	317	391	330	154
	(% product)	29·1	15·4	10·8	44·7	..	30·6	20·4	25·2	23·8	..
Total home-produced income	(000's)	13,930	2755	385	2830	19,900	12,113	3307	1035	2000	18,455
	(£m.)	728	158	130	831	1,847	1,434	376	522	1174	3,506
	(% product)	39·4	8·6	7·0	45·0	..	40·9	10·7	14·9	33·5	..

* These figures include 275,000 independent workers within this field of industry who employ no staff, largely in the building and clothing trades, who are not covered by the Census of Production. Their income, amounting to about £35–40 millions a year, is included with profits, and appears to have been so treated by Professor Bowley in the calculation for 1911.

† Excluding railway workshops.

It is in commerce and allied activities that the increase in the numbers and income of salary-earners has been most remarkable, and also the decline in the absolute and relative income going to capital and land. The share taken by wage-earners has remained almost the same. If we exclude the wages of domestic servants, the share of the income of these industries going to wage-earners is 20·4 per cent in 1911 and 23·1 per cent in 1930. A large part of the increase in the relative share and absolute total of incomes going to salary-earners is due to the increasing amount of State and municipal services, exclusive of mere transference of income such as unemployment benefits, pensions, etc., but including education, public health, armaments, etc. Expenditure on these consists mainly, but not entirely, of wages and salaries. Excluding highways, the total spent in this direction, as given later in Table 56, rose from £186 millions in 1913 to £383 millions in 1930. The incomes of Government and other public officials included in the gross tax assessments in 1933–4 were no less than £107 millions (including wage-earners with incomes over £125).

Turning to the general totals, we again get the results which we had previously established, showing as their main feature a transfer of income from profits, etc., to salaries. The share of capital in the national income had fallen from 45 per cent in 1911 to 33·5 per cent in 1930. But this was accompanied by an appreciable decline in the numbers of " capitalists ", including a strong decline in the numbers of small working capitalists and farmers (partly due to the severance of the Irish Free State). The activity in which the largest proportion of income goes to capital, curiously enough, is agriculture. This share largely took the form of low average incomes to a large number of small capitalists. Next after agriculture in 1911 came railways, in which 52 per cent of the income produced went to capital. This has been transformed to 25 per cent.

But in industry proper, namely, manufacture, mining and building, the same relation has held throughout, whereby almost exactly a third of the net produce in each year was taken by rent, interest and profit. Here Carlyle's famous quotation seems to have been not only figuratively but arithmetically correct.[1]

This chapter may be concluded by a more detailed examination of the distribution of the product in the principal industries. The figures which follow refer only to firms employing over ten persons, in Great Britain. The sources of information are the Census of Production, 1930, and the inquiries made under the Import Duties Act relating to the years 1933 and 1934. A wage inquiry was held in conjunction with the 1930 Census of Production, and by making certain assumptions it is possible to analyse the output of each industry in the following manner:

Gross value of sales.
Cost of materials, fuel and work given out.
Wages of manual workers.
Salaries (including income attributed to independent employers).
Employers' contributions.
Other expenses.
Surplus, i.e. rent, interest and profit, if the preceding data are correct.

The income of salary-earners, including employers, is calculated from the averages of £270 for each male and £125 for each female given above. These are based on general averages, and the results may be wrong in industries employing particularly highly paid or particularly lowly paid grades of salary-workers.

Employers' contributions, which are small relative to total costs, can be calculated from the size of the staff employed. Other costs of production, as analysed in

[1] "A widow is gathering nettles for her children's dinner; a perfumed seigneur, lounging delicately in the Œil de Bœuf, has an alchemy whereby he can extract from her every third nettle, and calls it rent, interest and profit."

Table 54, include depreciation, local rates, advertising, postal, travel and other office expenses. In 1911 Professor Bowley assumed these to be 10 per cent of the net output of industry. The general average for 1930 is 6·7 per cent. In default of more detailed information, it is assumed that these other costs represent 6·7 per cent of the net output in each industry. This figure will be invalid in the case of industries whose expenditure on advertising, or on depreciation, is much above or below the average.

Subject to these qualifications, it is possible to analyse the output of the principal industries in 1930.

Measured as a percentage on turnover, profits seem to be highest in the chemical and allied trades, food, drink and tobacco trades, the paper and printing trades, and miscellaneous manufactures. Measured as a percentage on the wages bill, the same four groups of industries are found to give the highest profits; in other words, these are the industries in which capital gets the highest and labour the lowest share of net output. Lower profits, both on turnover and as a percentage of the wage-bill, are found in iron and steel, textiles, building and coal-mining. The non-ferrous metal trades appear to make a small profit on turnover but a comparatively high profit in proportion to the amount paid in wages. The engineering and timber trades have been at a somewhat more profitable level than those trades just enumerated.

As pointed out previously, the profits of any trade in which expenditure on advertising is abnormally high will probably be overstated in this table. This applies particularly to the food, drink and tobacco trades. The amount of profit involved, however, is £107 millions, and it is likely that only a small fraction of this will represent the additional expenditure on advertising. In a certain section of the chemical trades, namely, the manufacture of patent medicines, there is also considerable advertising expenditure. The profits of other trades, whose advertising expenditure is very small, will be correspondingly higher than the figures given in Table 56.

TABLE 56

COSTS AND PROFITS OF INDUSTRIES IN 1930, GREAT BRITAIN ONLY

(£s million)

	Sales	Materials	Wages	Salaries	Employers' Contributions	Other Expenses	Rent, Profit and Interest	Profits as % of Turnover	As % of Wage-bill
Iron and steel	237·7	146·0	58·4	11·5	2·1	6·0	13·7	5·8	23
Engineering, shipbuilding and vehicles	451·7	225·7	119·5	38·3	4·5	15·2	48·5	10·7	40
Non-ferrous metals*	68·8	45·3	12·2	3·4	0·5	1·6	5·8	8·4	47
Textiles†	409·6	268·8	84·1	14·9	4·3	9·4	28·1	6·9	33
Leather and leather goods	36·0	25·8	4·8	1·2	0·2	0·7	3·3	9·2	69
Clothing and boots	177·0	100·3	40·1	9·5	2·1	5·1	19·9	11·2	50
Food, drink and tobacco†	576·9	391·2	45·6	18·6	2·0	12·4	107·1	18·5	234
Chemicals and allied trades†	175·9	103·3	19·3	9·7	0·8	4·9	37·9	21·6	197
Paper and printing	175·7	73·3	45·2	13·7	1·6	6·9	35·0	19·9	77
Timber and furniture	68·0	36·8	18·3	3·1	0·7	2·1	7·1	10·4	39
Building materials	71·2	26·5	25·0	7·5	1·0	3·0	8·2	11·5	33
Building and contracting	191·3	98·7	63·8	5·9	1·9	6·2	14·8	7·7	23
Miscellaneous industries	91·7	48·9	17·7	6·0	0·7	2·9	15·5	16·9	88
Coal mines	166·8	28·1	104·3	4·8	4·0	9·3	16·3	9·8	156
Other mines and quarries	20·4	4·2	10·7	0·9	0·4	1·2	3·0	14·7	71

* The value of gold and silver refined, which is a large and fluctuating total, is included only on the basis of net value added.

† Excluding Excise duties.

When we wish to make comparisons with the figures for more recent years, we must use a slightly different list of industries, owing to the exclusion of thirty-six industries from the Import Duties Act Inquiries, 1933 and 1934. The industries excluded are as follows :

*Motor vehicles
Shipbuilding
Carriage, cart and wagon
*Watch and clock
Flock and rag
Textile packing
Fellmongery
Tailoring, dressmaking, millinery, etc.
Fur
Bread, cakes and pastries
Cocoa and sugar confectionery
Bacon-curing and sausage
Sugar and glucose
Fish-curing
Ice
Brewing and malting
Spirit distilling
Spirit rectifying, compounding and methylating
Aerated waters, cider, vinegar and British wine
Wholesale bottling
Tobacco
Petroleum refining
Match
Printing, bookbinding, stereotyping, engraving, etc.
Printing and publication of newspapers and periodicals
Manufactured stationery
Cardboard box
Pens, pencils and artists' materials
Furniture and upholstery
Cane and wicker furniture and basketware
Wood crates, cases, boxes and trunks
Coopering
Manufactured fuel
*Scientific instruments, appliances and apparatus
*Musical instruments
*Cinematograph film printing

* Included in 1934 but not in 1933.

In addition, the mining and quarrying and building and contracting trades were excluded, and also the public utility services (which had not been included in Table 56 on the grounds that many of them make their returns on a " costs only " basis).

It is necessary, therefore, to give a new table for 1930 in which these industries are excluded, for comparison with the tables for 1933 and 1934 which follow. It should be noticed that these and subsequent tables refer to Great Britain and Northern Ireland.

The period from 1930 to 1933 was at any rate one of decline, from 1933 to 1934 one of rapid increase, in profits. The increase in the profits of the iron and steel industry, nearly all sections of which are covered by the Import Duties Act Inquiries, is noticeable. There was also a considerable increase in the profits of the chemical group of industries. In the textile industries the recovery of output and profits appears to have come much earlier than in most other industries, at the end of 1931. Profits had recovered to 10 per cent on turnover in 1933, and showed a slight decline in 1934. The same applied to the leather industry.

The figures for the clothing industry only covered small sections and cannot be taken as representative. The most important section covered is the boot and shoe manufacture.

A little more than half of the industries in the food, drink and tobacco group are covered by the recent inquiries. The excluded industries include some of the most highly profitable, such as the tobacco, brewing and other drink industries. The remainder showed a profit of 12·4 per cent on turnover, or 158 per cent on the wage-bill, in 1930, 15·4 and 166 per cent in 1933, and about the same in 1934. Unless there has been a decline in the profits of the excluded sections of the food trade, we must conclude that the already high level of profits in this group has been again considerably increased. Certain other comparisons can be made between 1930 and 1933. The engineering trades appear to have maintained approximately the same rate of profit on turnover with diminishing sales and employment. All the other sections, including the chemical trades, show an increase in the rate of profit to turnover between 1930 and 1933. The only declines are in non-ferrous metals and clothing.

[TABLE

TABLE 57

ANALYSIS OF COSTS AND PROFITS IN INDUSTRIES COVERED BY THE IMPORT DUTIES ACT INQUIRY, UNITED KINGDOM, 1930, 1933 AND 1934

	Sales	Materials	Wages	Salaries	Employers' Contributions	Other Expenses	Rent, Profit and Interest	Profits as % of Turnover	As % of Wage-bill
	1930								
Iron and steel . . .	237·4	146·0	58·6	11·5	2·1	6·3	12·9	5·7	23
Engineering, shipbuilding and vehicles	252·1	114·2	62·5	24·9	2·8	9·2	38·5	14·4	57
Non-ferrous metals* . .	68·1	44·7	11·9	3·3	0·5	1·6	6·1	9·7	51
Textiles†	411·9	266·7	88·0	15·2	4·5	9·7	27·8	6·7	32
Leather and leather goods .	32·7	23·1	4·6	1·2	0·2	0·6	3·0	9·2	65
Clothing and boots . .	62·1	35·6	15·6	2·7	0·7	1·8	5·7	9·2	36
Food, drink and tobacco† .	152·1	112·8	11·9	5·5	0·5	2·6	18·8	12·4	158
Chemicals and allied trades† .	160·1	94·5	17·7	9·4	0·7	4·4	33·4	21·0	189
Paper	40·2	25·5	6·8	1·1	0·2	1·0	5·6	13·9	82
Timber	18·0	11·5	4·0	1·3	0·2	0·4	0·6	3·3	15
Building materials . .	70·6	26·2	25·0	4·6	1·0	3·0	10·8	15·3	43
Miscellaneous . . .	68·1	38·7	12·3	4·2	0·5	2·0	10·4	15·3	84
Total . . .	1573·4	939·5	318·9	84·9	13·9	42·6	173·6	11·0	54·4
Motor and cycle trade . .	109·7	64·3	24·8	6·4	0·8	3·0	10·4	9·5	42
Other trades not covered by 1933 inquiry	23·0	9·7	5·6	1·8	0·2	0·9	4·8	20·9	86
Total, including trades not covered by 1933 inquiry	1706·1	1013·5	349·3	93·1	14·9	46·5	188·8	11·1	54·0
	1933								
Iron and steel . . .	201·6	117·0	50·2	11·2	2·0	5·7	15·5	7·7	31
Engineering, shipbuilding and vehicles	191·1	82·3	48·4	24·4	2·6	7·3	26·1	13·1	51

Clothing and boots . .	52·0	28·5	15·0	2·5	0·7	1·6	3·7	7·1	25
Food, drink and tobacco .	134·4	91·3	12·5	6·4	0·6	2·9	20·7	15·4	166
Chemicals and allied trades .	152·2	82·6	16·4	10·0	0·8	4·7	37·7	25·2	230
Paper	36·6	21·1	6·9	1·3	0·3	1·0	6·0	16·4	87
Timber	16·4	10·5	3·4	1·2	0·1	0·4	0·8	4·9	23
Building materials . .	66·5	24·1	23·4	4·8	1·0	2·8	10·4	15·6	44
Miscellaneous . . .	59·1	30·5	11·1	4·5	0·6	1·9	10·5	17·8	95
Total . . .	1373·1	776·6	280·6	85·3	13·9	40·0	176·7	12·9	63·0
					1934				
Iron and steel . . .	250·4	146·7	56·9	11·7	2·3	6·9	25·9	10·2	45
Engineering, shipbuilding and vehicles	236·0	104·5	59·9	26·7	2·8	8·8	33·3	14·1	56
Non-ferrous metals* . .	65·4	39·2	11·8	3·4	0·5	1·8	8·7	13·3	74
Textiles†	399·5	251·6	82·0	14·7	4·7	9·9	36·6	9·2	45
Leather and leather goods .	28·3	19·2	4·4	1·2	0·2	0·6	2·7	9·5	61
Clothing and boots . .	51·4	28·0	14·8	2·5	0·7	1·6	3·8	7·4	26
Food, drink and tobacco† .	138·2	93·8	12·8	6·8	0·6	3·0	21·2	15·3	166
Chemicals and allied trades† .	158·7	83·1	17·7	10·2	0·8	5·1	41·8	26·2	235
Paper	41·6	24·6	7·4	1·4	0·3	1·1	6·8	16·3	92
Timber	17·8	11·5	3·7	1·2	0·2	0·4	0·8	4·5	22
Building materials . .	75·3	27·5	25·0	4·7	1·1	3·2	13·8	18·3	55
Miscellaneous . . .	67·8	36·1	12·9	4·4	0·6	2·1	11·7	17·3	91
Total for comparison with 1933	1530·4	865·8	309·3	88·9	14·8	44·5	207·1	13·5	66·9
Motor and cycle trade . .	117·2	69·5	28·5	5·9	0·9	3·2	9·2	7·8	32
Other trades not covered by 1933 inquiry	20·6	8·8	5·2	1·7	0·2	0·8	3·9	18·9	75
Total for comparison with 1930	1668·2	944·1	343·0	96·5	15·9	48·5	220·2	13·2	64·2

* See footnote to Table 56.

† Excluding Excise.

CHAPTER VI

REDISTRIBUTION OF INCOME THROUGH TAXATION

In the previous chapter figures have been collected together giving all the available information as to the way in which the product of industry is distributed, and the changes which have taken place in recent years. But one of the salient features of the distribution of income in recent times has been the high rate of progressive taxation falling upon the larger incomes, a considerable part of the proceeds of which are redistributed in the form of unemployment benefit, old-age pensions and social services. On the other hand, we must not lose sight also of the high burden of indirect taxation, and the amount of public income which is redistributed in the form of interest on the National Debt, which largely goes to augment the higher incomes.

The net effects of redistributive taxation can only be judged if we take into account local as well as national taxation, and also the quasi-taxation involved in the compulsory Health and Unemployment Insurance contributions. We also require to note how much of the proceeds of these taxes have been redistributed, how much have been spent on social services, whose benefit can largely, though not entirely, be credited to certain classes of the community, and how much has been spent on general administration or services calculated to benefit the community as a whole.

Apart altogether from the difficulty of deciding into which of these classes each category of expenditure should be put, considerable confusion arises owing to the transfer of sums between one taxing authority and another. Thus a considerable part of Government expenditure consists of grants to local authorities, to which they add revenue from local sources to provide for expenditure on various objects.

The cost of unemployment benefit is partly met by contributions and partly by grants from the Exchequer calculated on a varying basis.

If our object is to study the effects, rather than the administration, of the public revenues and expenditure, it is most expedient to construct a consolidated revenue and expenditure account in which all inter-authority transfers are eliminated. We thus take as sources of revenue direct and indirect taxation levied by the Government, local rates, contributions to compulsory insurance, and certain miscellaneous revenues. When sums of money are transferred from one authority to be expended by another, only the latter is shown as expenditure.

Two of the sources of public incomes have already been enumerated in Tables 34 and 35. In the table which follows, the total paid in local rates shown in Table 35 is analysed into rates paid on private houses and on business premises. (The decline in the latter between 1928–9 and 1930–31 is accounted for by the derating of agricultural and manufacturing hereditaments.)

The other sources of public income are the various forms of direct taxation specified under that heading, with which should rightly be included Workers' Insurance Contributions, the sources of Government income described under Table 34, and certain other revenues. The net profits of local authorities from trading services were not included in Table 34, owing to the fact that they have already been assessed to income-tax. These net profits in fact during recent years have been equal, within one or two millions, to the amounts required for the payment of sinking funds on the trading services, the policy of most local authorities being to adjust their charges so as to bring about this equality. This income must be included here, and also the income derived by the Government from " miscellaneous revenue ".

The Government's income from miscellaneous revenue (excluding fee and patent stamps, which in the form of accounting in force since 1928 have been set off against the expenditure of the departments concerned) amounted to only £1·2 millions in 1913, £39·7 millions in 1924–5, rose to £59·7 millions in 1927–8, and during recent years has been between £15 and £25 millions.

On examination, however, these figures are discovered to consist, almost entirely, either of items which have already been included in Table 34, or else capital receipts. The following analyses may be made, for instance, of the miscellaneous revenue receipts in 1927–8 and in 1934–5 :

TABLE 58

MISCELLANEOUS REVENUES

(£s million)

	1927–8	1934–5
Receipts already covered under Table 34 :		
Bank of England profits on note issue	0·2	2·8
Post Office Savings Bank surplus of interest	2·9	4·3
Repayment of loans from Colonial and Allied Governments	3·4	..
Reparations	14·5	..
Items no longer treated as revenue :		
Teachers' superannuation contributions	2·9	..
Capital Receipts :		
From accumulated balance of Road Fund	12·0	3·1
Surrender of undrawn credits by Greek Government	3·4	..
Currency notes Investment Reserve Account	6·6	..
Enemy debts, clearing office surplus	3·8	..
Irish Free State compensation for damage to property before the truce	0·3	0·2
Disposal of War stores and shipping	3·6	0·3
Repayment of loans made by Ministry of Labour	1·1	..
Other capital receipts	0·9	0·7
Total of above	55·7	11·4
Miscellaneous revenue (other than Fee and Patent stamps) not covered above	4·0	3·7

The remarkable devices [1] to which the Government

[1] The most curious item is that of the Greek book credits above. These appear to have been book credits for the Greek Government opened, but never used, during the War, yet they are added to Exchequer revenue when they are surrendered.

A more recent financial exploit, less remarkable because more candidly admitted, was the raiding of £10 millions of unexpended balance of War Loan Depreciation Fund in 1933.

has had resort, in order to increase the nominal totals of revenue and sinking fund, deserve a certain amount of consideration, and serve to draw attention to the need for a more accurate system of the national accounts, in which capital and revenue transactions are kept distinct.

It is thus seen that the amount of revenue not already covered is no more than £4·0 millions in 1927–8 and £3·7 millions in 1934–5. The same results are obtained from analysis of the figures for each of the past ten years.

The inclusion of £3 millions under this head in each year, together with the trading profits of local authorities and the items specified under Table 34, makes up the total income received by all public taxing authorities.

Consolidated figures for expenditure are shown, irrespective of the spending authority. They are divided into two main categories. The first consists of transfer incomes, which are redistributed directly to individuals. The second consists of expenditure on all other public services and administration. The costs of administering certain forms of transfer income (e.g. unemployment benefit, pensions, etc.) are included under administration and not under transfer incomes.

The amount spent on " other services " is obtained by difference from the totals of public expenditure given in *Financial Statement, 1936–7*. In this financial statement, but not in previous issues, a table is given showing the total of public expenditure, compiled on a comparable basis, for the years 1913–14 and from 1924–5 onwards, including Exchequer contributions to and borrowings on behalf of social insurance funds. By adding to this the amount raised in Social Insurance contributions, we can determine consolidated expenditure as now defined.

By comparing this total of expenditure with the public income as determined above, we can determine a true net figure of the amount available for sinking funds—not including capital receipts as revenue, as has been done by the Treasury in the past. Finally, manipulations such as the accumulation of the Rating Relief Suspense Account in

1928–9, and its subsequent disbursement, will be treated as savings in the earlier years and as expenditure in the later years. We thus obtain a net figure of the amount of savings, or excess of expenditure over revenue, of the Government and of local authorities. To make this a true net figure, however, we must make allowance for the capital expenditure on roads which has been met out of revenue. This is determined by deducting from the total expenditure on roads the amount required for maintenance, as given in Table 36.

The whole operations of State and Local Government finance are summarised in this table, and its main features may be considered line by line.

Direct taxation rose from £85 millions in 1913 to a maximum of £482 millions in 1931, or from 3·8 to 12·4 per cent of the national income. But since that date it has fallen both absolutely and relatively, and was only 9·8 per cent of the national income in 1935. The direct taxation falling on wage-earners, namely, workers' contributions to Health and Unemployment Insurance, has risen nearly sixfold during the same period, and now stands at 2·4 per cent of their incomes.

The revenue from local rates and from other forms of indirect taxation has already been analysed in Table 35. It will be noticed that in 1913 the three types of revenue—direct taxation, local rates, indirect taxation—contributed approximately equal sums. In 1931–2 direct taxation contributed nearly half of the whole public revenues. By 1935–6 the contribution of direct taxation had fallen, of local rates had risen slightly, and of indirect taxation had risen considerably.

The Excess Profits Duty and the Corporation Profits Tax nominally became extinct in 1921 and 1924 respectively, but small amounts of revenue have continued to be derived from them for many years. They are placed in Table 35 with indirect taxation, for the reason that payments of these taxes were allowable as business expenses in computing assessments for income-tax.

The amount collected in direct and indirect taxation and in local rates in 1913 was £262 millions, or about 11 per cent of the national income. In 1929–30 it was £942 millions, or 21·5 per cent of the national income, and the share of the national income taken in taxation reached a peak in 1931–2 and 1932–3 at about 25 per cent of the national income. Since then the absolute total has risen to £1023 millions, but as a percentage of the national income it has dropped to 23 per cent.

In the Emergency Budget speech of September 1931, the Chancellor stated that a third of the national income was taken in rates and taxes and this ratio has been widely quoted. The basis of this calculation has never been revealed.

On the expenditure side, the principal division is into "transfer payments", where the payments directly benefited particular individuals, and various kinds of public services and administration. Among the public services it is possible to identify some, such as housing and education, which largely benefited the poorer classes, and others such as highways which largely benefit the wealthier classes.

Expenditure under many of these heads passes through either local authorities or social insurance.

The balance of revenue over expenditure calculated from this table is a true balance which does not count as revenue the various capital appropriations mentioned above, and in which borrowing and repayments by the Unemployment Insurance Fund are amalgamated with those of the Treasury. It may be noted that the major part of the saving is done by the local authorities through their sinking funds and other repayments of capital,[1] which

[1] As is pointed out in a later chapter, these capital repayments by Local Authorities, which continue year by year independent of changes in business prosperity, provide a substantial proportion of the whole national savings, and have a considerable effect on the business cycle and the level of unemployment. The figures for Scotland and Northern Ireland are readily available, but for England and Wales have been only published in a very obscure form in *Local Taxation Returns*. A continuous series of data, however, is now available in Sir Gwilym Gibbon's paper in *J.R.S.S.*, 1936 (Part III), p. 498. But the official attitude of

TABLE 59

Consolidated Revenue and Expenditure Account of Government, Local Authorities and Social Insurance

(£s million : Years ended 31st March)

	1913–14	1924–25	1925–26	1926–27	1927–28	1928–29	1929–30	1930–31	1931–32	1932–33	1933–34	1934–35	1935–36	1936–37
Income														
Direct Taxation :														
Income-tax	43·9	273·8	259·4	234·7	250·6	237·6	237·4	256	287·4	251·5	228·9	228·9	238·1	259
Super-tax and surtax	3·3	62·7	68·5	65·9	60·6	56·1	56·4	67·8	76·7	60·6	52·6	51·2	51	56·5
Death duties	27·4	59·5	61·2	67·3	77·3	80·6	79·8	82·6	65	77·1	85·3	81·4	87·9	89
Private motor-cars	..	8	9	11	13	13	14	14	13	13	15	15	14	15
Inhabited House Duty	2	0·5	..	..	..	..	..	..	..	..	..	..	..	..
Workers' insurance contributions	8	31	35	33	38	38	39	38	40	42	43	46	46	..
Total	85	435	433	412	439	425	427	458	482	444	425	422	437	..
Indirect Taxation :														
Local Rates :														
Private houses	40	91	95	102	106	107	109	113	113	112	115	118	123	..
Business premises	43	71	74	80	85	84	68	57	55	53	53	55	61	..
Customs and Excise	75	234·5	238	240·5	250·8	253	247·4	245·4	256·1	288·1	286·2	289·7	303·3	317·5
Stamp duties	10	22·8	24·7	24·8	27	30·1	25·7	20·7	17·1	19·2	22·7	24·1	25·8	..
Commercial vehicles	..	8	9	10	11	12	13	14	14	15	16	17	17	..
Excess Profits Duty and Corporation Profits Tax	..	18·8	13·7	8·5	1·8	1·7	2·2	3	2·5	2·2	1·8	2·3	1·3	..
Employers' contributions	9	40	40	46	49	49	49	48	49	51	51	53	54	..
Total	177	486	495	511	530	537	515	501	506	541	546	560	586	..
Income from international transactions, trading services, and miscellaneous revenue	19	11	23	40	40	57	67	63	59	50	46	55	45	..
Total Income	281	932	951	963	1009	1019	1009	1022	1047	1035	1017	1037	1068	..

Expenditure														
Transfers:														
National Debt Interest	16	278	288	279	284	283	278	265	274	260	212	211	210	..
Unemployment benefits and assistance	..	40	44	52	36·5	46·7	45·9	92·2	110·9	104·6	88·6	86	84·3	..
War pensions	0·8	71·3	70·4	65·8	62·3	58·7	56·2	54·6	52·1	49·5	48·6	46·8	45·8	44·8
Old-age pensions (70 and over)	12·4	25·9	28·1	31·2	34·1	35·4	36·2	38	39·2	41	41·7	43·1	44·6	45·6
Contributory Pensions (Widows and orphans: Old-age pensions, 65-70)	..	..	..	8·4	11·4	23·3	25·8	34	39·2	40·4	41·7	42·8	44	..
Public assistance	14·9	35·7	39·3	49·6	39·9	38·3	38·9	36·2	35	38	42	46	46	..
Sickness and disablement benefit	6·9	14·8	15·8	19·7	20·8	18	20·2	19·0	17·6	17·8	17·8	16·6	17	..
Total	51	466	486	505	489	503	501	539	568	551	492	492	492	..
Expenditure on public services and administration:														
Armaments	77·2	114·7	119·4	116·7	117·5	113·5	113	110·5	107·3	103	107·9	113·9	136·9	178·2
Education	37	89	91	92	93	97	100	104	102	99	102	106	111	115
Highways (excl. loan exp.)	19·5	48	51·5	52·4	55·1	54·4	58·1	60	60·1	54	51	50	530	..
Housing	0·4	10·2	11·4	13	14·7	15·8	16·2	17·4	17·8	18·2	18·6	19	18·2	19·8
Hospitals, maternity and child welfare	3·1	9·5	9·8	10·5	10·5	10·8	11·2	13·4	15·1	16	16·3	17	17	..
Other services	68·8	142·6	141·9	150·4	148·2	136·5	127·5	137·7	134·7	126·8	131·2	143·1	164·9	..
Services and administration	206	414	425	435	439	428	426	443	437	417	427	449	501	..
TOTAL EXPENDITURE	257	880	911	940	928	931	927	982	1005	968	919	941	993	..
Net Sinking Funds:														
Local	19	28	33	34	38	42	43	46	47	51	53	55	57	..
State	5	24	7	*−11*	43	46	39	*−6*	*−5*	16	45	39	18	..
Capital expenditure on roads met from revenue	..	4	6	6	8	6	10	14	14	10	7	5	8	..
TOTAL	24	56	46	29	89	94	92	54	56	77	105	101	83	..

are mainly statutory rather than voluntary. Rather less than half of the sinking funds are on trading services, and a large amount is on housing. The payment of these sinking funds now absorbs about 40 per cent of the produce of local rates, and loan charges (interest and sinking fund taken together) are equivalent to 70 per cent of the produce of local rates, as now diminished by the derating of industrial premises. The financial dependence of local authorities on the Central Government has therefore increased.

The only years in which an appreciable net amount was put to sinking fund by the Central Government were 1927–1930 and 1933–5.

A number of attempts have been made to estimate the burdens of taxation on various levels of income, and the relative amounts which different income classes contribute to the public revenues.[1] In the calculation which follows, no attempt is made to specify exactly the amount of direct and indirect taxation falling on persons on each income level. Too many arbitrary assumptions are involved. In this calculation, no more is attempted than to assess the incidence of taxation on the two main classes of the community, namely, those with incomes above and below £250 (£160 in 1913). As has been shown, the national income is divided roughly into two equal halves at this point. For convenience, we may describe all people with incomes below this level as " the working classes ".

The incidence of direct taxation is clear. Other than workers' contributions, only an inappreciable amount of direct taxation falls on incomes below £250 (except for Inhabited House Duty in 1913). The burden on working-class families of the taxes on drink, tobacco, tea, sugar, entertainments and other forms of expenditure was carefully examined by the Colwyn Committee. Their calculations are based on the estimated consumption of taxed

indifference to the wider economic aspects of these payments is also indicated by Sir Gwilym's comments on pp. 477-80.

[1] Sir Herbert Samuel, *J.R.S.S.*, 1919 ; Committee on National Debt and Taxation, 1927 ; D. Caradog Jones, *J.R.S.S.*, 1930 ; D. M. Sandral, *J.R.S.S.*, 1931.

commodities by a family of five. They compiled tables showing the burden on such a family when its income is £100, £150, £200 and £500 a year.

Unfortunately, or perhaps rather fortunately, a working-class family of five persons depending on one income is the exception rather than the rule. It is more convenient to regard the Colwyn Committee's data as showing the average expenditure on taxed commodities of families with 7s. 6d., 11s. 6d., 16s. and 37s. 6d. per head per week respectively. From data compiled in Table 50 we know approximately the relative frequencies of these types of the family income in working-class families. "Working class" is now defined so as to include about 85 per cent of the population, and a considerable number of families (where there are several earners) with incomes in the neighbourhood of £2 per head per week will be included. The four income classes examined in the Colwyn Report are therefore weighted as follows :

£100	1	£200	3
£150	1	£500	3

With this basis, it is possible to reckon the consumption, and hence the tax paid on drink, tobacco, etc., by the average working-class family. The Colwyn Report deals with the consumption of a constructive family of five. We can therefore determine the factor by which the tax burden on their "average" family must be multiplied in order to obtain the absolute aggregate burden of taxation on the whole working-class population.

From the Colwyn Report these data can be obtained relating to the years 1913 and 1925. No fresh data regarding consumption are available. It is assumed that the burden of indirect taxation on the working classes in respect of each particular commodity has changed, since 1925, proportionately to movements in the total revenue obtained from that commodity ; in other words, that the proportion borne by the working class of the whole burden of tax on each commodity has not changed.

Certain other forms of indirect taxation probably are incident on the well-to-do. These include that part of the petrol tax estimated to fall on private motoring, a considerable part of the silk tax, Excess Profits Duty and Corporation Profits Tax, and also employers' contributions and rates on business premises. These two latter are of an ambiguous nature. Some economists would hold that they are probably " charged into prices " of commodities in general, and thus partially fall upon the working classes. A minority would go further and state that all direct taxation is also largely " charged into prices " and thus falls upon the working-class consumer rather than the rich income-earner.

At any rate, it will be generally agreed that the following forms of taxation are diffused in their incidence throughout the whole price structure, and probably fall on the working classes in proportion to their consumption; namely, stamp duties, taxes on commercial vehicles, and general import duties other than on the commodities already specified. An appreciable part of the rates on business premises, and of employers' contributions, is possibly a " diffused tax ", but it has here been regarded entirely as a tax falling on the well-to-do.

The average rates of tax per working-class family, weighting the Colwyn Report figures as above, were as follows:

TABLE 60

BURDEN OF INDIRECT TAXATION, 1913 AND 1925

	1913–14			1925–6		
	£	s.	d.	£	s.	d.
Drink	3	0	0	10	13	6
Tobacco and matches . .	1	11	0	4	10	0
Tea	0	13	6	0	12	6
Sugar	0	7	2	2	4	6
Entertainment . . .		..		0	7	0
Other indirect taxes . .	0	2	6	0	6	6
Total . .	5	14	2	18	14	0

Between 1925 and 1935 there was a 5 per cent increase

in population. The average tax burden per working-class family fell by 9·5 per cent, mainly owing to the heavy drop in the consumption of beer and spirits. The burden of the sugar duty per family fell by 26·9 per cent, owing to the consumption of an increasing proportion of tax-remitted sugar from imperial and home sources. The burden of the beer duty on the average family fell by £1 : 12s., and of the spirits duty by £1 : 6s., owing to decreased consumption. The burden of the tobacco duty, however, increased by £1 : 15s., and there were also increases in the burden of the wine and entertainments duties, owing to increased working-class outlay in these directions.

We can now analyse the whole incidence of national and local taxation for the three years 1913, 1925 and 1935.

TABLE 61

Incidence of National and Local Taxation, 1913–14, 1925–6, 1935–6

1913–14

On Working Class	£s million	Diffused	£s million	On Well-to-do	£s million
orkers' contributions	8	Stamp duties .	10	Direct taxation .	76
nhabited House Duty	1	Other Customs and Excise	5·6	Petrol . .	0·8
ndirect taxation at £5 : 14 : 2 per family	47·6			Rates on business premises	43
hare of diffused taxation	8·6			Employers' contributions	9
ates on dwellings	25			Share of diffused taxation	7
				Rates on dwellings	15
				Other indirect taxes	21
Total . .	90·2	Total .	15·6	Total .	171·8

Share borne by working class . . 34·3 per cent.

[Table—*contd.*

L

1925–6

On Working Class	£s million	Diffused	£s million	On Well-to-do	£s million
Workers' contributions	35	Stamp duties .	24·7	Direct taxes .	398
Indirect taxation at £18 : 14s. per family	142	Tax on commercial vehicles	9	Rates on business premises	74
Share of diffused taxation	22	Other Customs and Excise	8	Employers' contributions	40
Rates on dwelling-houses	66			Excess Profits Duty and Corporation profits	14
				Share of diffused taxation	19
				Rates on dwellings	29
				Other indirect taxes	89
Total . .	265	Total .	41·7	Total .	663

Share borne by working class . . 28·6 per cent.

1935–6

On Working Class	£s million	Diffused	£s million	On Well-to-do	£s million
Workers' contributions	46	Stamp duties .	25·8	Direct taxes .	391
Indirect taxation at £16 : 18s. per family	135	Tax on commercial vehicles	18	Duties on silk .	4
Share of diffused taxation	69	Other Customs and Excise	73	Duties on petrol for private cars	10
Rates on dwellings	88			Rates on business premises	61
				Employers' contributions	54
				Excess Profits Duty, etc.	0
				Rates on dwellings	35
				Share of diffused taxation	48
				Other indirect taxes	86
Total . .	338	Total .	116·8	Total .	685

Share borne by working class . . 33·0 per cent.

The situation in 1925 differed enormously from that of 1913. All forms of taxation had been increased, but the working classes were bearing a lower proportion of the whole. Taxation on consumers of beer and spirits had risen very greatly, but other working-class families had escaped comparatively lightly from the general increase in taxation.

During the last decade the absolute amount of revenue required has again increased. A much higher proportion of this increased total is now levied in taxation falling on the working classes, and the ratio has nearly gone back to the pre-War figure.

We can select the following transfers and services as covering the major part of the public expenditure designed directly to benefit the working classes :

Unemployment benefits and assistance,
War Pensions,
Old Age Pensions,
Widows' and Orphans' Pensions,
Public Assistance,
Health Insurance benefits,
Education,
Public Health services,
Housing,

and the following as mainly benefiting the well-to-do :

National Debt interest,
Highways.

The expenditure in these two classes has been :

TABLE 62

Allocation of Expenditure, 1913, 1925 and 1935

	£s million	
	Beneficial to Working Classes	Beneficial to Well-to-do
1913–14	75·5	36
1925–6	310	336
1935–6	429	263

In 1913 it appears that the working classes contributed more than the cost of the services from which they were the direct beneficiaries, leaving a surplus contribution to general revenue. In 1925 working-class taxation contributed 85 per cent of the cost of these specified beneficial expenditures; in 1935, 79 per cent. Between 1925 and 1935 working-class taxation increased by £73 millions, but expenditure on services beneficial for the working classes increased by £119 millions. This considerable increase comprises the following:

TABLE 63

Increases in Public Expenditure, 1925–35

	£s million
Unemployment benefit	40
Old Age Pensions	40
Widows' Pensions	24
Housing	8
Education	20
Public Assistance	10

—together with a decrease of £25 millions in war pensions.

The net effect of taxation and local rates in 1935 can be described as a redistribution of £91 millions from the rich to the poor in the form of services, other than those provided for from the proceeds of working-class taxation. The £685 millions paid by the rich in indirect and direct taxation provides £263 millions of services beneficial to themselves, £91 millions for transfer as above, and the whole cost (£331 millions) of general administration and of public saving not covered by miscellaneous revenue.

CHAPTER VII

INDEPENDENT DETERMINATION OF THE NATIONAL INCOME

THE results so far obtained are all based upon income statistics of one sort or another—Inland Revenue returns of assessable income, wage statistics, and a number of miscellaneous sources. It is probably the case that the most accurate and complete statistics of national income can be obtained in this way. On the other hand, it is certainly desirable that we should have a completely independent check. Such an independent determination can be made from statistics relating to the spending (or investment) of the national income.

This field has been thoroughly explored by Mr. A. E. Feaveryear,[1] who compiles figures from a number of separate sources showing the amount devoted to all the possible different objects of expenditure. To this he adds a rough estimate of savings, giving a figure which should correspond to the national income.

At first sight it appears that the total thus obtained differs widely from that obtained by an examination of income-tax and wage statistics. Some interesting and important points in the reconciliation of these figures are, however, cleared up in an article by Miss Myra Curtis.[2] She has corrected some theoretical misconceptions on the part of both of us relating to Government revenues from direct and indirect taxation, investment and savings, and has, as it were, drawn up an agreed standardised form for the national accounts.

In the provisional figures analysed by Miss Curtis, and in the final figures given below, it is found that the totals of

[1] *Economic Journal*, March 1931 and March 1934.

[2] *Ibid.*, September 1935.

incomes determined from the side of spending and from the side or earning differ by about £100 millions or 3 per cent (the estimates of outlay exceeding the estimates of income). This figure about represents a reasonable range of error. It may possibly be held to indicate that the amount of evasion (probably the most uncertain item in the whole calculation) is greater than has hitherto been estimated.

Mr. Feavearyear's latest and most comprehensive figures relate to expenditure in the year 1932. This was a year of comparative stability (at the bottom of the slump) and serves very well as a basis for comparison. In Mr. Feavearyear's analysis, a little over half of the national expenditure represented the purchase of goods at retail, and the remainder payments for services, rents, taxes, etc. Of the retail expenditure, nearly half was on food.

In the analysis which follows, I have rearranged Mr. Feavearyear's figures so as to distinguish "services" properly so called from retail purchases. It is thus possible to compile a figure showing the total value of retail sales. Mr. Feavearyear has used different methods for food and for other commodities. For food he has obtained figures of the physical quantities of all the principal foodstuffs consumed, and has multiplied these directly by their average retail prices, making allowances in the case of goods which are partially wasted in the course of distribution (e.g. meat, fish, fruit).

In the case of other commodities, he has used data of values at wholesale obtained from the Census of Production, adjusted for imports and exports, showing the values of consumable manufactured goods available for sale. He has increased these by appropriate ratios to allow for the costs and profits of distribution. I have ventured to revise some of these latter calculations in the light of some more recent information available. This information is based on some fuller calculations which have been supplied to me regarding the value of consumable output in 1930, and of the average gross distributors' margins in recent years, by certain authorities in this field of investigation.

The various categories of consumable goods have been arranged on a classification which accords with the nine classes used by the Bank of England and the Incorporated Association of Retail Distributors in preparing their monthly statistics of retail trade activity. In the case of motor-cars, I have differed slightly from Mr. Feavearyear's procedure. He has allowed one-sixth of the capital value of all cars at present in existence as a kind of depreciation allowance, but I have included with retail sales all sales of new cars. In the case of petrol and lubricating oil, I have included only the amount (as estimated by Mr. Feavearyear) consumed in private cars.

The amount of retail sales, comprehensively defined, is found to have been £2296 millions in the year 1932. Miss Iris Douglas [1] has pointed out the very great discrepancies between a number of estimates, hitherto quoted, of the aggregate value of retail sales. The situation is not quite as bad as it seems, because many of these discrepancies can be accounted for by the fact that different authors define " retail sales " in different ways. Drink, tobacco, coal, motor-cars, petrol or newspapers are sometimes excluded, or various combinations of these, while some authors have quoted figures of the value of retail sales exclusive of the Customs and Excise duties incorporated in the selling value of the goods.

It is possible to analyse the statistics of output in 1930 in order to show the wholesale value of goods retailed during that year. The Final Report of the Census of Production [2] gives £2606 millions as the value at works (or place of import) of all goods available for consumption

[1] *J.R.S.S.*, 1935.

[2] Pp. 52-55. In this Report it is assumed that the net output of agriculture in the U.K. in 1930 was £190 millions. From data given in Table 29 *et seq.* it appears that the net output of agriculture, if defined in the Census of Industrial Production manner, should be about £160 millions. The estimate of £72 millions for the cost of transport and distribution of industrial materials included in the Board of Trade's total should be increased by £14 millions to allow for the cost of distribution of goods used by farmers (on the basis previously suggested). There is thus a net reduction in the total of £16 millions, to £2590 millions.

TABLE 64

RETAIL SALES IN 1932

	£s million
Piece goods	70
Women's wear	139
Men's wear	115
Boots and shoes	55
Furniture	95
Hardware	60
Stationery, drugs and fancy goods	123
Sport and travel goods	31
Foodstuffs	1054*
Other groceries	30†
Drink	232
Tobacco	136
Petrol and oil	21
Car and cycle	40
Newspapers	30
Coal	65
Total	2296

* Mr. Feavearyear's total, *less* net value added by service in hotels and restaurants.
† Soap, matches, oil and candles, which are classified with foodstuffs in the retail trade statistics.

or investment in 1930. This figure is obtained, not by scrutiny of the individual headings showing the output of finished goods, but by the more precise method of adding the net output of industry to the value of basic materials used. It is possible, however, to obtain a result in close agreement by means of analysis of the returns of the output of finished products.

In the case of the food and perishables (including other groceries commonly classified with them) we have the data given in Table 65.

Table 66 identifies the values of finished produce available for sale to the consumer, or sold in other ways, e.g. investment goods, coal for railways and shipping, etc. The figure for the value of capital or investment goods sold anticipates the results obtained on p. 177 below.

One item in Table 66 requires explanation, namely, the inclusion of advertisement revenue of newspapers.

TABLE 65

WHOLESALE VALUE OF FOOD SALES, 1930

	£s million
Value of output of manufactured food, drink, groceries and tobacco returned in the Census of Production	586·5
Product of agriculture, fishery, horticulture, *Less* agricultural, etc., products used by industry	230
Customs and Excise duties on food and drink not already included	54·8
Retained imports, *Less* exports valued at works	297
Total . .	1168

This is necessitated by the method by which the statistics of output of the newspaper printing industry are compiled. Net output is here defined as the excess over the cost of materials of the gross revenue from sales *plus advertisements*, and as a result the statistics of finished output include both the selling value and the advertising revenue of newspapers. When this advertising space is purchased by other industrialists, it is not reckoned by them for Census purposes as cost of materials, and it represents a form of " output " which is not sold directly to the consumer.[1] Other forms of output which must be accounted for are sales of gas, water and electricity other than those used in industrial production, goods supplied for Government use, and fuel used neither for private nor industrial consumption (i.e. for transport services).

This total agrees very closely with the figure of £2606 millions (or £2590 millions) directly computed on page 151.

It is estimated that the retail selling value in 1930 of food, drink, tobacco and groceries was £1596 millions, and

[1] It is probably correct to say that it is sold indirectly to the consumer, by enhancing the price of distributive services, but does not " enter into " the wholesale selling price of industrial produce.

TABLE 66

WHOLESALE VALUE OF GOODS SOLD, 1930

	£s million
Food, drink, tobacco and groceries (Table 65)	1168
Other goods for retailing . . .	653
Investment goods	607
Gas, water and electricity . . .	90
Coal, oil and petrol for railways, shipping and commercial road vehicles	33
Advertising revenue of newspapers .	35
Goods for Government use . .	20
Reduction of Stocks . .	−25
Total . .	2581

of other articles £932 millions. The gross cost of distribution was thus £428 millions or 36·6 per cent of wholesale value in the case of food and perishables, and £279 millions or 43 per cent in the case of other goods. Isolated examples of high distributive margins are of course well known, but many will be surprised that the averages are so high.[1]

We may now compile from Mr. Feavearyear's figures a final estimate of the value of consumption in 1932. As pointed out above, I have rearranged his figures so as to include all commodity consumption under retail sales, and segregated pure " services " consumption. I have added to his figures an estimate for the value of domestic service, which he has not covered, and also for the services supplied by hotels other than the preparation of food. I have also made an entry of £20 millions for subscriptions paid to clubs, trade unions, etc., and a similar sum for fees paid to local authorities for a number of miscellaneous services (schools, parks, etc.). The only other appreciable change which I have made is the entry of £40 millions for the net

[1] It appears that there was some fall in retailers' margins in the years subsequent to 1930. So far as the financial returns of retailing concerns go, the high aggregate gross margins of 1930 were offset by the necessity for writing down stocks during that year owing to the rapid fall in prices.

expenditure on betting. This is based on two articles in *The Economist* [1] in which a careful examination is made of the turnover of various sections of the betting industry and the net amount retained by bookmakers and other promoters. I have quoted a somewhat lower figure for 1932 than their estimate for 1935, in view of the fact that football pool betting was much less a few years ago than it is now.

The figures relating to direct taxation were taken from Table 59 above.

TABLE 67

AMOUNTS SPENT ON GOODS AND SERVICES, 1932

	£s million	£s million
Rail, tram and bus travel *	158	
Domestic service	150	
Entertainment other than betting	57	
Betting	40	
Hotel and restaurant	78	
Medicine	45	
Postal services *	35	
Religious organisations	33	
Laundry	25	
Private education	25	
Fees to local authorities	20	
Clubs, trade unions, etc.	20	
Undertaking	8	
Other services	20	
Total		714
Rent, rates, repairs and mortgage interest on houses	363	
Gas, electricity and private water supply *	85	
		448
Direct taxation and social insurance contributions	..	444
Garaging, insurance, etc., of private cars	..	35
Retail sales previously given	..	2296
GRAND TOTAL	..	3937

* Refers to private expenditure only and excludes business expenditure.

One other type of outlay must now be considered which has not hitherto been included either with consumption or investment. This is the outlay on services connected with

[1] 29th February and 7th March 1936.

the transfer of property from one person to another—such as the incomes earned by stockbrokers, lawyers and auctioneers, together with the stamp duties charged on such transfers. When such services are rendered to business concerns or to landlords, they are regarded as an element in costs of production or maintenance, and allowed as such in the computation of taxable income. When they are rendered to an individual, however, he regards them as expenses necessarily incidental to the outlay of capital.

The numbers engaged can be determined from Census records under the following industrial classifications :

No. 680. Auctioneering, Valuing, House and Estate Agency.
No. 686. Moneylending and Pawnbroking.
No. 688. Land and Estate Development.
No. 689. Stockbroking and Jobbing.
No. 698. Other Finance.
No. 731. Law.
No. 741. Architecture.

Banks, Insurance Companies and Building Societies are not included, the reason for which can best be explained by the following illustration. If a man has £1000 in a bank, he does not say, " I get an income of £35 from this, but my outlay on banking services is £25, so there is only £10 left ". He says, " I get £10 from this ", and fills in his income-tax form accordingly. But if he does £1000 worth of transactions through an estate agent, he reckons that he has to find (say) £25 for fees and stamp duty out of his own pocket, and this is not a deductible expense in the computation of income-tax liability. In other words, the expenses of Banks, Insurance Companies and Building Societies can best be regarded as having been already deducted from the gross incomes of those who have invested money through them.

In the other industries specified above, assuming that half of those engaged in Industries Nos. 680 and 731 are working for businesses,[1] we find the following numbers employed in Great Britain in 1931 :

[1] Or for landlords, who treat their outlay under these heads as a deductible expense under Schedule A.

Employers and managers		23,500
Branch and office managers		4,500
Workers on own account :	Male	8,000
" "	Female	500
Clerks and operatives :	Male	54,400
" "	Female	29,700

The following estimate can be made of the value of the services rendered by these industries :

	£m.
Profits and salaries	35
Rents and other expenses	10
Stamp Duties	19
	64

Using the data of Table 67 regarding consumption and taxation, and anticipating figures given in the next chapter regarding outlay on investment goods (to which the above outlay of £64 million may be added), we can now " balance the accounts " in the form which Miss Curtis has suggested.

TABLE 68

ANALYSIS OF OUTLAY, YEAR 1932

	£s million		£s million
Consumption	3493	Incomes (including trading incomes of State and local authorities)	3303
Taxes and workers' contributions	444	Depreciation and maintenance	366
Gross investment and expenditure on transfer of property	478	Transfer incomes	551
		Savings by public authorities	77
Total	4415	Total	4297

PART OF ABOVE TRANSACTIONS WHICH BECAME INCOME

	£s million		£s million
Spending (*less* indirect taxation incorporated in selling values)	2971	Private incomes	3253
Net investment	48	State and local authority incomes	50
Public services paid for by taxation*	357		
Outlay on transfers of property	45		
Total	3421	Total	3303

* Excluding services paid for out of State and local authority trading incomes.

The discrepancy (which is the same in both tables, as the results of the second table are obtained by making certain deductions from either side of the first table) amounts to £118 millions. It may be the case that evasion is greater than hitherto estimated. This comparison provides a quite independent check on the accuracy of the work which has been done previously. At present we cannot make so detailed a check for any other year than 1932.

The amount spent on goods and services for consumption may be put at £3900 millions in 1932. This includes the whole value of consumable services supplied by State and local authorities (£417 millions, *less* £10 millions value of capital work done on roads) whether paid for out of taxation or out of trading revenues.

There are a considerable number of indications to show the trend of consumption since the year 1932. Retail trade figures, analysed into a number of departments, have been compiled by the Bank of England and the Incorporated Association of Retail Distributors since 1930. The results are given in a rather peculiar form. The returns from different traders in each month are combined into a weighted average, showing the average percentage rise or fall of sales in that month compared with the corresponding month in the previous year. Since 1933 the crude figures have been corrected by the compilers to allow for the varying number of selling days in the different months ; in the figures which are quoted below similar adjustment is made to the earlier data. Publication of the figures began in August 1930, giving comparisons with August 1929. In the table which follows, the year 1930 is taken as base, and index numbers are given showing changes in retail sales by departments in subsequent years. Sales in the twelve months ended 31st January (i.e. covering the after-Christmas sales period) may be regarded as corresponding most closely to output in the previous calendar year. The figures given for 1929 relate only to the six months from August 1929 to January 1930, and for 1936 only to the three months February to April inclusive :

TABLE 69

RETAIL SALES INDEX NUMBERS, 1929–1936

	(6 months) 1929	1930	1931	1932	1933	1934	1935	Feb.–April 1936
Piece goods . .	101·6	100	95·0	85·2	85·6	82·9	81·2	78·4
Women's wear . .	100·5	100	95·5	90·9	92·4	94·3	98·0	100·7
Men's wear . .	103·3	100	95·5	90·1	93·3	96·6	103·2	106·2
Boot and shoe . .	104·2	100	94·1	87·8	88·1	92·6	97·2	100·9
Furniture . .	107·3	100	98·7	93·2	96·7	103·7	108·0	110·8
Hardware . .	104·8	100	95·7	95·3	103·5	106·6	112.0	120·5
Stationery, drugs and fancy goods	104·0	100	93·6	92·9	95·3	98·1	103·3	109·7
Sport and travel .	108·7	100	92·1	90·3	89·3	92·2	96·2	99·8
Food and perishables	103·7	100	94·8	91·6	90·3	93·3	100·8	110·1
Miscellaneous . .	105·2	100	95·3	92·3	89·7	93·4	101·0	108·9

It will be seen that sales of most goods fell to a minimum in 1932 and have subsequently risen to varying levels. The most remarkable contraction is to be found, however, in the case of textile piece goods, sales of which have shown a strong persistent downward trend. Presumably this is partly accounted for by increasing purchase of ready-made clothing, as opposed to home-made.

The level of sales of food is now considerably in advance of what it was in 1929, in spite of much lower prices. This can be largely accounted for by the purchase of better quality goods, and also by the largely increased quantities consumed of both home-produced and imported products.[1]

The other two departments in which sales have risen to a high level are hardware and furniture. Hardware includes electrical goods of all kinds. The high level of furniture sales can easily be accounted for by the large number of new houses which have recently been built, but the very rapid expansion of hardware sales is more difficult to understand. In general, it is probably true to say that hardware covers a number of articles of a lower

[1] In this department, a useful check on the validity of the figures is provided by a new direct estimate for 1934 made by Mr. Feavearyear in *Food, Health and Income*. This was £1075 millions or 2 per cent above the 1932 level, as against a rise of 1·9 per cent in food sales shown in the above table.

degree of urgency in people's scale of purchases, as compared with, say, boots and shoes or clothing, and therefore shows a greater proportionate rise during a period of recovery. As compared with 1929, several departments show evidence of a secular upward movement, which can be explained by the rise in standard of living of many sections of the community.

We can also obtain certain evidence about the trend of the consumption of services from the movement of employment in the relevant industries. These employment figures are obtained from the Ministry of Labour returns of the numbers of insured workers and unemployed in each industry. The number of insured workers attached to each industry, as counted in July of each year, is interpolated to give monthly figures, and the number of unemployed in each month deducted from them. Employment figures thus calculated are averaged for the twelve months. We obtain in this way results less liable to chance fluctuations than those based on the numbers employed in a single month in each year.

The following figures show the numbers employed in four of the principal "service industries" in 1924 and in the years 1929–35, and in the first four months of 1936. These figures are likewise reduced to index numbers on 1930 as a base.

TABLE 70

EMPLOYMENT IN SERVICE INDUSTRIES, 1924–36

(Base 1930 = 100)

	1924	1929	1930	1931	1932	1933	1934	1935	1936 (1st 4 months)
Professions	85·8	96·8	100	103·4	110·0	114·9	116·2	119·3	121·5
Entertainment and sports	86·2	100·2	100	111·0	119·4	132·1	139·8	148·8	155·5
Hotel, catering, boarding-house, etc.	82·2	100·2	100	103·1	104·4	109·6	117·1	122·2	124·2
Laundries	79·5	99·2	100	102·8	107·0	110·3	109·8	112·6	115·9

It is in these forms of consumption that we have evidence of a most rapid rise during the last six years. In the various forms of professional service, the workers in which are covered by employment insurance, the rise in employment during the five years covering the slump (1929–34) was over 20 per cent, which compares remarkably with the rise of 13 per cent in the five years 1924–9. Still more remarkable figures are shown in the entertainment and sports industries. In the hotel and catering industry (covering also employment in boarding-houses, clubs, colleges, etc.), the rate of expansion seems to have continued fairly steadily, being slightly less in the quinquennium 1929–34 than it was in 1924–9. In the laundry industry, which was expanding rapidly from 1924 to 1929, there appears to have been a definite slowing down of the rate of growth.

The above figures provide a useful indication of changes in the direction of consumption during recent years, but do not provide us with any figures from which changes in the aggregate value of consumption can be estimated in detail. Information is, however, available, covering a large part of the field of consumption, from which annual and quarterly estimates, for the period 1929 to 1936, can be made with a fair degree of accuracy.

Our principal source of information is of course from the retail-trade statistics previously mentioned. The figures for sales in each department can be weighted from the results given in Table 64 above. A difficulty, however, arises in obtaining quarterly series from these data, owing to the form in which they are compiled, showing only the percentage changes from the corresponding month of the previous year. This difficulty is avoided by the following procedure. In the first place, an arbitrary assumption is made as to the value of retail sales in each of the four quarters (or the twelve months) of the basic year. By applying the published figures of percentage changes to this arbitrary basis, we obtain a series of figures showing retail sales in each of the succeeding years, the figures for each quarter (or month) containing an arbitrary error. This error will be the same year by year in any given quarter. When the results for several years are available, this arbitrary error can be eliminated by exactly the same technique as is used for the elimination of seasonal variations. We thus obtain a series of index numbers giving a close estimate of the actual sales in each period, and which incidentally is free from the strong seasonal variations to which the original data are subject.

After retail sales, the next largest item shown in Mr. Feavearyear's table is that covering expenditure on rent and rates of houses. This figure shows a fairly strong upward trend, due to the building of new houses, rent increases and derestriction, and some increases in local rates. It is assumed that the total spent on rent and rates, gas and electricity, continues to rise at about the same rate as during the period 1927–32.

The next large item consists of expenditure by means of tax payments on public services of various kinds. The annual value of these services can be obtained from Table 54, and quarterly figures estimated by interpolation.

Another important group of expenditures, not covered to any great extent by the retail trade statistics, are those on drink, tobacco and entertainment (which does not include expenditure on betting). The taxation of these three luxuries provides, however, the principal part of the Customs and Excise revenue. Quarterly figures are available showing the amount of Customs and Excise revenue, though it is only annually that an analysis is given showing the amounts derived separately from taxation of drink, of tobacco and of entertainments. The principal source of Customs and Excise revenue other than under these three heads is from the taxation of petrol and oils. From the figures published monthly by the Board of Trade of the quantity of petrol paying tax, the revenue under this head can be estimated quarterly. There remains to be eliminated a figure of revenue collected under the Import Duties Act, Irish Free State

Special Duties Acts, and other headings. The following is an example of the calculations involved for the year 1935 :

TABLE 71

ANALYSIS OF CUSTOMS AND EXCISE REVENUE, 1935

(£s million)

	1st Quarter	2nd Quarter	3rd Quarter	4th Quarter
Customs and Excise revenue	68·1	73·7	75·8	81·7
Of which :				
Hydrocarbon oils . .	9·9	11·6	12·4	10·8
Import Duties Act, etc. .	17·0	18·7	18·7	18·7
Drink, tobacco and entertainment	41·2	43·4	44·7	52·2
Do. (at 1929 rates*) .	40·4	42·6	44·7	52·2
Corrected for seasonal variation	43·1	46·1	45·1	45·7
Estimated total expenditure on drink, tobacco and entertainment	103·4	115·0	112·5	114·0

* In this case, the only correction involved was for the higher level of Entertainment Duty in force in the first six months of 1935.

Under the headings above, we have now covered something like 75 or 80 per cent of the whole consumptive expenditure of the community. We are left with a residue consisting mainly of services and certain commodities, largely of the nature of non-essential purchases. We have the following seven statistical series which may be held to be indicative of movements of expenditure in this latter field :

Registrations of new motor-cars.
Petrol consumption.
Railway passenger revenue.
Tram and bus revenue.
Postal receipts.
" Miscellaneous " retail sales.[1]
Number of car licenses current.

The number of new cars registered may be taken as a good measure of the level of " luxury " or postponable

[1] This figure, whose scope is perhaps variable, is designed to cover sales of coal, newspapers, catering, hairdressing, etc., i.e. very much the field which we require to cover.

purchases. Petrol consumption and the number of car licenses in existence serve as indicators of the steadier categories of consumption. In this latter series, motor-cycle licenses current are included on the basis of three motor-cycles equivalent to one car. Statistics of tram and bus receipts are obtained from the accounts of the L.P.T.B. and the Area Traffic Commissioners, and are kept up to date by use of published figures of the traffic receipts of certain municipal authorities.

It is assumed that these seven series can give a satisfactory measure of the level of consumption of the miscellaneous services and commodities not already included, and they are weighted as follows :

Registration of new motor-cars	9
Petrol consumption	8
Railway passenger receipts	14
Tram and bus receipts	15
Postal receipts	10
Miscellaneous retail sales	25
Number of cars and cycles licensed	19
	100

We then have the following quarterly figures of consumption free of seasonal variation from the middle of 1929 to the first quarter of 1936:

[TABLE

TABLE 72

QUARTERLY FIGURES OF CONSUMPTION, 1929–36 (£s million)
(Seasonal variations eliminated)

	Retail Sales	Rent and Rates, Gas and Electricity	Public Services	Drink, Tobacco and Entertainment	Other Services and Commodities	Total
1929 :						
i	..	..	..	..	..	..
ii	..	..	..	..	..	..
iii	493·1	104·3	102	122·1	215·8	1037·3
iv	501·5	105·0	102	117·3	211·8	1037·6
1930 :						
i	497·2	105·6	102	119·1	215·0	1038·9
ii	462·0	106·2	102	118·9	210·6	999·7
iii	485·5	106·8	102	117·0	212·7	1024·0
iv	479·8	107·5	102	115·8	209·6	1014·7
1931 :						
i	487·0	108·1	102	117·0	206·7	1020·8
ii	456·5	108·7	102	107·1	204·8	979·1
iii	462·5	109·3	102	115·3	203·3	992·4
iv	449·7	109·9	99	107·1	201·2	966·9
1932 :						
i	452·0	110·6	99	106·2	204·0	971·8
ii	448·5	111·3	99	107·8	203·2	969·8
iii	440·8	112·0	99	108·0	202·8	962·6
iv	446·2	112·7	99	103·6	211·6	973·1
1933 :						
i	431·2	113·1	99	97·2	206·5	947·0
ii	453·7	113·7	99	104·3	209·0	979·7
iii	435·2	114·3	99	105·6	208·1	962·2
iv	456·2	115·0	99	105·6	214·8	990·6
1934 :						
i	450·0	115·6	99	105·8	223·5	993·9
ii	462·7	116·2	100	109·1	216·9	1004·9
iii	450·4	116·8	103	105·0	218·5	993·7
iv	469·8	117·5	106	104·8	227·7	1025·8
1935 :						
i	471·7	118·1	109	103·4	236·9	1039·1
ii	484·6	118·7	112	115·0	234·9	1065·2
iii	483·2	119·3	115	112·5	235·5	1065·5
iv	507·3	120·0	118	114·0	246·6	1105·9
1936 :						
i	510·7	120·6	121	114·4	255·1	1121·8
ii	523·2	121·2	121	115·0	253·8	1134·2

A number of interesting features in this table will be dealt with in a later chapter.

CHAPTER VIII

THE ACCUMULATION OF CAPITAL

THE amount of income saved every year and devoted to the purpose of capital accumulation has for a long time been the subject both of speculation and of measurement. There are two sides from which the problem can be approached, generally described as the " money " approach and the " real " approach. The former studies new capital issues, the disposition of bankers' assets and so forth, in an attempt to estimate the annual *net* flow of money into the purchase of new securities, representing the additions to capital. The " real " approach was first made possible when information as to the output of various classes of goods became available from the Census of Production, and was first used by Sir Alfred Flux in 1912 in interpreting the results of the Census of Production, 1907. For many years, ideas as to the extent of capital accumulation in Britain in recent years were based on an estimate prepared for the Colwyn Committee on National Debt and Taxation by Dr. W. H. Coates, making use of the " money " method.

This method depends on an examination of new capital issues, of the purchase of investments by the banks, of the financing of private house-building, the undistributed profits of companies, and other principal sources of the " flow of savings ". The general conclusion nowadays is, that the more carefully one examines the details of this method, the greater the difficulties become. A large part of the money raised in new capital issues is in fact not used at all for new capital investments, but is used for the purchase of existing assets, the vendors of which may or may not reinvest the money received. The undistributed profits of companies may be used to purchase new issues, or may even find their way indirectly into the financing of private house-building. There are so many possibilities of overlapping between the different items that a net total is quite unobtainable.

On the other hand, with the greater frequency and comprehensiveness of the present Census of Production, and with the accumulation of supporting data relating to the output of various classes of capital goods, the determination of investment from the " real " side should, as time goes on, become more prompt and accurate.

In 1933–4 a detailed investigation into this question was made by the present writer, using the results published and available at that time.[1] At the time of writing, only preliminary reports of the 1930 Census were available, and no results from the 1933 Import Duties Act Inquiry. The publication of the full data necessitates revision of the figures hitherto given for 1930.

The accumulation of capital can be comprehensively defined and classified under the following three heads :

(1) *Fixed Capital*

Work of construction, installation, maintenance and repair done on buildings, plant and machinery, transportation equipment and roads, telephones and telegraphs, gas, water and electricity supply equipment.

(2) *Working Capital*

Investment in working capital, which may be either positive or negative, consists of net additions to the quantity of stocks-in-trade and work in progress during any period. During the period when the price of goods in stock has changed, the net addition or subtraction to working capital is of course not measured by the *change in value* of the quantity of stocks, but by the *current value of the change in quantities* which has taken place during the year.

[1] London and Cambridge Economic Service, Special Memorandum No. 38, " Investment in Fixed Capital in Great Britain ", September 1934.

(3) *Foreign Investment*

This form of investment, which may also be negative, is the amount by which the value of goods and services exported exceeds the value of goods and services imported, reckoning interest on overseas investment as a service exported, and not counting gold as a commodity (i.e. the accumulation of gold is treated as a form of foreign investment).

This definition, including all maintenance and repair work, refers to gross investment, and to determine net investment it is necessary that a deduction should be made for the cost of depreciation and maintenance. In the determination of the national income (Table 36) the actual current expenditure on depreciation and maintenance was reckoned, in view of the great difficulties of estimating the amount of depreciation "attributable" to any one year. For the purpose of estimating the amount of net investment, it is necessary to make a closer estimate. It appears that in one or two directions, particularly on the railways, renewals and maintenance expenditure during recent years have fallen short of the amount properly attributable. Also during certain years, particularly 1931 and 1932, the fact that many businesses were making losses precluded them from claiming wear-and-tear allowances, whence the totals shown under this head in the Inland Revenue statistics are too low for these years. For the years subsequent to 1929, the following figures were taken as representing the necessary minimum of depreciation and maintenance work necessary:

	£s million
Wear and tear	100
Railway maintenance	50
Road maintenance	35
Depreciation and maintenance of other untaxed properties	18
Other maintenance work	70
	273

—together with maintenance and depreciation of buildings (Schedule A allowances) as given.

These Schedule A allowances include certain maintenance work done on tramways, waterworks, etc., but no overlapping is involved, as these are not provided for elsewhere in the table. The rapidly rising maintenance costs of buildings shown in Table 36 (Schedule A allowances, unlike those of Schedule D, are granted to firms making losses and their course was therefore not affected by the slump) are a noticeable and accurately measured effect of the great additions to the number of buildings which have been made during recent years. In all, the cost of merely maintaining intact the existing stock of capital had risen by 1935 to £394 millions a year, or 8·5 per cent of the gross value of home-produced income. In 1924, when the stock of capital was lower but maintenance costs were higher, it was £341 millions, or almost the same proportion (8·3 per cent) of the national income. In 1907 (as estimated below) it was £139 millions. The gross home-produced national income in that year, measured by the same method as the post-War figures, was in the neighbourhood of £2030 millions, of which depreciation and maintenance of the stock of capital required only 6·8 per cent.

The Census of Production is fortunately arranged so that the output of finished capital goods, for new investment and for meeting depreciation and maintenance, consists of the output of five Census industries. These are building and contracting, mechanical and electrical engineering,[1] railway carriage- and wagon-building, repair and construction work done by railway companies, shipbuilding, and commercial vehicles produced by the motor industry.

We require the total output of goods of these types, whether returned on the schedules of the industries concerned or elsewhere, and we must deduct the exports and

[1] The output of *marine engineering* is included in the output of the shipbuilding industry, and of *constructional engineering* under the output of the building and contracting industry.

add imports of goods of these types. We must exclude goods of other types produced by these industries.

Warships and military aircraft are not regarded as forms of investment.

Building and Contracting

The output of building and contracting work coming within the scope of the Census of Production in 1930 is recorded in the *Census of Production*, Part 4, p. 188, including work done by other trades, and by local authorities and Government departments, in addition to work done by the building trades.

TABLE 73

BUILDING AND CONTRACTING WORK DONE, 1924 AND 1930

(Figures in 000's)

Kind of Work done	1924	1930
Construction, alteration, repair or maintenance of—		
Buildings	151,311	181,920
Railways and light railways	24,560	22,337
Tramways	5,013	2,689
Highways	45,727	52,668
Sewers and sewage disposal works	5,489	6,502
Harbours, wharves, docks and piers	5,684	4,039
Canals and waterways	1,676	1,292
Sea walls and embankments	564	1,008
Waterworks, etc.	6,908	6,705
Gas mains and works (other than buildings)	15,137*	9,083
Telegraphic and telephonic lines and works	13,086	13,027
Electric power and lighting lines (including installation and erection of generating plant and appliances)	11,541	19,015
Electrical repair and maintenance work, not separately distinguished	1,627	1,676
Recreation and sports grounds	..	2,674
Other and unclassified works†	2,614	9,906
Total	290,937	334,541
Iron and steel constructional work	15,720	21,301
GRAND TOTAL	306,657	355,842

* Including £6,034,000, work done by employees of gas undertakings on buildings, plant and machinery and on gas mains and works, not separately distinguished.

† Including, in 1930, work of all kinds done on subcontract. In 1924 this work was included against the appropriate headings.

In order to avoid overlapping with other headings, we must at this stage exclude the work done on electrical lines and works, and work done by or for railway companies. We have the following final estimate for the gross value of building and contracting work done in the United Kingdom in 1930 :

	£s million
Recorded for Great Britain in above table . .	355·8
Work done by firms employing under 10 men in the building trade	55
Northern Ireland (including small firms) . .	3·4
Work done by small firms in other trades . .	1
Maintenance work done by manufacturers . .	10
Duplication	−23
Electrical contracting	−32
Railway companies	−30
	340

The subdivision of the total according to the type of work done is very difficult, owing to the fact that repair and maintenance work is often not specified separately from new work, or work on buildings distinguished from work on other constructions. In the output figures, dwellings are not distinguished from other types of buildings, and the proportion of new buildings represented by dwelling-houses has to be partially estimated from data published (for 1924 and for 1930) by the Inland Revenue, showing the proportion of the annual value of new buildings which was represented by dwelling-houses, supported by evidence of the annual value of all plans passed for various types of buildings in certain areas.

Sir Alfred Flux made an estimate of the value of new houses built in 1907, but he appears to have included site values with the cost of construction, and his figure cannot be substantiated from the Census of Production returns. The following are the best estimates which can be made of the allocation of building and constructional expenditure, in the three Census years, covering work done by all firms and public authorities, excluding railway and electrical contracting:

TABLE 74

TOTAL OF BUILDING AND CONTRACTING WORK DONE

(£s million)

	1907	1924	1930
New dwelling-houses . . .	35·0	80·0	95·0
Other new buildings	8·0	36·0	36·5
Construction and maintenance of highways	13·5	47·0	54·0
Other contracting	30·0	40·0	37·5
Repair and maintenance work . .	37·5	85·0	117·0
Total . .	124·0	288·0	340·0

General Engineering

From the output as recorded we must exclude railway, marine, constructional and electrical engineering, the output of heating and ventilating apparatus and similar goods used by the building trade (and thus included in the statistics of the finished output of that trade), and certain minor non-engineering products produced by the engineering trades. We have the following figures for 1930 :

	£s million
Output of engineering products (recorded by all trades) excluding changes in work in progress	128·7
Repair and jobbing work	10·7
Repair work done by manufacturers . . .	13·5
Marine engineering	– 21·0
Heating and ventilating engineering . . .	– 6·4
Railway engineering	– 8·3
Other non-engineering products and duplication .	– 6·7
Output of small firms (other than above excluded products)	5·0
Output of Northern Ireland (other than above excluded products)	1·6
Total . . .	116·9

During the year there was a decline in the amount of work in progress of £2·8 millions, and therefore the true value of work done during the year on engineering products was £114 millions.

The figures compiled for the year 1933 under the Import Duties Act Inquiry show a very considerable reduction in output below this level. The output during the year may be given as follows :

	£s million
Recorded output of products covered	64·8
Repair work by engineers	9·0
Work done by small firms	5·0
Repair work by manufacturers	9·7
Addition to work in progress	0·5
Total	89·0

The items of repair work, and of work done by small firms, have had to be estimated. The Import Duties Act Inquiry of 1934 shows a remarkable increase in output. Allowing also for some increase in the production by small firms and of repair work, we obtain a figure of £108 millions of output, and of £3·7 millions addition to work in progress.

The following are the figures of exports and of retained imports of engineering products, and of the estimated value (at the producers' works) of machinery taken by the home market. Exports are reduced by 6 per cent to convert f.o.b. values to " values at works ".

TABLE 75

Imports, Exports and Home Consumption of Machinery

(£s million)

	1907	1924	1930	1933	1934
Exports	30·7	39·4	40·6	24·5	29·1
Retained imports	4·7	8·3	14·7	7·6	10·1
Home consumption	45·0	100·0	93·5	73·0	91·0

Electrical Engineering and Contracting

Care must be taken not to duplicate entries under this head. The main part of the output consists of work done on electrical lines and works, and on telegraph and telephone lines and works, a large part of which is recorded by electricity supply companies, building and contracting firms, and the Post Office, rather than by firms manufacturing electrical equipment. The values thus recorded of " work done " will include the value of cables, etc., supplied, and these must not be added in twice. The output, free of duplication, of the capital goods under this head is taken to consist of:

(1) Work done on power, lighting, telephone and telegraph lines by all types of firms and public authorities.
(2) Production of electrical machinery, instruments and non-portable accumulators.
(3) Value of installation work on machinery, etc. (recorded net).
(4) Repairs.

Domestic electrical goods such as lamps, wireless sets, etc., are excluded.

Full figures are only available for the Census of Production years, as the 1933 and 1934 inquiries do not cover the building and contracting trades, electricity supply companies or the Post Office, and the main part of installation work was therefore unrecorded. Estimates of the value of such work done in later years (on lighting and power lines) can be made from the annual figures of loans sanctioned by the Electricity Commissioners. These loans include certain sums for the purchase of machinery, and thus overlap with the other output data. On the other hand, they do not cover equipment purchased and the value of work done to meet depreciation and maintenance, which represents a substantial part of the work done. For the value of work done on telephone and telegraph lines, the annual capital outlay under the Post Office (Money) Acts can be used; this figure is open to the similar objection of not covering maintenance expenditure. It is assumed that the absolute changes in the sum of these two loan-expenditure figures will provide a measure of the absolute changes in the value of work done (i.e. that work done to meet depreciation and maintenance, and the extent of duplication, either did not change, or changed in the same direction).

We have the following figures :

TABLE 76

ELECTRICAL ENGINEERING

(£s million)

	1924	1930	1933	1934
Output :				
Electrical machinery	17·6	21·2	16·2	20·2
Telegraph and telephone apparatus .	3·9	6·1	3·8	4·0
Stationary accumulators . .	1·3	0·9	0·7	0·7
Repair work	1·6	1·6	1·6	1·6
Value of work done :				
Post Office lines	13·1	13·0	8·0	9·0
Lighting and power . . .	12·0	19·6	13·6	19·2
Retained imports	1·0	1·7	0·5	0·7
	50·5	64·1	44·4	55·4
Deduct exports (*less* 6 per cent) . .	6·1	7·6	4·4	5·8
Goods supplied and work done for home market	44·8	56·9	40·2	49·9

Shipbuilding and Marine Engineering

Considerable difficulties are involved here owing to the fact that the output fluctuates very rapidly and that the building of a ship is rarely completed in a year. As a result, the value of work done during a particular year may differ very widely from the value of ships completed. The value of work done during the year, which is recorded by the Census of Production, provides the best measure for our purposes. Construction and repair of warships is excluded. We have the following data :

TABLE 77

SHIPBUILDING

(£s million)

	1907	1912	1924	1930
Work on new construction . .	24·7	31·4	36·3	41·8
Repair work	8·4	9·9	17·5	16·5
	33·1	41·3	53·8	58·3
Deduct exports of ships . . .	9·5	6·3	5·5	19·4
Total .	23·6	35·0	48·3	38·9

These figures of course do not represent the general trend of shipbuilding. All four years happen to have been abnormally active. In 1930 a large number of ships were launched, much of the work on which had been done during previous years, and nearly half of which were for export. In the years from 1930 to 1935 scarcely any new ships were built.

Commercial Vehicles

Under this heading are included commercial motor vehicles (lorries, buses and taxis), horse-drawn carts, tram-cars and trolley-buses. Output under these two latter heads has been very small since 1924. There are considerable difficulties in obtaining a figure of the value of repair work done on commercial vehicles.

Aircraft are not included, as almost the whole of the output during recent years has been for military purposes.

The output of motor vehicles was covered under the 1934 Import Duties Act Inquiry, but not in 1933.

TABLE 78

(£s million)

	1907	1912	1924	1930	1934
Commercial vehicles output .	1·7	2·1	6·6	11·3	11·0
Repair work	1·3	1·7	5·1	7·0	8·0
Less net exports . . .	..	..	1·1	1·5	0·6
Total . .	3·0	3·8	10·6	16·8	18·4

Railway Permanent Way and Rolling-stock

We have two separate sources of information on this subject. The first is from the Census of Production, which gives the value of the goods made and work done by the engineering and permanent-way staffs of the railway companies. To these we must add the work done for the railway companies, firstly, by building firms and others in the maintenance of permanent way, stations, etc., and secondly, by engineering and wagon-building firms in the provision of locomotives and rolling-stock (but not covering wagons supplied to private owners).

The other source of information is from the railway companies' own published financial accounts. The amounts spent each year on maintenance and renewals of way and works and of rolling-stock are shown. From the capital accounts we can determine the increase in the railway companies' capital during the year, and we can deduct the amounts which are due to the purchase of land, ships and similar purchases, leaving a residue which represents the expenditure on railway engineering work.

For each of the three years for which these informations can be compared—namely, 1907, 1924 and 1930—we find that the amount allowed for maintenance expenditure, plus the recorded capital expenditure, fell short by £8 millions in each year of the amount of work actually done for the railway companies. It appears, therefore, that approximately this amount of renewal work every year must be done by the railways, but charged to accounts other than the ordinary maintenance and renewal accounts.

We are now in a position to enumerate the gross value of investment in each of the three Census years :

TABLE 79

Output of All Capital Goods for Home Market

(£s million)

	1907	1924	1930
Building and contracting	124·0	288·0	340·0
Engineering	51·4	103·2	90·7
Electrical engineering	11·2	44·8	56·9
Shipbuilding	23·6	48·3	38·9
Vehicles	3·0	10·6	16·8
Railway work	36·0	79·9	63·9
Total	249	575	607

These represent the value of the work actually done during the year, and not necessarily the value of completed capital goods becoming available. In 1907, for instance, they include increments to work in progress in engineering and shipbuilding, representing goods which do not become available until a later year, while in 1930 the reverse is the case. They have all been adjusted for imports and exports of capital goods.

The amount of maintenance and repair work included above can be identified as follows :

TABLE 80

MAINTENANCE AND REPAIR WORK

(£s million)

	1907	1924	1930
Building and contracting :*			
Work done directly by manufacturers .	5	10	10
Work done by builders, etc. . .	32·5	75	107
Roads and bridges	12	39	36
Engineering :			
Work done directly by manufacturers .	13·9	24·6	20
Work done by engineers, etc. . .	6·7	16·3	14
Electrical machinery and equipment .	0·3	2·1	2
Ships	8·4	17·5	16·5
Road vehicles	1·3	5·1	7
Railway rolling-stock and permanent way	21	52·9	47
Total . .	101·1	242·5	259·5

* These totals include :

	1924	1930
Maintenance of plant covered by Schedule D . .	22	13
Maintenance of untaxable properties (Post Office, etc.) .	8	9

After deducting these from the totals shown above, we are left with a sum which has to provide for depreciation and obsolescence as well as for new home investment. This amounts to £148 millions in 1907, £333 millions in 1924 and £348 millions in 1930.

Besides these years, we have information for the output of certain of the trades only for the years 1933 and 1934. We can obtain, however, information of changes in the numbers of insured workers in employment in these industries year by year, or month by month, and these figures will serve as an approximate basis for interpolation and extrapolation. In the case of the building trade, which provides more than half the total, a somewhat better basis of interpolation can be obtained from the statistics of the value of building plans passed in 146 municipalities, which are collected by the Ministry of Labour. The value of maintenance and new capital work done on the railways can be determined year by year from their accounts. For commercial vehicles, monthly figures are available showing the number of new vehicles licensed.

The figures of the value of building plans passed are used by the Board of Trade for computing the index for the volume of building output used in their general index number of industrial production, but the details of their method are not given. It is here assumed that the value of work currently performed on the building of dwelling-houses corresponds to the value of the plans which were being passed three months earlier; in the case of commercial buildings, to the value of the plans passed six months earlier. As has been seen, however, the building and contracting industry contains a comparatively large stable element, in the shape of repair work, and work on the roads, etc., and an index number based on the construction of new buildings alone will tend to overstate its fluctuations.

An attempt is now made to calculate annual and quarterly estimates of the value of output of capital goods, for the years since 1929. The bases of interpolation are as described below. In the case of the building trade, the value of plans passed for new buildings (appropriately ante-dated) are compared with the value of the work actually done in 1924 and 1930. It is found that the value of plans passed for dwelling-houses (which now represent about 75 per cent of the value of all new buildings) had a slight upward bias of about 1 per cent per annum when compared with the actual figures. It is assumed that this bias continued. The value of building plans for commercial buildings had a much stronger upward bias of nearly 5 per cent per annum. This is also extrapolated, but less precision can be claimed for the result. Repair work is assumed to increase linearly at the same rate as during the period 1924–30. Finally, the value of contracting work is assumed to be approximately constant, except during the period 1931–3, when public contracts of all kinds were delayed during the economy campaign.

The cause of this upward bias is probably due to the exclusion of rural districts and small towns, and possibly also to the inclusion of returns from rapidly growing boroughs in Outer London.

The returns for the four principal types of buildings are each multiplied by a factor which gives the correct total for the year 1930, and the seasonal variation is removed from each series.

The accuracy of this method can be tested when the results of the 1935 Census become available. The results of the extrapolations so far made indicate that the value of all building and contracting work done, including work done by small firms, work returned on schedules for other trades, and including as before an allowance for the repair work done by the manufacturers, should equal almost exactly £400 millions for 1935.

In the engineering trade, a considerable number of those recorded as engineers under Unemployment Insurance are in fact engineers employed by the railway companies. Their numbers can be obtained from the railway companies' annual staff returns, and deducted from the insurance statistics. On comparing these figures with the value of engineering output as previously calculated, the average gross output per insured worker in employment is found to be £319 for 1924, £301 for 1930 and £305 for 1933. The returns for 1934 show a sudden jump of 15 per cent in output per insured worker as compared with 1933. This is perhaps not so surprising as it seems, in view of the rapid expansion of output which was then taking place, for the first time in many years. For interpolation purposes, it is assumed that the old ratio held up to the end of 1933 and that since then the new ratio has held.

For shipbuilding and electrical engineering, where the

output involved was smaller, the 1930 ratio is used throughout. In the former industry the average output per worker is much lower than in 1924, in the latter higher.

In 1934 the output of commercial vehicles was much higher than in 1930 when measured in number, but about the same when measured in value. Interpolation is effected in the basis on the number of new vehicles licensed during each quarter, with an allowance for the downward trend in average values, and a constant addition for repairs.

Imports are added at price c.i.f. When the deduction is made for exports, 6 per cent is deducted from the f.o.b. value of exports and re-exports, to allow for cost of transport and merchanting between place of production and seaport.

It is convenient to reckon the value of investment at this stage. But in the case of machinery (not buildings or ships) some further allowance, possibly up to 10 per cent of its value at maker's works, should be made for the cost of transport, merchanting and installation.

We must now convert these into net figures by the deduction of depreciation and maintenance charges. The estimate of maintenance charges is derived from page 86 above, and has already been quoted. It is necessary, however, to construct a similar figure for the year 1907.

Sir Alfred Flux, in the calculations made at the time of the first Census of Production, estimated £180 millions as representing the cost of depreciation and maintenance of all home capital in that year. When compared with calculations made by the same procedure as was used for the post-War years, this figure seems to be considerably too high.

The pre-War Schedule A figures do not provide so precise a measure of the cost of maintenance of buildings and of agricultural land, owing to the comparatively high income-tax exemption limit in force at that date. About

15 per cent of the gross income from property was then exempt from income-tax, owing to its ownership by

TABLE 81

QUARTERLY FIGURES OF OUTPUT AND HOME CONSUMPTION OF CAPITAL GOODS (SEASONAL VARIATION ELIMINATED), 1929–36

(£s million)

	Home Sales: Commercial Vehicles	*Output:* Engineering	Shipbuilding	Electrical Engineering	Railway Maintenance	*Building:* Dwelling-houses	Factories and Workshops	Shops and Offices	Public Buildings, etc.	Repair Work	Contracting	Net Exports of Machinery and Ships	Total consumed in Home Market
1929:													
i	4·3	32·1	13·9	13·3	15·7	20·0	4·75	2·49	3·30	28·2	23	12·7	148·2
ii	4·6	32·2	14·8	13·6	15·5	17·5	3·47	3·67	3·62	28·4	23	12·9	147·5
iii	4·6	32·1	15·0	14·0	15·5	25·4	2·88	1·82	3·45	28·6	23	12·4	154·0
iv	4·5	32·0	15·6	14·2	15·5	22·6	5·95	3·33	4·84	28·8	23	12·0	158·3
1930:													
i	4·4	30·7	15·2	14·4	16·0	23·3	2·78	2·07	3·53	29·0	23	10·3	154·1
ii	4·2	29·6	14·7	14·4	16·0	21·9	3·78	2·60	3·76	29·2	23	13·6	149·5
iii	4·1	28·4	13·8	14·4	15·9	26·1	4·57	2·59	3·14	29·4	23	11·6	153·8
iv	4·2	26·4	12·2	14·4	15·8	23·6	2·42	1·99	3·27	29·6	23	10·1	146·8
1931:													
i	4·2	24·9	10·1	13·6	13·3	22·6	2·06	2·01	3·88	29·7	24	7·5	142·8
ii	4·2	23·7	8·7	13·5	13·5	19·4	1·98	1·85	5·58	29·9	24	8·0	138·3
iii	4·1	22·9	8·2	13·3	13·3	21·3	2·05	1·92	3·69	30·1	24	6·9	137·9
iv	4·0	23·1	7·3	13·2	13·0	24·2	1·36	1·95	3·30	30·3	21	5·5	137·2
1932:													
i	3·8	23·0	6·4	13·0	14·0	15·6	1·23	1·59	3·28	30·4	21	5·1	128·2
ii	3·7	22·3	6·3	12·8	13·4	18·5	1·55	2·36	2·49	30·6	21	8·0	127·0
iii	3·6	21·7	6·1	12·5	13·4	25·5	1·38	1·40	2·23	30·8	21	5·1	134·5
iv	3·7	21·3	5·8	12·3	13·2	21·0	1·52	1·43	2·18	31·0	21	5·0	129·4
1933:													
i	3·6	21·2	5·3	11·7	12·5	26·9	1·97	1·54	1·30	31·2	21	5·4	132·8
ii	3·9	21·9	5·8	11·5	12·5	25·5	1·60	2·54	1·99	31·4	21	4·8	134·9
iii	4·0	22·6	6·4	11·6	12·5	31·7	2·07	1·38	3·85	31·6	22	4·6	145·1
iv	4·2	22·9	6·7	11·7	12·5	33·2	1·65	1·56	2·27	31·8	22	5·4	145·1
1934:													
i	4·4	26·4	6·5	13·1	12·0	31·2	1·35	1·26	2·24	32·0	23	4·8	148·6
ii	4·2	27·0	7·2	13·3	12·6	31·3	2·44	1·49	1·50	32·2	23	5·5	150·7
iii	4·0	28·9	9·1	14·3	12·6	36·8	3·20	1·40	2·34	32·3	23	5·1	162·8
iv	4·2	29·2	9·1	14·4	12·8	32·1	2·59	1·54	2·82	32·5	23	6·8	157·4
1935:													
i	4·3	29·0	8·6	15·0	13·0	33·8	2·94	1·87	2·33	32·7	23	7·0	159·5
ii	4·0	29·4	9·1	15·2	13·2	34·5	2·99	1·38	1·63	32·9	23	6·8	160·5
iii	3·9	29·8	9·6	15·5	13·4	38·7	3·98	1·87	3·40	33·0	23	6·4	169·7
iv	4·0	30·8	10·3	15·8	13·6	37·7	2·90	2·34	3·42	33·2	23	6·7	170·4
1936:													
i	4·5	31·0	10·3	15·8	13·8	39·0	3·90	2·38	3·85	33·4	23	6·0	174·9
ii	4·2	31·6	10·8	16·0	14·0	33·5	3·44	2·82	2·95	33·6	23	5·6	170·3

persons of low incomes or by religious and charitable institutions, and the published total of repair allowances must be raised accordingly. An addition of 5 per cent is made to the value of allowances under Schedule D, to account for small businesses exempt from tax. The total is obtained as follows :

TABLE 82

MAINTENANCE AND DEPRECIATION IN 1907

	£s million
Schedule A allowances adjusted .	46·5
Schedule D allowances adjusted .	21·0
Railway maintenance . . .	21·0
Roads, Post Office and other untaxed property	20·0
Other maintenance	30·5
Total .	139·0

Sir Alfred Flux's higher total was obtained from a rough estimate of the value of capital employed in industry and transport, which was assumed to require 4 per cent per annum allowance for depreciation and maintenance. The total of Inland Revenue allowances gives a considerably lower figure. This is not attributable to any change in the scale on which the Inland Revenue allowances were reckoned. The evidence of the Board of Inland Revenue to the Royal Commission on Income-Tax, 1920,[1] describes the circumstances under which wear-and-tear allowances and allowances under Schedule A were given. From 1878 to 1897 they were assessed by local commissioners, but from the latter date onwards they were allowed nationally. Examination of the scale of allowances printed in the above evidence shows that the same rate of depreciation on the principal types of machinery was allowed then as now. Since 1897, moreover, the obsolescence allowance has been in force (under which a manufacturer can claim the unexhausted value of a machine which is scrapped before wear-and-tear allowances have written it down to scrap value), and a uniform rate of allowances under

[1] See particularly Appendix III to the Minutes of Evidence.

Schedule A was in force. It is interesting to note the very rapid growth in the total of wear-and-tear allowances, and the much slower growth of Schedule A allowances.

TABLE 83

MAINTENANCE AND DEPRECIATION, 1901–34

(£s million)

	Wear-and-Tear Allowances	Schedule A Allowances
1901–2	11·5	34·3
1907–8	20·0	39·5
1913–14	34·9	43·4
1920–21	51·7	47·0
1924–5	55·9	74·8
1934–5	105·0	110·0

The second column can be fully explained by the increase in building costs and in the number of buildings, but the first column can only be explained on the assumption of progressive introduction of the shorter-lived types of machinery, as a result of which a rapidly increasing proportion of the produce of industry is required to meet the depreciation of existing capital.

We are now in a position to enumerate the whole total of capital investment. The totals of overseas investment are taken from estimates prepared by the Board of Trade. Investment in working capital is calculated in Appendix III for the years 1931–3. For earlier years it is taken from *The National Income, 1924–1931*. For 1934 and 1935 there is certain evidence, which will be dealt with in a later publication, to show that movements have been very small.[1]

[1] This evidence is derived from a comparison of the output of imports and exports of finished and semi-finished goods. At a time when working capital is being accumulated, this must take the form of a relatively high output on the part of the industries producing semi-finished goods. Independent data are also now available of changes in retailers' stocks. Calculations along these lines are used to interpolate the data in changes in working capital in the years 1929–33.

TABLE 84

CAPITAL INVESTMENT,* 1907–35

(£s million)

	1907	1924	1929	1930	1931	1932	1933	1934	1935
Fixed capital, gross .	249	576	623	607	560	526	556	619	662
Fixed capital, net .	110	235	255	235	178	141	168	228	268
Working capital .	..	20	−44	−84	−40	−61	−107	−2	0
Overseas investment	138	72	103	28	−104	−51	0	−2	37
Total net .	248	327	314	179	34	29	61	224	305

* The deductions for maintenance and depreciation in this table, for the conversion of gross investment to net, are calculated on a basis of the amounts properly attributable to each year, rather than the amounts actually spent (as in Tables 36 and 37).

The course of these figures is very interesting. Investment as a percentage of the national income was as follows:

1907 . .	12·2	1929 . .	7·2
1924 . .	8·1	1935 . .	6·9

During the period 1931–3 the net additions to capital were exceedingly small. Net additions to fixed capital, though heavily diminished, remained, at any rate, well on the positive side throughout the slump. But this was offset by considerable decumulation of stocks from 1929 to 1933 and a heavy negative trade balance in 1931 and 1932.

A comparison of changes in the *proportion* of national income saved in various years does not give such interesting results as a comparison of the relationship between the *absolute* variations of investment and of income. The results of this comparison will be discussed in a later chapter.

Having prepared a fairly full analysis of investment from the "real" side, we may turn now to examine some of the relevant factors from the "money" side; with the proviso that the traditional method of examining the problem, through statistics of new capital issues, must be regarded as quite useless owing to duplication.

It is well known that the principal source of savings under modern conditions is in the undistributed profits of companies and firms (including private companies). In the Colwyn Report the building of private houses is treated as a form of saving, on the assumption that it is always privately financed, but it would be difficult to maintain this contention today. Repayments of principal to building societies are of course an important channel of private saving, but these amounts are by no means equivalent to the value of new houses built during the year, and will be dealt with below.

In default of fuller information, an estimate of year-by-year changes in the amount of undistributed profits can be derived from *The Economist's* analysis of company profits and losses. *The Economist's* figures cover all companies in their records, without any attempt at weighting. The result is that companies operating abroad and certain speculative industries are seriously over-weighted, and several other trades such as retail distribution are under-weighted. *The Economist's* figures also include the results of a number of investment trusts, thus introducing an element of duplication. Their results, however, are much more comprehensive than any possible alternative source. In July of each year *The Economist* publishes an aggregate covering the trading results of all the companies in its files whose accounts had been published during the past twelve months, i.e. companies whose terminal date averages somewhere near the end of the previous December, thus corresponding fairly well with the "income-tax year". In the table which follows, the figures are set against the years in which the profits are estimated to have been made.

We have no knowledge of the amount of undistributed profits of private companies and individual traders, and we must assume that the proportion of their profits saved each year is the same as that of public companies. This will probably have the effect of exaggerating our total of savings. On the other hand, the inclusion of a number of investment trusts in *The Economist's* figures will probably work in the opposite direction. In Table 39 above we calculated by difference the aggregate amount of profit and interest in each of the years from 1924 to 1935. In a number of years this figure must differ considerably from what would be regarded as profits in drawing up a company's accounts, owing to the question of revaluation of stocks during the period of falling prices. From our definition, it will be remembered, the amounts thus written off in inventories are not deducted from profits. In the table below, a revised figure for profits is shown after deduction of these sums. It will be noticed that *The Economist* covers a substantial and increasing proportion of the whole total of profits, and their ratio of undistributed to distributed profits is used to calculate the total amount of undistributed profits.

TABLE 85

UNDISTRIBUTED PROFITS, 1924–35

	Profits and Interest (£s m.)	Profits, Interest and Rent after writing down Stocks	% covered by *The Economist* sample	% of Profits Undistributed	Estimated Total Undistributed Profits (£s m.)
1924	834	834	18·0	22·3	186
1925	1014	793	20·8	21·1	167
1926	823	749	23·9	17·9	134
1927	853	765	22·7	20·6	158
1928	801	778	25·4	20·3	158
1929	821	740	26·8	18·6	138
1930	902	651	28·8	15·8	103
1931	620	518	26·9	5·5	28
1932	590	539	25·5	8·8	47
1933	642	642	24·8	17·2	110
1934	781	749	27·0	20·9	156
1935	949	949	..	24·0	228

The figure for 1924, although worked out quite independently, agrees very closely with the official figure (£194 millions) quoted in the Colwyn Report. For no other year have we any check. The very considerable rise shown during recent years is in accord with common experience.

There is also considerable information about the savings of the middle and working classes through certain well-known channels. Much the most important of these is now in the form of repayments of principal to building societies. We are not entitled to assume, what may have been the case in the past, that deposits with and shares in building societies represent mainly working-class and middle-class savings. On the other hand, principal repayments to building societies must mainly represent savings of these classes. The amount of such repayments can be estimated by comparing the value of new mortgages granted during the year with the net increase in the value of mortgages outstanding between the beginning and end of the year. In a period when defaults are not numerous, the amount by which the latter falls short of the former probably represents repayments of principal made during the year. These have risen from £20 millions in 1924 to £72 millions in 1934. During this period, however, the amount advanced on mortgage during the year has increased threefold (from £40 millions to £124 millions), and mortgages outstanding from £120 millions to £476 millions.

The net savings through life insurance can be defined as the amount by which the income of the life assurance and industrial assurance companies exceeded their outgoings during the year, transfers to and from reserve not being included. The foreign business done by British insurance companies is almost exactly balanced by the British business done by overseas insurance companies. In this construction, the insured person is regarded as saving, not only his actual premium payments, but also the interest received on the insurance companies' invested funds, less the companies' expenses and profits.

Other forms of working-class savings are through the Post Office and Trustee Savings Banks, through National Savings Certificates, and through " Provident Societies ". The net annual addition to the assets of these latter has averaged nearly £15 millions a year over the last eight years, and savings through savings banks have been of the same order of magnitude. We have the following figures of working-class and middle-class savings :

TABLE 86

WORKING- AND MIDDLE-CLASS SAVINGS
(£s million)

	Repayments of Principal to Building Societies	Life Insurance	Other Working-class Savings (Savings Banks, Provident Societies, Savings Certificates)	Total
1924	19·7	42·3	24·9	86·9
1925	23·7	53·3	14·4	91·4
1926	26·8	51·8	12·4	91·0
1927	29·3	48·9	22·3	100·5
1928	28·8	50·2	35·4	114·4
1929	34·1	49·2	12·5	95·8
1930	40·6	41·0	41·2	122·8
1931	50·5	45·6	21·9	118·0
1932	54·0	57·2	50·7	161·9
1933	68·0	55·9	40·7	164·6
1934	71·9	54·6	45·9	172·4

A considerable number of life insurances represent the savings of the well-to-do, but the remainder of the life insurance, and the other forms of saving dealt with above, consist entirely of working-class and middle-class savings.

Another form of saving, if saving be defined as excess of income over consumption, consists of the writing down of stocks described previously. This is a concealed form of saving, but represents an important manner in which, at certain periods, dividends distributed to shareholders are made to fall short of the net income earned by industry as defined for national income purposes.

We are now in a position to bring together the whole total of savings.

Trading losses are included with investment in this comparison, for the reason that such losses must be met, in some way or another, by sale of assets, and hence by the using up of the monetary savings of others.

In the years prior to 1929 the items of saving specified just about equalled the whole total of losses and investments. During the slump years, investment fell heavily, a large part of this decline being balanced by a rise in trading

TABLE 87

TOTAL INVESTMENT COMPARED WITH SAVINGS FROM CERTAIN SOURCES, 1924 AND 1927–35

(£s million)

	1924	1927	1928	1929	1930	1931	1932	1933	1934	1935
Savings:										
Undistributed profits .	186	158	158	138	103	28	47	110	156	228
Working- and middle-class savings	86·9	100·5	114·4	95·8	122·8	118	161·9	164·6	172·4	..
State and local authority savings	56	89	94	91	54	56	77	105	101	83
Written off inventories	..	88	23	81	251	102	51	..	32	..
Total .	328·9	435·5	389·4	405·8	530·8	304	336·9	379·6	461·4	..
Investment . . .	327	330	360	314	179	34	29	61	224	305
Trading losses . .	30	30	30	30	100	165	140	120	50	30
Total of investment and losses*	357	360	390	344	279	199	169	181	274	335

* Expenses arising out of the transfer of property from one owner to another, which are probably treated as capital outlay in most cases, were estimated at £64 millions in 1931–2, and help to explain the discrepancy between the figures of saving and investment.

losses. The figures relating to savings did not drop to a similar extent. It is possible that *The Economist* figures for the slump years are slightly too high owing to the omission of some of the companies making losses or paying dividends out of reserves. But at the same time it is clear that a considerable amount of this discrepancy can be accounted for, during the slump years, by individuals spending out of capital at a time when their incomes fell very sharply.

Private savings, it will be noticed, are not included at all in Table 87.

During the last four years, it appears that the sources of savings specified have been adequate to account for the whole total of investment ; in other words, that private saving has not recovered to the modest level which it occupied in the years prior to 1929, and in fact private individuals are probably still on balance spending from their capital.[1]

The outstanding fact of the situation is that three channels of saving—namely, the obligatory saving funds of local authorities, trading profits held back by company officials, and savings for security by the working and middle classes—provided enough to meet nearly the whole of investment requirements in recent years, and more than enough at the present time. Large private incomes have ceased to count as a source of saving. Opinions may differ as to whether this is due to the present level of taxation, low interest rates or lack of investment opportunities ; and whether an increase in taxation would lead to lowered consumption on the part of the rich, or an increasing rate of decumulation.

These conclusions may appear startling, but they are broadly confirmed by some recent figures published by Mr. Feavearyear.[2] From an examination of Death Duty

[1] Or spending the proceeds of capital appreciation of securities, which is equivalent to spending capital from the social, if not the individual, point of view. The figures dealt with relate to *net* private saving after provision for taxation and Death Duties.

[2] *Economic Journal*, June 1936.

statistics he has made estimates of the change in the aggregate value of *private* fortunes in Great Britain during recent years, deflating by a specially constructed index number to allow for changes in the price of securities and other assets. His broad conclusion is that in the years up to 1929 private capital, measured at a given level of security values, was increasing at the rate of about £300 millions per annum. From 1930 to 1933 it showed a decline. In 1934 the decline was arrested, but no increase was shown.

This chapter may be closed with some figures about the outlay of invested capital during the years for which information was available. One of the principal sources of capital requirement has always been the construction of dwelling-houses for an increasing population, or to give a higher standard of accommodation to a given population. A somewhat kindred need is in the provision of roads and of other public utility requirements. Many of these are covered by local-authority activities. Figures of the capital outlay of local authorities are shown for the various years. For the last two years, detailed figures not being available, estimates have had to be made on the basis of published figures of loan sanctions granted by the Ministry of Health. These are not very satisfactory, as a considerable number of local authorities obtained sanction for loans from private Acts of Parliament and in other ways. Municipal capital expenditure is shown exclusive of work on housing, roads, electricity supply and transport. Capital expenditure for electricity supply is derived from the Electricity Commissioners' Reports (estimated for 1907 from Municipal Statistics), and capital expenditure by the Post Office from borrowing sanctioned under the Post Office (Money) Acts. After meeting these various housing and public utility requirements, the residue available for industrial and commercial capital is calculated by difference.

TABLE 88

CAPITAL OUTLAY

(£s million)

	Net Home Investment in Fixed Capital	Houses	Roads	Electricity	Other Municipal Outlay (excluding Transport)	Post Office	Industrial and Commercial Capital
1907	110	35	2	5	18	1	49
1924	235	80	18	13	33	10	81
1928	240	75	19	29	35	11	71
1929	255	85	28	22	37	11	72
1930	235	95	34	24	44	11	27
1931	178	87	34	21	48	10	−22
1932	141	80	21	23	39	7	−29
1933	168	117	17	18	40	6	−30
1934	228	131	15	24	50	7	1
1935	268	145	..	..	..	..	25 ?

CHAPTER IX

PRICES, REAL INCOME AND SHORT-PERIOD DETERMINATION OF THE NATIONAL INCOME

"When between two dates prices have undergone large changes, a mere comparison of money incomes does not tell us much. We instinctively try to penetrate the money façades and to discover what has happened to the 'real' incomes behind them. If the quantities of all the various types of goods and services that become available in a year had changed in the same proportion, this proportion would show in an unambiguous way how real incomes had changed. But when, as, of course, happens in actual life, the quantities of different types of goods and services have altered in very various proportions, real income becomes a shadowy concept. It is no longer a physical entity, susceptible of direct measurement, but a sum of money divided by some index of general prices. Moreover, there are alternative ways of constructing index numbers for this purpose, between which it is not possible to say that this one is right, that one wrong. Over a considerable range the choice can only be arbitrary."[1]

The difficulties of measurement notwithstanding, an instinctive desire to "penetrate the money façades" remains, and though we have to measure the national income in money terms, the results are for most purposes of little use to us unless we can translate them into "real" terms. Some of the ambiguity to which Professor Pigou refers is due to the fact that we ourselves are not precisely clear as to the purpose for which we wish to use the measurements.

There are two principal uses to which measurements of real income can be put. The first type of measurement, or of index number suitable for converting money to real

[1] Prof. A. C. Pigou, Royal Economic Society, Memorandum No. 60.

measures, sets out to determine the changes in utility or welfare obtained by the consumer from a unit of money income, due to changes in prices. This is a fairly clearly marked concept. The principal difficulty involved is when, as is always the case to some extent, the relative quantities of different commodities and services consumed have changed during the period in question. Often, however, these changes have no appreciable effect on the calculations. Where they are large, there is no better formula than that suggested by Professor Pigou himself,[1] which also incidentally provides a method for comparing the standard of living in different countries as well as at different times.

When, however, we are dealing, not with consumption, but with income as a whole, a further difficulty is involved owing to the fact that a proportion of the income is invested. One possible treatment is to calculate the real value of such an income, on the basis of its real purchasing power if it had all been consumed and none invested ; this is the method which has been adopted in the Royal Economic Society Memorandum mentioned above.

A very different concept is introduced when we attempt to measure " real production " rather than " real consumption ". It might be thought that these two quantities will necessarily be the same or almost the same. But in a country such as Britain this is by no means the case. A considerable proportion of our output is exported, and of our consumption is imported ; and during a period in which the terms of trade have changed, as for instance during recent years, a diminished output for export may actually exchange for an increased quantity of imported goods for consumption.

In my previous book I have developed the concept of a price index applicable to output as a whole. The form of this index was largely determined by the practical considerations of the form in which statistics of the prices of consumption goods were available, rather than on any

[1] *Economics of Welfare,* chapter vi.

new theoretical principle. The basic idea is, that such an index should incorporate an index number of the current prices of goods and services for consumption, and that weighted additions should be made for the prices of visible and invisible exports, and of home investment goods, and that then a negative weight should be given to the price of imports. In this manner, the index number reflects as closely as is practicable the price of *output* rather than of any other variable.

Goods and services available for consumption represent very clear and definite concepts, and we can make very accurate index numbers of their average prices, provided we have enough data. But the measurement of the price of " goods and services produced " involves much greater difficulties, for the reason that much production consists of a net addition to value. For example, take the case of a loaf of bread or a cotton shirt—a substantial proportion of whose value consists of imported material, and the remainder of " net output " of home manufacturers and distributors. The selling price of this " net output " can only be determined by subtracting, on certain assumptions, a figure indicative of material costs from the actual price of the finished article. Very similar difficulties arise when attempts are made to make direct measurements of changes in the quantity of output by means of index numbers. The Board of Trade index number of industrial production compromises on this point. The figures of the gross or final outputs of the various products are used, but each is weighted proportionately to the net value added by the industrial process in question.

The following are the average prices obtained :

[TABLE

TABLE 89

PRICES OF OUTPUT

(1930 = 100)

	Consumption	Exports	Capital Goods	Retained Imports
1929 :				
i	103·2	105·5	101·0	113·0
ii	102·7	103·7	101·9	113·8
iii	102·2	105·3	101·9	114·2
iv	102·1	104·2	102·1	112·1
1930 :				
i	101·9	103·2	101·9	107·9
ii	100·3	100·3	99·7	101·5
iii	99·8	99·5	99·6	99·0
iv	98·1	96·4	98·1	92·2
1931 :				
i	96·8	93·2	98·6	84·4
ii	96·0	90·8	97·8	81·7
iii	95·3	87·8	96·9	78·6
iv	92·1	86·1	96·8	78·6
1932 :				
i	92·8	84·2	95·2	78·0
ii	96·0	84·3	95·4	74·5
iii	94·4	82·0	94·1	72·2
iv	93·5	82·5	94·1	73·9
1933 :				
i	92·8	81·7	94·0	70·2
ii	91·9	80·8	93·5	70·0
iii	91·9	81·9	93·2	71·7
iv	92·9	82·8	92·4	73·5
1934 :				
i	91·9	82·1	92·4	73·0
ii	92·3	82·6	93·6	73·1
iii	93·2	82·2	93·7	73·4
iv	92·6	82·0	94·1	75·6
1935 :				
i	92·6	81·7	93·7	74·4
ii	93·2	81·2	93·6	73·4
iii	93·7	82·1	93·5	74·6
iv	93·7	82·2	94·0	77·6
1936 :				
i	94·4	82·1	94·0	77·2

The following are the weights used in the calculation of a general price index number, now based on the year 1930 :

	£s million
Consumption Goods :	
Retail food prices	1173
Other retail prices	757
Rent and rates	350
Fuel and light	150
Beer *	185
Petrol	20
Motor-cars	35
Other tobacco and drink, services, etc.	444
Public services †	400
Unknown	545
Investment Goods :	
Building	360
Iron and steel	100
Machinery ‡	130
Commercial vehicles	21

* The price of this article was taken as constant except during the period of increased duty from September 1931 to April 1933.

† The price of these services was assumed to be reduced by 3 per cent during the period of Government and Municipal salary abatements from September 1931 to July 1934, and by 1½ per cent during the ensuing year.

‡ Derived from export prices.

The principles of weighting described above were used previously in the construction of a price index number applicable to output as a whole, but it will be seen below that they break down when big changes of prices are involved, particularly when the price of one class of goods moves very differently from that of another, as in the following example :

TABLE 90

PRICE INDEXES

	Values in Base Year	Price Index in Later Year	Values in Later Year	Calculation of Weighted Price Index	Income in Later Year revalued at Prices of Base Year
Home consumption and investment	4500	90	4000	4050	4444
Exports	700	80	350	560	438
Retained imports (*deduct*)	1000	60	800	600	1333
Invisible exports	400	90	250	360	278
Total	4600	..	3800	4370	3827

This is drawn from the experience of Hypothetica, a

country not unlike our own, which before the slump had a national income of £4600 millions, £100 millions of which was invested overseas in the form of an export surplus. During the slump its income fell to £3800 millions. Owing to the abnormal cheapness of imports and favourable terms of trade, the quantity of imports consumed rose and exports fell. Calculating our price index number applicable to home output, we obtain a result of $\frac{4370}{4600}$, or 95·1. Their income of £3800 millions therefore apparently corresponds to an income of £3995 millions at prices of the base year. If, on the other hand, we reconvert each of the four items back to quantities (measured at base year prices) by means of the appropriate index number, we reach the conclusion that the value of output at base year prices was only £3827 millions.

In Britain the fluctuations have not been quite so extreme, and if they had been tabulated would not have illustrated the point quite so neatly. But we may be satisfied that there is a danger of appreciable inaccuracies in using such an index number of prices over a period such as the present. The only safe procedure is to take separately the value of consumption, investment, imports and exports and revalue each of them at the price of some base year. The Board of Trade index number of prices is now based on the year 1930, for the reason that we have for that year a Census of Production. Although it has undoubted drawbacks as a base year, owing to the rapid fall of the prices and production which was taking place, it has at any rate the merit of standing half-way between the two very different periods 1924–9 and 1931–6. A base year situated in one of these quinquennia might have caused serious distortion in the measurement of phenomena in the other period.

The measurement of real income therefore involves the revaluation of annual and quarterly series relating to the value of consumption and investment (the revaluation of imports and exports at 1930 prices has already been done by the Board of Trade). But there is an alternative method giving figures almost as comprehensive, i.e. proceeding direct from statistics of output.

A comprehensive index number of industrial output has been calculated by the Board of Trade since 1928, and in 1935 it was revised and enlarged. The results of the 1930 Census of Production show that over the period 1924–30 the index provided a good measure of changes in the output of industries which it purported to cover. Its principal omissions at that time were of building and similar work (by private builders and by local authorities), which omission has been partially repaired in the recent index.

The items to be included in a general index number of the quantity of production are as follows :

Industry

Board of Trade index number of production.
Allowance for building not covered by index number.
Allowance for additional value of dutiable goods.[1]

Agriculture

Special index number constructed from returns under Corn Sales Acts, and Ministry of Agriculture records of cattle, sheep and pigs sold in principal markets.

Transport

Tonnage of general merchandise carried on railways.
Tonnage of fuel and minerals carried on railways.
Number of goods vehicles licenses current.
Tonnage of shipping entered and cleared (weight proportional to importance of shipping + docking).

Services

Dwelling-houses index number proportional to number of houses standing.
Government and local authority services from Table 59 (i.e. volume assumed to be the same as value except during the period of salary abatements).

[1] The weights given to the relevant industries (principally drink and tobacco) in the Board of Trade index number of production are based on their untaxed values.

Retail distribution—quantity of goods distributed, calculated by applying weight and price index number to retail sales figures.
Professions employment index.
Entertainment employment index.
Hotel and catering employment index.
Laundries employment index.

In the adjustments to the Board of Trade index of production, the addition for the value of dutiable products is based on the output of the food, drink and tobacco group. Up to the end of 1933, the entire estimated net output of building and contracting is added in. Since the beginning of 1934, the Board of Trade index has covered the value of new buildings, but a constant addition at the rate of £100 millions a year is made to allow for the net output created by repair work, local authority contracting and other sections of the trade which remain at a fairly constant level of activity and not covered by the Board of Trade index. We may now give the value of output, at 1930 prices, calculated in this manner. "Invisible exports" of all kinds are excluded, for the reason that, except in the case of shipping, it is impossible to use any price index to determine their volume.

The value of this index is clear. It enables us to obtain another measure, which can be kept up to date quarter by quarter, of the general level of activity. We have already obtained separate quarterly measurements of the value of consumption and of investment. The addition of these two series should give an up-to-date measurement of the money value of the national income. The problem now is to obtain a separate method of comparing this series, relating to the money national income, with the data relating to the real quantity of output given above.

The relationship can be established by means of the procedure of revaluing consumption, exports, imports and investment by means of appropriate price index numbers. We may at first confine ourselves to the data for the years

TABLE 91

OUTPUT AT 1930 PRICES (EXCLUDING SHIPPING AND OVERSEAS INVESTMENT), SEASONAL VARIATIONS ELIMINATED

(£s million)

	Board of Trade Index of Production	Board of Trade Index of Production (including building from 1934)	Building Repairs, Roads, etc.	Building before 1934	Add for Dutiable Drink, Tobacco, etc.	Agriculture	Dwellings	Railways, Fuel and Minerals	Railways, General Merchandise	Goods Vehicles	Docks	Retail Distribution	Professions	Entertainment	Hotel and Catering	Laundries	Government and Local Authority	Total
Weight																		
1930 :	1449·0	1534·0	100	185·0	206·0	180·0	310·0	46·0	43·0	50·0	25·0	640·0	75·0	60·0	80·0	25·0	400	3774·0
1924 :	1409·0	..	..	158·2	195·1	175·0	279·0	42·0	48·7	23·4	23·3	575·0	64·4	51·7	65·8	19·9	350	3480·5
1929 :																		
i	387·7	..	..	44·6	51·7	52·9	75·8	12·1	11·5	11·5	6·0	160·0	17·9	14·7	19·5	6·1	100	972·0
ii	388·4	..	..	47·3	52·6	50·4	76·1	12·5	11·9	11·7	6·3	160·0	18·1	15·0	20·0	6·1	100	976·4
iii	402·5	..	..	47·7	52·7	50·1	76·4	12·8	11·7	11·9	6·6	159·7	18·3	15·2	20·3	6·2	100	993·7
iv	391·9	..	..	46·8	50·8	51·3	76·7	12·6	11·4	12·1	6·3	163·1	18·4	15·1	20·4	6·3	100	983·2
1930 :																		
i	384·5	..	..	46·1	50·1	52·7	77·0	12·2	11·5	12·4	6·3	162·1	18·6	15·1	20·2	6·3	100	975·1
ii	362·8	..	..	46·3	52·1	50·2	77·3	11·5	11·1	12·4	6·3	155·0	18·7	15·0	19·8	6·2	100	944·7
iii	362·1	..	..	46·1	51·1	43·8	77·6	11·1	10·5	12·5	6·3	155·8	18·8	14·8	20·2	6·3	100	937·0
iv	339·6	..	..	46·5	52·7	40·2	78·0	11·2	10·0	12·7	6·1	167·3	18·9	15·1	19·8	6·2	100	924·3
1931 :																		
i	327·3	..	..	46·1	51·2	45·2	78·3	10·0	9·7	12·8	5·7	173·9	19·0	15·5	20·0	6·3	100	921·0
ii	324·1	..	..	48·2	50·9	44·2	78·7	10·4	9·7	12·9	5·7	165·3	19·2	16·2	20·5	6·3	100	912·3
iii	325·2	..	..	47·2	51·4	43·2	79·0	9·9	9·5	13·1	5·8	176·1	19·5	16·9	20·8	6·4	100	918·0
iv	331·9	..	..	45·2	51·3	39·6	79·4	9·1	9·5	13·1	5·7	169·0	20·1	18·0	21·2	6·6	100	918·7

1932 :																		
i	333·3	..	..	43·3	50·4	46·2	79·8	9·6	9·2	13·3	5·4	167·3	20·2	17·1	20·7	6·7	100	925·1
ii	322·4	..	..	43·3	47·9	50·8	80·2	8·9	8·3	13·3	5·2	165·4	20·5	17·8	21·2	6·7	100	911·9
iii	318·5	..	..	42·3	46·7	47·0	80·5	9·2	8·5	13·4	5·3	167·0	20·8	18·2	21·0	6·7	100	904·9
iv	324·1	..	..	42·3	46·2	53·5	80·9	9·5	8·4	13·4	5·1	173·1	21·5	18·5	20·7	6·7	100	923·9
1933 :																		
i	325·2	..	..	41·8	46·3	50·6	81·3	9·2	8·3	13·6	5·5	169·8	21·0	19·1	21·2	6·7	100	919·6
ii	337·8	..	..	47·5	50·7	50·7	81·7	9·3	8·6	13·7	5·6	178·7	21·4	19·7	21·8	6·8	100	954·0
iii	354·3	..	..	48·2	49·8	56·6	82·1	9·9	9·1	13·9	5·8	169·8	21·8	20·1	22·4	7·0	100	970·8
iv	366·3	..	..	50·1	51·7	51·7	82·7	10·1	9·0	14·2	5·5	178·3	22·0	20·2	22·3	7·0	100	991·1
1934 :																		
i	..	407·7	25	..	52·5	56·9	83·8	10·4	9·2	14·7	5·6	176·8	21·8	20·4	22·7	6·9	100	1013·9
ii	..	413·4	25	..	51·5	51·9	83·9	10·4	9·1	14·7	5·7	180·0	21·7	21·3	23·6	6·8	100	1019·0
iii	..	408·0	25	..	52·0	54·8	84·6	10·5	9·3	15·0	5·8	172·6	21·7	21·1	23·9	6·8	103	1014·1
iv	..	408·0	25	..	54·5	56·7	85·2	10·6	8·7	14·7	5·6	182·3	21·9	21·2	23·4	6·8	106	1032·0
1935 :																		
i	..	436·0	25	..	53·5	61·0	85·8	10·2	9·0	15·4	5·6	184·0	22·0	21·6	23·7	6·9	109	1068·7
ii	..	447·5	25	..	54·8	56·4	86·4	9·9	8·9	15·4	5·8	186·0	22·3	22·1	24·5	7·0	112	1084·0
iii	..	432·0	25	..	55·4	59·9	87·0	9·9	9·0	15·6	6·0	184·0	22·5	22·1	24·8	7·1	115	1075·6
iv	..	440·5	25	..	58·0	63·6	87·6	11·1	9·2	15·6	5·8	193·1	22·6	22·9	24·3	7·2	118	1104·5
1936 :																		
i	..	469·0	25	..	57·1	62·9	88·2	10·7	9·2	16·3	6·4	192·5	22·7	23·1	24·6	7·2	121	1135·9

up to 1933, for which we have income-tax data for the national income.

TABLE 92

OUTPUT AT CURRENT AND 1930 PRICES

(£s million)

	1924	1929	1930	1931	1932	1933
At current value :						
Gross national income	4376	4765	4698	4264	4210	4334
Gross investment .	668	682	551	416	414	449
Consumption (by difference)	3708	4083	4147	3848	3796	3885
Consumption directly ascertained	..	..	4087	3961	3878	3879
Mean of two above results	..	..	4117	3905	3837	3882
At 1930 prices :						
Consumption . .	3382	3960	4117	4070	4045	4210
Home investment .	558	562	525	554	482	486
Exports . . .	662	707	517	437	438	449
Retained imports .	870	985	957	984	864	878
Output (excluding invisible exports)	3732	4244	4256	4077	4101	4267
Do. from output index .	3480	3925	3781	3670	3666	3836
Percentage of output covered by index	93·3	92·5	88·9	90·0	89·5	89·9

These results appear to show, as might have been expected, a slight downward trend in the coverage of the output index, due to the increasing importance of services. Apart from the year 1930, during which conditions were abnormal, the ratio between the two figures has been fairly steady during recent years, and it is assumed that, on the average, the figures given by the output index represent 89·9 per cent of the real national income, measured at 1930 prices, during recent years.

We now have two series which can be used to give quarterly data of the national income :

(A) Based on output statistics.

(B) i. Money incomes, obtained by adding consumption and investment figures.

ii. The above converted into real incomes by use of appropriate price indexes.

A quarterly comparison of (A) and (B) ii shows results which are very close throughout the period covered. The maximum divergence is about 2½ per cent and throughout the last three years the series have rarely differed by more than 1 per cent.

For convenience we also wish to convert (A) into a money series. The best way in which this can be done is to take the figures of (B) i and deduct from them invisible exports. We may then raise or lower this figure by the same proportion as that by which (A) exceeds or falls short of (B) ii in that quarter. We may then add back the figure of invisible exports to obtain an alternative quarterly estimate of the money value of the national income.

The agreement between these two series, calculated by quite independent methods, entitles us to assume that we have succeeded in obtaining a satisfactory method of making fairly close estimates of short-period changes in the national income.[1] The two estimates for money national income are plotted quarter by quarter in a diagram given in the next chapter, for the purpose of comparison with changes in the amount of investment, and the closeness of their agreement can readily be seen.

We may now make a determination of the production of real income per head throughout the period 1924 to the beginning of 1936. For 1929 and earlier years, the price index applicable to output as a whole previously calculated[2] is used. For subsequent periods, the mean is taken of the two determinations of national income at 1930 prices and an addition made for invisible exports proportional to their relative importance in money income.

[1] Quarterly estimates of the National Income have been prepared on these lines by the present writer for publication in a quarterly brochure issued by Messrs. Pritchard Wood and Partners, Incorporated Practitioners in Advertising, and these figures will be kept up to date in this publication.

[2] *The National Income, 1924–1931*, p. 125.

TABLE 93

QUARTERLY FIGURES OF NATIONAL INCOME FREE OF SEASONAL VARIATIONS

(£s million per quarter)

	National Income at Current Prices		National Income at 1930 Prices (excluding Invisible Exports)	
	Consumption plus Investment	Calculated from Output Statistics	Revaluation of Investment and Consumption	Output
1929 :				
iii	1229	1248	1087	1105
iv	1222	1228	1086	1094
1930 :				
i	1181	1195	1071	1085
ii	1148	1171	1028	1051
iii	1170	1147	1065	1042
iv	1141	1117	1052	1028
1931 :				
i	1135	1091	1070	1024
ii	1098	1084	1028	1015
iii	1107	1091	1037	1021
iv	1065	1085	1001	1022
1932 :				
i	1067	1074	1028	1029
ii	1086	1065	1036	1014
iii	1083	1056	1034	1007
iv	1081	1063	1047	1028
1933 :				
i	1038	1036	1025	1023
ii	1067	1070	1058	1061
iii	1091	1092	1079	1080
iv	1128	1120	1111	1102
1934 :				
i	1135	1139	1124	1128
ii	1150	1148	1135	1133
iii	1158	1156	1130	1128
iv	1194	1169	1173	1147
1935 :				
i	1217	1196	1211	1189
ii	1238	1227	1216	1205
iii	1250	1225	1222	1196
iv	1286	1259	1257	1229
1936 :				
i	1301	1292	1273	1263
ii	1302	1343	1258	1300

The number of occupied persons in work is made up of three items :

(1) Wage-earners and salary-earners in receipt of incomes below £250 from Table 28.
(2) Employers and higher salary-earners, whose numbers are assumed to remain constant at 1,625,000.
(3) Independent workers, taken at 1,310,000 in 1931, whose numbers are assumed to be rising by 7000 per annum throughout the period.

These figures, as shown in Chapter II, are in agreement with the Census total of occupied persons for 1931, and for other dates, even if the above assumptions are wrong, they will probably only have the effect of placing persons in the wrong category, and will not affect the totals.

Calculations can be made both of *total income* per head and of *home-produced* income per head. The latter is of course a more precise measurement of changes in productive capacity. It will be noticed that the method of calculation is such that money income is reduced to real income by means of a price factor applicable to output and not to consumption. In other words, an improvement in the terms of trade is not reckoned to raise real income. It is possible to include the effects of terms-of-trade by substituting a consumption-price index for the price factor actually used, and the results are given in a separate column.

Results are given per person in work and not per head of population, for the reason that, as indicated in Chapter II, the proportion of occupied to total population is at present rapidly changing. A calculation which is, however, of some interest is one which shows the output per head of occupied population *including* unemployed, as compared with output per head of occupied population *excluding* unemployed. This latter shows a tendency to rise much more slowly than the former. In other words, the increasing real output obtainable from the labour of those in work, whether by increasing productivity at home or by improvement in the terms of trade, is largely wasted in the form of increasing unemployment.

TABLE 94

REAL INCOME PER HEAD, 1924–35

	Occupied Persons in Work. Millions	Occupied Persons, including Unemployed.* Millions	Net National Income at 1930 Prices. £s million	Real Income per Person in Work; Home-produced (£)	Real Income per Person in work. Total (£)	Real Income per Person in Work at Consumption Prices (i.e. including Effect of Terms of Trade) (£)	Real Income per occupied Person, including Unemployed (£)
1924	18·05	19·75	3679	189·5	203·8	202·4	185·0
1925	18·22	20·06	3947	201·1	216·6	214·2	194·3
1926	17·76	19·96	3817	199·0	214·9	215·3	191·2
1927	18·80	20·48	4040	199·5	214·9	214·3	196·8
1928	18·89	20·68	4117	202·1	217·9	214·0	195·2
1929	19·19	20·95	4337	209·8	226·0	221·9	203·4
1930	18·79	21·39	4318	215·2	229·8	229·8	202·0
1931	18·44	21·94	4026	207·1	218·3	219·4	184·4
1932	18·38	22·08	3995	207·5	217·4	220·4	183·4
1933	18·75	22·11	4160	211·3	221·9	228·8	194·2
1934	19·43	22·30	4445	217·7	228·8	235·2	204·8
1935	19·96	22·70	4735	225·7	237·2	240·8	211·8
1936: i	20·13	22·76	4960	234·6	246·3	251·2	221·8

* With an estimate for unregistered unemployed.

The most significant column to which attention must first be turned is the home-produced income per person in work. This showed a rapid rise from £189·5 per head in 1924 to £215·2 in 1930, a rise of 13·4 per cent in six years. During the years of the slump it fell back. But in 1933 the advance was resumed. In 1934 the previous high record was overtaken, and by 1936 it had risen to a figure of £238·3, or a 26 per cent rise on the level of twelve years earlier.

Inclusive of income from overseas, the rise was not so rapid, owing to heavy losses of real income from this source during the years subsequent to 1930. In 1924 the income produced by each occupied person in Britain was supplemented by £14·3 (at 1930 purchasing power) of income from overseas, or a 7½ per cent addition, and by 1929 this had risen to £16·2. During recent years the addition has been on the average £11.

The change in the terms of trade has also had a remarkable additional effect during recent years. If we had wished to consume our whole national income (which at present we are not far from doing), the quantity of goods and services which we could have obtained in return for each person's work has been rapidly raised by means of the fall in consumption prices relative to the selling price of British output. In 1929, and in earlier years, the quantity of consumption goods which the average income would purchase, at 1930 prices, was £2 to £4 less than the value of that income measured in terms of real output. In 1933 it was £6 to £9 more. During the last three years the terms of trade have moved slightly against this country, but there still remains a difference of nearly £5 between the income measured at consumption prices and the real output per head.

To summarise the changes which have taken place between 1929 and 1936. The quantity of goods and services produced by a year's labour was worth then, on the average, £210. Now the quantity produced is considerably greater and is worth £234·6 at the same price-level. Owing to loss of income from overseas investment, about £4·5 of this increase have been lost, leaving an increase of £20·3. Owing to the improvement in the terms of trade, however, the value of goods and services which we on the average (of those in work) are able to consume has risen by £29·3, an increase of no lesss than 13·2 per cent. A large part—£10·9—of this we have thrown away, in the form of keeping an additional 3–4 per cent of our working population in unemployment.

CHAPTER X

HISTORICAL STATISTICS OF NATIONAL INCOME

THE first inquiry into the national income of England was made by Gregory King, Lancaster Herald, in the year 1696. Some of the detail of his investigations is given below, and from their thoroughness and consistency it appears that his estimate is by no means a guess, but a carefully compiled and checked total based on all the information then available.

After Gregory King we have a long gap with only the scantiest information. From the middle years of the nineteenth century onwards we have statistical series continuous with our own times. Professor Bowley's calculations of the wage-rates and aggregate earnings of the working-class population have been carried back to 1860, and Sir Josiah Stamp's carefully adjusted series [1] showing the amount of taxable income are carried back to 1847. For the earlier years of the nineteenth century we have a number of isolated and divergent estimates made by different writers.

Gregory King's pioneer estimate was undoubtedly a work of genius. In the words of his biographer, "Gregory King produced his *Political Conclusions*, in 1696, though his modesty did not publish those curious efforts of art and sagacity. He allowed Doctor Davenant, a well-known writer of those times, to peruse, and to garble his *political conclusions*." The *Natural and Political Observations and Conclusions upon the State and Conditions of England, 1696*, a short memorandum of only forty pages, was not published till over a century later. It was published by Sir George Chalmers as an annex to his own work, *An Esti-*

[1] *British Incomes and Property.*

mate of the Comparative Strength of Great Britain,[1] and he also included a biography of Gregory King. The father of English statistical science seems to have been a man of great versatility in his activities and studies, and a most colourful character.

Born in Staffordshire in 1648, Gregory King was the son of a land surveyor who paid " more attention to *good fellowship*, than mathematical studies generally allow : but with all his laxity of *company-keeping* was extremely attentive to the education of his children ". Gregory King began to earn his living at the age of eleven as a pupil teacher, and at fourteen became clerk to Dugdale, a well-known Herald and Antiquary. After this he practised for a time in his home town as an independent genealogist, artist and draughtsman, and schoolmaster, and then became steward and auditor of an estate at Sandon. At the age of twenty-three he moved to London and became assistant to the *Royal Cosmographer*, an office whose powers and functions are no longer known. But King's duties appear to have been the engraving of seals and the preparation and printing of maps. Gregory King was the first cartographer to prepare a large-scale map of London, and prepared maps of many other counties. The funds for this work were at that time raised by a series of lotteries, which it fell to King to manage. He also carried on his professional practice as a surveyor, and drew the plans for Soho Square and the adjacent streets.

In 1674, while lodging in St. James's Street, Covent Garden, Gregory King married his landlady, a marriage which " laid a good foundation of future competence, though fruition was somewhat retarded by his liberal manner of living ". Some other details have been preserved of his private business activities. He seems to have dealt in land and lent money on mortgage, and record has been preserved of one interesting transaction, in which he

[1] Published by J. Stockdale, London. First edition 1801, second edition 1804. There are copies in the library of the Royal Statistical Society and in the Pryme collection at Cambridge.

TABLE 95 (from *Political*

A SCHEME OF THE INCOME AND EXPENSE, OF THE SEVERAL

Number of Families	Ranks, Degrees, Titles and Qualifications	Heads per Family
160	Temporal Lords	40
26	Spiritual Lords	20
800	Baronets	16
600	Knights	13
3,000	Esquires	10
12,000	Gentlemen	8
5,000	Persons in offices	8
5,000	Persons in offices	6
2,000	Merchants and traders by sea	8
8,000	Merchants and traders by land	6
10,000	Persons in the Law	7
2,000	Clergymen	6
8,000	Clergymen	5
40,000	Freeholders	7
140,000	Freeholders	5
150,000	Farmers	5
16,000	Persons in Sciences and Liberal Arts	5
40,000	Shop-keepers and tradesmen	$4\frac{1}{2}$
60,000	Artizans and handicrafts	4
5,000	Naval officers	4
4,000	Military officers	4
511,586		$5\frac{1}{4}$
50,000	Common seamen	3
364,000	Labouring people and out-servants	$3\frac{1}{2}$
400,000	Cottagers and paupers	$3\frac{1}{4}$
35,000	Common soldiers	2
849,000		$3\frac{1}{4}$
..	Vagrants	..
849,000		$3\frac{1}{4}$
	So the GENERAL	
511,586	Increasing the wealth of the kingdom	$5\frac{1}{4}$
849,000	Decreasing the wealth of the kingdom	$3\frac{1}{4}$
1,360,586	Net Totals	$1\frac{1}{20}$

Conclusions of Gregory King)

FAMILIES OF ENGLAND CALCULATED FOR THE YEAR 1688

Number of Persons	Yearly Income per Family		Total of the Estates or Income	Yearly Income per Head		Expense per Head			Increase per Head			Total Increase per Annum
	£	s.	£	£	s.	£	s.	d.	£	s.	d.	£
6,400	2,800	0	448,000	70	0	60	0	0	10	0	0	64,000
520	1,300	0	33,800	65	0	55	0	0	10	0	0	5,200
12,800	880	0	704,000	55	0	51	0	0	4	0	0	51,000
7,800	650	0	390,000	50	0	46	0	0	4	0	0	31,200
30,000	450	0	1,200,000	45	0	42	0	0	3	0	0	90,000
96,000	280	0	2,880,000	35	0	32	10	0	2	10	0	240,000
40,000	240	0	1,200,000	30	0	27	0	0	3	0	0	120,000
30,000	120	0	600,000	20	0	18	0	0	2	0	0	60,000
16,000	400	0	800,000	50	0	40	0	0	10	0	0	160,000
48,000	200	0	1,600,000	33	0	28	0	0	5	0	0	240,000
70,000	140	0	1,400,000	20	0	17	0	0	3	0	0	210,000
12,000	60	0	120,000	10	0	9	0	0	1	0	0	12,000
40,000	45	0	360,000	9	0	8	0	0	1	0	0	40,000
280,000	84	0	3,360,000	12	0	11	0	0	1	0	0	280,000
700,000	50	0	7,000,000	10	0	9	10	0	0	10	0	350,000
750,000	44	0	6,600,000	8	15	8	10	0	0	5	0	187,000
80,000	60	0	960,000	12	0	11	10	0	1	10	0	40,000
180,000	45	0	1,800,000	10	0	9	10	0	0	10	0	90,000
240,000	40	0	2,400,000	10	0	9	10	0	0	10	0	120,000
20,000	80	0	400,000	20	0	18	0	0	2	0	0	40,000
16,000	60	0	240,000	15	0	14	0	0	1	0	0	16,000
2,675,520	67	0	34,495,800	12	18	12	0	0	0	18	0	2,447,100
												Decrease
150,000	20	0	1,000,000	7	0	7	10	0	0	10	0	75,000
1,275,000	15	0	5,460,000	4	10	4	12	0	0	2	0	127,500
1,300,000	6	10	2,000,000	2	0	2	5	0	0	5	0	325,000
70,000	14	0	490,000	7	0	7	10	0	0	10	0	35,000
2,795,000	10	10	8,950,000	3	5	3	9	0	0	4	0	562,000
30,000	..		60,000	2	0	3	0	0	1	0	0	60,000
2,825,000	10	10	9,010,000	3	3	3	7	6	0	4	6	622,000
ACCOUNT is :												
2,675,520	67	0	34,495,800	12	18	12	0	0	0	18	0	2,447,000
2,825,000	10	10	9,010,000	3	3	3	7	6	0	4	6	622,000
5,500,520	32	0	43,505,800	7	18	7	11	3	0	6	9	1,825,100

laid out £1260 (most of which he had borrowed) in purchasing a thirty-three-year lease of sixty houses, whose aggregate rent was £220 a year, in the parish of St. Catharine's (? near the Tower of London). The price of the lease seems very low, but we are informed that shortly after the purchase (about 1690) rents fell and taxation rose, which " two unlooked for circumstances reduced a good bargain to little value ".

In 1677 he was appointed to the heraldic post of *Rouge Dragon*, and in 1688 (on payment of £160) to the higher post of *Lancaster Herald*, posts at that time of greater dignity and remuneration than they are today. It appears that the tenure of these offices gave King access to records of all the estates of England and Wales, which served as a basis for his estimates of the annual and capital value of landed property, the principal source of wealth at that time.

He was in charge of the ceremonies for the coronations of James II and of William III, and in 1689 paid a leisurely and magnificent visit to Berlin to bestow the Order of the Garter on the Elector of Brandenburg. Returning by Hamburg, " our herald was entertained nobly by the English merchants who, in doing honour to the King's heraldic representative, on a splendid embassage, tried to do honour also to the nation ". Later he also performed ceremonial investitures at The Hague and Dresden, at the latter of which " it was resolved to outdo the Elector of Brandenburg, in magnificent expence, and munificent rewards. Such carousals, as were on this occasion displayed, had seldom been seen."

But, after all this varied experience, King's final qualification for writing on the national income was his appointment, under the terms of an Act first passed in 1692, as Secretary of the *Commissioners for stating the Public Accounts*, which post he held till he died in 1712. The duties of this post apparently corresponded, in a primitive form, to those of Secretary of the Treasury and Chairman of the Board of Inland Revenue at the present day.

At that time, William III was engaged in a long and exhausting war with France. Gregory King's primary concern, it appears, was to prepare estimates of the possible yield of new taxes, and of the extent to which existing taxes were being evaded. For this purpose he made estimates of the consumption of ale, meat and other commodities. But the economic situation seems to have been so serious that he felt the need to investigate the more fundamental factors of population, national income, savings and taxation, the amount of liquid capital, and the question of how long the economic drain of war could continue. He prepared such estimates, not only for England, but also in a less detailed form for France and Holland. Though these results are also of great interest, we have in this case unfortunately no means of checking the extent of Gregory King's knowledge or the sources of his information regarding these countries.

For England and Wales, Gregory King first prepares an estimate of the population from the numbers of assessments to Hearth-tax, making a careful estimate of the extent of evasion, numbers of sailors, vagrants, etc. The average numbers of people per house were determined by sample inquiries in different districts, and his conclusion is :

Population in 1690

London and adjacent parishes	530,000
Other cities and market towns	870,000
Villages and hamlets	4,100,000
	5,500,000

It is interesting to notice the great size to which London had already grown by that date, containing as it did nearly 10 per cent of the population. 75 per cent of the population of England and Wales was rural (not necessarily, it will be seen, engaged in agriculture). Compared with the rest of the urban population, London's predominance was very marked.

From statistics of the taxes levied on baptisms, marriages and burials King prepares an estimate of the birth-

and death-rates and the age-composition of the population. King's estimate of age-composition, so far as I am aware the first that was ever prepared, may be tested in various ways and its results appear probable. 40 per cent of the population was below the age of 16, and the average age of the population was only 27·5. The death-rate was 30·9 per 1000, the birth-rate 34·6, and the infant mortality about 160. In comparing the first two figures with those prevailing at the present day, the effects of the different age-composition of the population must be borne in mind. The annual number of births per 1000 women (married and unmarried) between the ages of 16 and 45 was as high as 190.

Both the crude birth-rate and the crude death-rate were then much higher in London than in the rest of England (King gives London a death-rate of no less than 70 per 1000). He analyses the birth-rate figures and shows that they are fully explained by the high proportion of young married people in the population of London. The average number of children born to each marriage in London is found to be less than in the country, to account for which Gregory King suggests five possible reasons :

(1) From the more frequent fornications and adulteries.
(2) From a greater luxury and intemperance.
(3) From a greater intenseness to business.
(4) From the unhealthfulness of the coal smoke.
(5) From a greater inequality of age between the husbands and wives.

Modern readers may smile, but they should be told that modern statisticians know, if anything, less than Gregory King did about the causes of differential fertility.

Our author then makes one or two interesting but highly speculative digressions. He estimates the population of the entire world at 700 millions, of whom 230 millions were in China. (Here again our present-day knowledge is quite as uncertain as his was.) Reckoning the population of England to have been 2 millions at the time of *Doomsday Book*, King shows that his estimates of the growth of population in England, and of the world, are not inconsistent with the re-peopling of the world by eight persons after the Flood at about 2300 B.C. He suggests that England was probably first colonised by a few hundred people in about 1500 B.C., at which time the number of Noah's descendants populating the world had risen to 5 millions. (On these matters we now think we know better.) King also digresses to make an estimate of the stock of gold and silver in Europe, which he puts at only £45 millions in 1490, before the discovery of America, but at £225 millions in his own time, of which £39·4 millions was held in France, £17·8 millions in England and £12·8 millions in Holland.

The determination of the national income of England is made by dividing the population into families and making an estimate of the average income of each type of family. The details of his calculation are shown in Table 95, reprinted verbatim from his book. We may trust that King's official posts enabled him to make satisfactory estimates of the income, at any rate of the landed families.

Thorold Rogers confirms King's estimate of £15 a year as the average earnings of labouring men, and is quite prepared to accept his estimate showing nearly half the population partially dependent upon alms or poor relief; but is of the opinion that King has understated (at £400 a year) the average incomes of merchants by sea.

King estimates the capital value of land and buildings at £234 millions (he reckons as much as eighteen years' purchase of the rents) and gives a somewhat inflated figure of £330 millions for the capitalised value of "trades arts and labours". The genuine liquid capital of England (including gold and silver), the true "sinews of war", he put at £86 millions, of which £25 millions was in live-stock. He estimated that the effect of the war up to 1695 had been to reduce this to £73 millions and "that the Kingdom does now yearly decrease 3 millions sterling ". He estimated that up to 1698 was the longest period for which the war could be carried on without complete economic breakdown.

The remainder of King's work consists of detailed statistics of the production and consumption of a number of commodities, and estimates of the income and liquid capital of France and Holland, which latter bear some signs of having only been very approximately estimated. He estimated that the economic strain of the war was greater on France than on England, but that Holland was continuing to add to her capital.

It is impossible to make much use of Gregory King's results unless we have some idea of the level of prices prevailing at the time. Fortunately, we can obtain very full data from Thorold Rogers' *History of Agriculture and Prices in England*, and it is possible, with some reservations, to re-express in terms of present-day prices the value of goods consumed per head of the population in 1688. Weighted according to seventeenth-century consumption, the purchasing power of money seems to have been then about four times its present purchasing power.

Gregory King's definition of National Income seems to have been almost identical with that now used, with one exception. He did not include the incomes, in cash and kind, of domestic servants (whom he treats as members of their employers' families). He gives their numbers as 260,000 men and 300,000 women, and assuming that their earnings and keep are about equal to those of low-paid outside wage-workers, their incomes would be £5,700,000, making a total national income of £49,200,000.

Gregory King makes an analysis of the distribution of expenditure which gives us the necessary weights for a revaluation of the whole national income at prices of the present day. He gives figures of the actual quantities consumed in the case of ale and of all varieties of meat, and we can therefore directly multiply these quantities by present-day prices.

TABLE 96

EXPENDITURE OF NATIONAL INCOME, 1688

Food and Drink :		
Bread, cakes, flour, etc.	£4,300,000	..
Meat and poultry	3,900,000	..
Butter, cheese and milk	2,300,000	..
Fish and eggs	1,100,000	..
Fruit, vegetables and garden produce	1,200,000	..
Salt, oil, spices, grocery, confectionery, etc.	1,100,000	..
Beer and ale	5,800,000	..
Spirits and wines	1,300,000	..
		£21,000,000
Rent of houses and gardens	..	2,500,000
Apparel	..	10,400,000
Domestic service	..	5,700,000
Other consumption	..	5,550,000
Taxation	..	2,000,000
Saving	..	1,800,000
		£49,200,000

These consumptions are re-expressed at present-day prices by use, where possible, of Thorold Rogers' data for the decade 1683–92 (to avoid the fluctuations to which prices for a single year are liable).

The average present-day prices of foodstuffs are taken from the tables prepared by Mr. Feavearyear, relating to the year 1934, in *Food, Health and Income.*

Meat

Mr. Feavearyear's figures cover the average retail price, including waste, and are adjusted to give the average price of meat actually sold.

Bread and Flour

As nearly all bread was home-baked, we can take flour prices as a basis of comparison. Thorold Rogers gives 52s. per quarter as the price of flour in 1683–92 as compared with 1s. per 7 lbs. as the present retail price.

Butter, Cheese and Milk

Butter and cheese sold at 5s. 8d. and 3s. 9d. per dozen lbs.

respectively, as against 11s. 1d. and 11s. 5d. at the present day. The price of milk was very uncertain, but appears to have been about 5d. per gallon in the few recorded transactions.

Fish and Eggs

Eggs have risen from 3s. 7d. to 18s. 5d. per gross. The only fish prices quoted by Thorold Rogers are for herrings (3s. 9d. per 100) and salt cod (10½d. each). The average price of fish appears to have risen two- or threefold.

Fruit, vegetables, etc.

Practically no information. The price of apples was 20s.–40s. a quarter according to season, peas 50s. a quarter, beans 65s. The order of magnitude of the price increase seems to have been twofold.

Salt, Oil, Spices, etc.

The price of salt was then £1 per quarter and is now £2 : 8s. per ton. Olive oil sold at 4s. a gallon as against its present wholesale price of 3s. Ginger sold at 7½d. per lb., currants at 5d., raisins at 4½d., prunes at 2¼d. and refined sugar at 9½d. We shall not be far wrong in saying that the general level of prices in this group was about the same as it is today.

It is interesting to present the results expressed in pence per head per week for comparison with those given by Sir John Orr for the present-day average, and also for comparison with the average dietary of the poorest 10 per cent of the population (those who have on the average 4s. per head per week to spend on food) at the present time.

Our ancestors seem to have enjoyed, averaged over the whole population, a diet which, except for meat, was inferior to that of the unemployed at the present time. But there were certainly great inequalities of expenditure at that time. A quarter of the population were "cottagers and paupers" whose total outlay was only 10½d. per head per week, and who must have had a far worse diet. Gregory King estimates that 1,020,000 persons only ate

TABLE 97

FOOD CONSUMPTION—PENCE PER HEAD PER WEEK

	Average of Population 1688	Ditto at Present Prices	Poorest 10% of Population 1934	Average of Population 1934
Bread and flour	3·61	5·9	9·0	8·1
Meat and lard	3·29	18·7	14·6	30·2
Butter, cheese and milk	1·94	7·1	9·5	18·2
Fish and eggs	0·90	3·2	2·7	9·4
Fruit and vegetables	1·00	2·0	6·4	19·2
Sugar, grocery, etc.	0·92	1·0	5·8	20·6
Total	11·66	37·9	48·0	108

meat once a week, and 1,280,000 only ate meat twice a week. The 2,700,000 (excluding infants, invalids, etc.) who ate meat regularly consumed 2 lbs. 13 oz. per head, or double the general average, and above the average of the present day.

We may next make some comparisons of the prices of clothing and textiles. The latter is very difficult as we have little idea of the qualities involved.

TABLE 98

PRICE COMPARISONS

TEXTILES	Price, 1688	Present Price as Multiple	CLOTHING	Price, 1688	Present Price as Multiple
	s. d.			s. d.	
Silk, yard	8 6	0·71	Blankets, pair :		
Flannel, yard	1 9	1·72	Best quality	35 0	1·43
Coarse linen, yard	1 4	0·75	Worst quality	24 0	1·25
Bed-linen, yard	2 6	0·8	Gloves, pair	2 0	2·0
Wool, yard :			Shoes, ,,	3 10	2·6
Best quality	5 0	1·2	Wool stockings, pair	4 0	1·5
Worst quality	2 6	0·8	Boots and spurs, pair	15 0	2·0
Geometric mean	..	0·94	..	..	1·75

TABLE 98—*Contd.*

Sundry Goods	Price, 1688	Present Price as Multiple	Building Materials	Price, 1688	Present Price as Multiple
	s. d.			s. d.	
Canvas, yard	1 0	1·5	Bricks, thousand	16 7	2·86
Rope, cwt.	70 0	0·49	Tiles ,,	18 8	4·38
Buckets, each	1 4	2·0	White lead, cwt.	28 0	1·43
Wheelbarrow, each	7 0	2·0			
Knife ,,	1 3	0·8	Geometric mean	..	2·61
Glasses ,,	0 3	1·0			
Broom ,,	0 10	2·4	Iron		
Mop ,,	0 11	2·2	Tyres, cwt.	32 6	0·65
Shovel ,,	1 4	2·0	Bar ,,	37 0	0·41
Soap, cwt.	37 0	0·65	Wire ,,	112 0	0·19
			Chain ,,	47 0	0·94
			Screws ,,	93 0	0·30
Geometric mean	..	1·29	Geometric mean	..	0·43

These data can be used to revalue the other consumption items, and present-day values may be placed upon the work of domestic servants (£150 a year for men, £75 a year for women and girls). There remains to be revalued our forefathers' expenditure on drink, and this gives some remarkable results.

Gregory King estimates that 23 million bushels of malt were brewed, giving 7·1 million barrels of small ale and 5·3 million barrels of strong, the ratio of their strengths, judged from the malt content, being 3 : 1. The amount of malt brewed in 1688 was four-fifths of the amount (including substitutes) brewed in 1930, which gave 21 million " standard " barrels (i.e. beer reduced to strength 1·055°). Our ancestors' small beer appears therefore to have corresponded in strength to our present-day mild beer, which retails at prices ranging from 4d. a pint in East Anglia to 5d. in other parts of the country and 6d. in the towns. Their strong beer must have been a liquor of the sort which we rarely drink now, of a quality approaching 5X or Audit. The average weekly consumption per head of the population, men, women and children, was 7 pints of small ale and $5\frac{1}{2}$ pints of strong, the price of which was in all 4·85 pence.[1] At present-day prices it would cost about 9s.

Consumption of wines and spirits amounted to a little over one-fifth of the consumption of beer and ale. Thorold Rogers gives the average prices of claret, sack and muscatel as 7d., 1s. 4d., 2s. 1d. per bottle respectively, i.e. between one-fourth and one-fifth of present-day prices. Brandy, in spite of the fact that England was nominally at war with France, could be purchased at 4s. a gallon during the last decade of the seventeenth century (as against approximately 90s. at the present time).

Wide changes in value are also apparent when we come to revalue the rents of houses. Gregory King gives the number of houses at 1,300,000, of which a million were in the country, and had on the average nearly an acre of garden each. About 550,000 of these (according to Davenant) only had one hearth, though this does not by any means necessarily mean that they were single-roomed cabins. According to the assessments for window-tax, 430,000 of the houses with more than one hearth had less than 10 windows, 270,000 had 10–20 windows, and 50,000 had over 20 windows. This is all the information we have to go on.

The houses with one hearth were probably very modest cottages, and a number may have been single-roomed huts. We may attribute to them an average present-day value of £5 a year. With regard to the next type of house, the present writer happens to be the owner of a house in Devonshire built in the latter part of the seventeenth

[1] In comparing the average diet of the seventeenth century with that of the present day some allowance should be made, strictly speaking, for the nutriment contained in beer. There was an average consumption of barley to the extent of 5 lbs. per week per head of population in this form. Part of the nutrient sugars were lost in fermentation, but the beer of that period was probably made from more nitrogenous barley, and contained more protein and vitamins, than the chemically treated beers of the present day. At an approximate estimate, the nutrition obtained from barley in this way may have been equivalent to about two-thirds of that given by a corresponding weight of flour, or valued at about $5\frac{1}{2}$d. per week at present-day prices—a 15 per cent addition to their diet.

century. It has subsequently been altered, but in its original form it had 8 windows. The present-day letting value of houses of that type (unaltered) is £20–25 per year. At the present time the most prosperous fifth (about $2\frac{1}{2}$ millions) of householders occupy houses worth on the average £50 a year each, and this would be the least present-day value which could be attributed to 320,000 houses with over 10 windows in Gregory King's time. The annual value of housing in 1688, revalued at present prices, must therefore be £28·4 millions, or $11\frac{1}{2}$ times its old value.

In computing the general level of real income, we must omit the items of Taxation and Saving and work out a general price index on the basis of consumption goods and services. For comparison with nineteenth-century data, it is also useful to re-express the figures in terms of 1913 prices.

The very great change in the prices of drink is mainly due to the imposition of indirect taxation, which of course throws some doubt on the suitability of this item for inclusion in the general revaluation. An alternative value is calculated, in which drink is reckoned at its untaxed present value.

TABLE 99

Revaluation of National Income, 1688

(£s million)

	Outlay, 1688	Outlay at Present Prices	Outlay at 1913 Prices
Rent	2·45	28·4	18·0
Food	14 2	46·2	37·0
Apparel	10·4	14·0	7·6
Other goods	5·55	7·9	4·6
Domestic service	5·7	61·5	30·7
Drink	7·1	125·0 (Untaxed, 43)	49·0
Taxes	2·0	..	..
Savings	1·8	..	..
Total	49·2	218–306	159

Thus the average income per head of population was

£29 at 1913 prices, or £40–55 at present-day prices, the uncertainty of the present-day pricing arising out of the fact that our ancestors spent a seventh of their incomes on drink. The average income per head of the population in 1913 was £51 (inclusive of indirect taxation).

Gregory King also had a very up-to-date notion of what is meant by net output. He has given us data in a form from which the net output of agriculture can be determined. He has excluded the agricultural produce used for seed and fodder, and he has included value of fodder supplied to non-agricultural horses, which was at that time an important element in output. It is possible to revalue the principal items in this output at present-day prices. King gives actual estimates of the quantity of cereals produced. He gives £2,300,000 as the value of dairy produce, which can be revalued on the basis of prices already quoted. He gives no estimate for the output of eggs, but at the present time the annual output of eggs is approximately three times the value of the poultry sold and on this basis we can calculate a figure. In the case of hay sold for the keep of horses, Thorold Rogers gives a price of 30s. a ton at that date as against £3 at the present time. In the case of tallow and hides King gives estimates of the numbers of beasts slaughtered, and we can use the estimate of the present-day value of the by-products given by Mr. G. R. White [1] of £4 a head for cattle and 10s. for sheep.

It is interesting to notice that even at that date crops only provided £12 millions (measured at present prices) or 22 per cent of the value of agricultural output. At the prices then prevailing the net produce of agriculture represented £22 millions, or less than half of the national income of £49·2 millions (including domestic service). About half the population seems to have been engaged in agriculture. Including fishery, forestry and horticulture with agriculture, we obtain a total net output of £23·5 millions. This is consistent with the data of individual incomes given in Table 95, if we assume that rather less than half the

[1] *J.R.S.S.*, 1932.

TABLE 100

NET PRODUCE OF AGRICULTURE IN 1688 REVALUED AT PRESENT PRICES

	£s million
Wheat ($1\frac{1}{2}$ mn. qtrs.)	1·56
Rye (1 mn. qtrs.)	0·9
Barley (3·1 mn. qtrs.)	4·83
Oats (2 mn. qtrs.)	1·74
Flax, hemp and other crops	1·5
Peas and beans	1·5
Butter, cheese and milk	8·5
Wool (40 mn. lb.)	1·5
Eggs	4·0
Horses	0·3
Meat and poultry	22·4
Tallow and hides	4·8
Hay sold off farms	2·0
Total	55·5

paid wage-workers were engaged in agriculture, and that half the income of the Church came from tithes.

TABLE 101

SOURCES OF INCOME IN 1688

	£s million
Rent of lands	10·0
Tithe	0·2
Wages	3·4
Farmers' incomes	7·7
Net output of agriculture, etc.	23·5
Rent of dwellings, mines and other buildings	3·0
Income of Forces and mercantile seamen	2·1
Law, professions, etc.	4·2
Traders and manufacturers	6·6
Non-agricultural wages	4·1
Domestic service	5·7
Total	49·2

This most interesting analysis of the sources of national income responds to tests of consistency and may be taken as fairly well established.

Right through the eighteenth century we have no data whatever about the national income or the produce of agriculture. A figure estimated by Sir Robert Giffen for 1785 is sometimes quoted, but this was nothing more than a rough guess for purposes of comparison with 1885. The introduction of the income-tax in 1801 caused a number of estimates to be made then and in subsequent years, but it is probable that evasion was very serious, and under-estimated by contemporary authors. The first serious calculation of the produce of agriculture was made in 1837 by MacCulloch, making use, however, of materials collected by Young thirty or forty years earlier.

MacCulloch estimated the net produce of agriculture in Great Britain at £143 millions after deduction of the cost of seeds and fodder. He estimated the national income of Great Britain at £297 millions, thus again giving agriculture a share of nearly a half.

It is this which makes MacCulloch's conclusions impossible to accept. We can use the results of the Census of 1841,[1] which, though imperfect, can be approximately interpreted, to give us the proportion of occupied persons who were engaged in agriculture. Booth shows that there were 1,297,000 persons occupied in agriculture and horticulture in 1841 in England and Wales, or approximately 1,450,000 in Great Britain, out of an occupied population of about 8 millions. The suggestion that 1½ million agriculturists could produce an output of £100 per head (at prices of that date), and the remaining 6½ millions of occupied persons only £24 per head, is ludicrous. MacCulloch's estimate of agricultural production is possibly too high, but there is no doubt that his general estimate of national income is far too low.

MacCulloch estimated the net agricultural production of Ireland at £39 millions, of which £3·5 millions represented

[1] The occupational tables in each census between 1841 and 1881 were made comparable by Charles Booth (*J.R.S.S.*, 1886, p. 314). His figures do not cover Scotland, but so far as the numbers of agricultural workers in that country are concerned, there are certain alternative figures.

rents to absentee landlords. The number of persons engaged in agriculture in Ireland in 1841 is given by Booth at 1,835,000, giving a productivity of only £21 per occupied person. He estimates the whole income of Ireland at £48 millions. At that time, according to Booth's total, exactly half the population of Ireland was engaged in agriculture, and it is clear that MacCulloch has put non-agricultural incomes at far too low a figure even for Ireland.

There are a considerable number of isolated estimates of national income for the years between 1800 and 1860, prepared by Levi, Farr, Smee, Colquhoun and others. Some of them give results fairly close to MacCulloch's, but they show little agreement among themselves. From an analysis of the statistics of output of industry and agriculture, made in a later chapter, better estimates can now be made for the average real national income in each of the decades 1830–60, which estimates, though they cannot claim precision, are approximately continuous with those of the years after 1860.

For the years since 1860 we can obtain a continuous annual series of data. Sir Josiah Stamp's adjusted figures of income-tax assessments are carried back to 1847. Professor Bowley [1] has given figures showing the estimated total paid in wages to the entire wage-earning population year by year since that date; these figures have been slightly modified in a subsequent publication. Professor Bowley has also made a systematic survey of the national income statistics for the years between 1880 and 1913, and made estimates of the two principal remaining quantities required for determination of the total national income—namely, the amount of income evading tax, and of incomes below £160 other than those of wage-earners.

To carry the data back to 1860 we require estimates of these quantities for the earlier years. The relative importance of the intermediate incomes was probably greater in the twenty years before 1880 than it was at later dates,

[1] *Economic Journal*, 1904.

and it is assumed that their absolute total remained constant. This is in accord with estimates prepared by Baxter and Levi during the 1860's.

Evasion was a more serious problem, both administratively and statistically, in the earlier years than it is now. For 1880, Professor Bowley estimates that the amount of income evading tax was equal to about one-quarter of the annual Schedule D assessments (this is the only schedule under which considerable evasion is possible). For earlier years we have two independent pieces of evidence. Professor Leone Levi, after an examination of the Inhabited House Duty statistics,[1] came to the conclusion that the amount of evasion of tax probably amounted to 50 per cent of the recorded Schedule D assessments. Sir Josiah Stamp quotes in his book an interesting (and unique) estimate of the amount of evasion prepared by the Board of Inland Revenue, relating to the year 1864. During the course of some extensive demolitions for public works in London, traders and manufacturers in that district submitted copies of their last year's trading results as basis for claims for compensation for disturbance. The Inland Revenue took the opportunity of comparing these with the returns sent in under Schedule D, and found that over three-quarters of the latter were defective. If these London traders were to be taken as representative, the Board of Inland Revenue concluded that the amount of income evading assessment was equal to 52 per cent of the recorded Schedule D assessments.

During the course of fifty years the opportunities for evasion were rapidly stopped up, and for 1913 Sir Josiah Stamp gives a much lower estimate than that suggested by Professor Bowley. In the following calculation we will accept Professor Bowley's estimate of the amount of evasion in 1880, and extrapolate linearly back to 52 per cent of Schedule D assessments for 1864.

With the addition of indirect taxation (Customs and Excise Duty including duties reserved to local authorities,

[1] *J.R.S.S.*, 1874.

Stamp Duties other than on wills, local rates) we can now calculate comparable annual series from 1860 to 1913. There is, however, one heavy drawback. Schedule D assessments throughout were made on the basis of the average earnings of the previous three (or in the case of certain enterprises five) years. This has a smoothing and delaying effect upon a series, and the data as they stand cannot be used for the study of industrial fluctuations.

It is, however, feasible to use these data for a study of the secular rate of growth of real income. The period from 1860 to 1913 is divided up into a series of periods of seven to ten years long—each, it will be seen, concluding some three years after one of the recognised " crisis years " of the trade cycle.

An appropriate price index is calculated with weights from the following :

	Weight
Cost-of-living index	80
Domestic and similar services	10
Exports	20
Building costs	7½
Iron and steel	7½
Imports	−25

For the cost-of-living index the Board of Trade index number is available back to 1880. This is reweighted so as to give a somewhat lower weight to food, the original weighting being based on working-class budgets in which food had a high weight. Prior to that G. H. Wood's index is used. The index figure of wage-rates is taken as representative of the price of domestic and similar services. For prices of imports and exports Silverman's series [1] are used back to 1880, and prior to that some series calculated by Mr. P. K. Debenham.[2] The index of building costs is that calculated by Mr. G. T. Jones.[3] The price index for iron and steel has been supplied to me by Mr. A. K. Cairncross of Glasgow University. The following gives the

[1] *Review of Economic Statistics, 1926.*

[2] Unpublished. A diagram based on this series is published in the *Economic Journal*, September 1931.

[3] *Increasing Returns*, 1932.

calculation of the general price index, taking the year 1913 as base :

TABLE 102

Price Index Number, 1860–1913

	1860–69	1870–76	1877–85	1886–93	1894–1903	1904–10	1911–13	1913
Cost of living .	84·0	86·6	81·6	71·8	70·2	74·9	78·8	80·0
Services .	6·5	7·8	7·8	8·3	9·0	9·4	9·8	10·0
Exports .	..	24·4	18·0	19·3	17·8	18·3	19·6	20·0
Iron and steel	..	11·8	9·4	6·0	6·5	6·6	7·2	7·5
Building .	7·1	7·6	7·5	6·8	6·8	7·5	7·2	7·5
Imports .	..	− 30·5	− 26·5	− 15·9	− 18·1	− 22·0	− 24·4	− 25·0
General index	98·0	117·7	97·8	96·3	92·3	94·7	98·2	100·0

We also require figures of the numbers of the occupied population who have been engaged in producing this income. For this purpose we can take the proportion of the population occupied at each Census and interpolate, the figures only moving slowly. The percentage of the population of Great Britain occupied at each Census since 1881 has been as follows :

1881	44·8	1911	44·9
1891	43·9	1921	45·2
1901	44·1	1931	47·0

It is clear that we are here dealing with a slow secular change due to the gradual increase in the average age of the population.

We are now in a position to compile a general table showing the amount of real income produced per head of occupied population between 1860 and 1913. It may be repeated that the price index has been calculated in such a manner as to exclude all effects due to changes in the terms of trade, and that this index refers only to wealth produced in Britain or drawn from capital investments overseas. The amount of real income available for consumption or investment in Britain may show a different movement during a period in which the terms of trade are changing.

Account must also be taken of changes in the amount of

unemployment. For the period up to 1913 we have only the Trade Union percentages. These figures only cover industrial workers, and exclude workers in agriculture, domestic service, retail trade, salaried work and other occupations where employment is more steady than in industrial work. On the other hand, the Trade Union returns probably give too low a figure for the industries which they purport to cover, owing to the exclusion of many of the unskilled, casual workers and others among whom unemployment may be very high. We have no knowledge about the order of magnitude of these considerations, or whether they balance each other and can only take the Trade Union figures as they stand. The figures taken are the adjusted series quoted by Sir William Beveridge in *Unemployment, A Problem of Industry*.

TABLE 103

REAL INCOME PER HEAD, 1860–1913

	National Income* (£s million)	Occupied Population (millions)	% Unemployed	Occupied Population in Work (m.)	Output per Occupied Person in Work (£)	Output per Occupied Person at 1913 Prices (£)	Output per Occupied Person including Unemployed at 1913 Prices (£)
1860–69	899	13·71	4·2	13·13	68·4	69·8	66·9
1870–76	1177	14·64	1·5	14·42	81·5	69·3	68·3
1877–85	1242	15·61	5·6	14·74	84·2	86·2	81·5
1886–93	1410	16·45	5·3	15·58	90·5	94·0	89·0
1894–1903	1666	17·82	4·0	17·11	97·3	105·4	101·2
1904–10	1940	19·49	5·7	18·38	105·6	111·3	105·0
1911–13	2241	20·58	2·8	20·00	112·0	114·0	110·9
1913	2339	20·80	2·1	20·36	114·9	114·9	112·5

* Inclusive of indirect taxes.

In order to make the series continuous between 1913 and the present day, a link is required in the price-index numbers between 1913 and 1924. The calculation of a general price index applicable to changes in the value of output between these two years is difficult owing to the large changes in relative prices and consumption. The method adopted is to revalue elements in 1913 output

DIAGRAM II

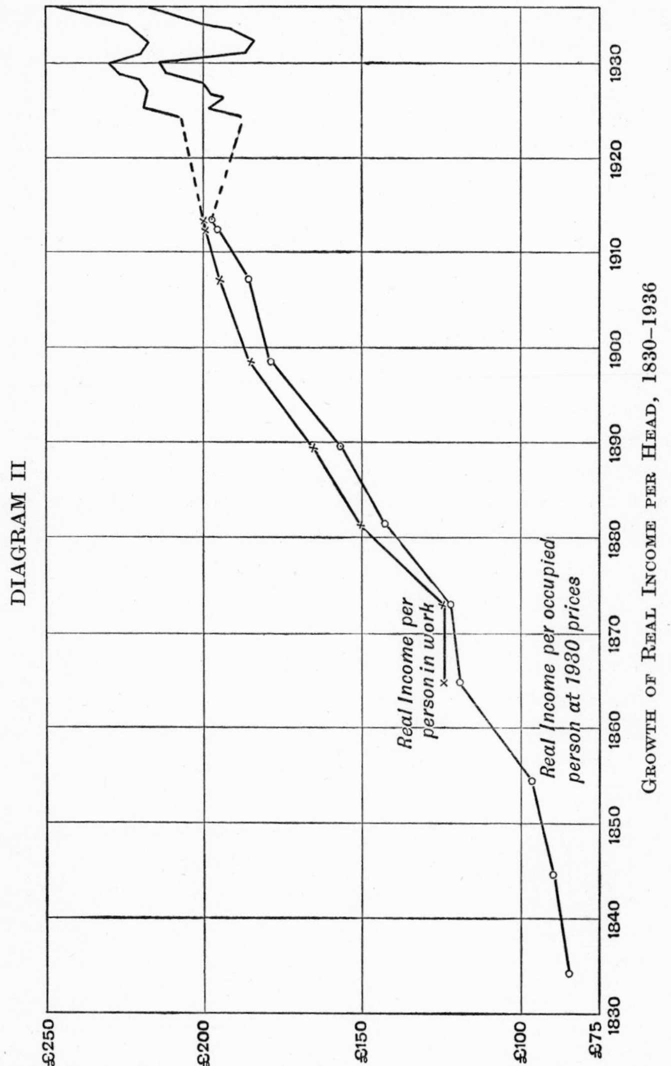

GROWTH OF REAL INCOME PER HEAD, 1830–1936

at 1924 prices, and in 1924 output at 1913 prices. The two methods give almost identical results.

As in the calculation of the previous index number, exports are given a positive weight and imports a negative weight. The prices of investment goods are represented by building costs and by the price of iron and steel (from the Board of Trade wholesale index number). The total expenditure on consumption each year is known by deduction of investment from the national income, but these figures of consumption have to be distributed under various heads. Expenditure on drink at current retail prices is given in the *Alliance Year-Book and Temperance Reformers' Handbook*, and of tobacco from the Census of Production. The change in retail prices of drink and tobacco between 1913 and 1924 is given in the Colwyn Report, and is between two- and threefold.

Expenditure on services other than distribution is estimated from Professor Bowley's tables for 1911, and from Mr. Feavearyear's for 1932. The price of services may be regarded as equivalent to the index of wage-rates.

There remain the five items, printed at the head of the list, covered by the cost-of-living index number. As this is a working-class index number, it very much understates the relative expenditure on " sundries ", and this item is given a much higher weight. The other items are, for 1913, weighted as in the original cost-of-living index number, and for 1924 estimated from current data.

Many of the data are approximate and conclusions cannot be drawn from individual items in the table.

[TABLE

TABLE 104

CALCULATION OF PRICE INDEX FOR 1924 ON 1913 BASE

	1913 Output, £ m.	1913 Output at 1924 Prices	1924 Output, £ m.	1924 Output at 1913 Prices
Food	900	1530	1300	764
Rent and rates	240	352	300	204
Clothing	180	405	355	158
Fuel	120	223	200	108
Sundries	200	360	480	267
Drink and tobacco	200	500	420	168
Services (excluding distribution)	400	760	600	316
Exports	425	945	801	445
Iron and steel	150	214	275	192
Shipping	85	111	140	107
Building	150	330	300	136
Imports (deduct)	660	990	1137	757
Total	2490	4740	4035	2108

1924 prices on 1913 base	190·3
1913 prices on 1924 base	52·3
Prices in 1924 on 1913 base (geometric mean)	190·5
Prices in 1930 on 1913 base	173·8

Bowley and Stamp deduced a price index of 176 for 1924 on a 1914 base. However, their index number was applicable to *consumption* rather than *output* ; that is, they did not discount the effect of the cheapness of imports relative to exports. Also, they did not add indirect taxation to the national income, and did not therefore require their index number to include the great rise in price of drink and tobacco. Excluding exports, imports, and drink and tobacco from the first two columns of the above table, we get a price rise of 176·5—an almost exact agreement.

CHAPTER XI

PRODUCTIVE SOURCES OF INCOME

In the investigation of the distribution of national income between factors of production, an analysis was made of the distribution of income in industry, agriculture and other economic activities in 1911 and 1930. The object of Table 53 was to show changes in distribution rather than to analyse the changing relative importance of the different sources of national income. We may restate the figures here analysed along these lines, for 1911, 1924, 1930 and 1934, from which we can obtain some idea of the trend. Table 106 shows the numbers occupied and the value of the net product of each of the six principal forms of economic activity, the share of the national income contributed by each, and the average net output per occupied person in each sphere. The figures for 1911 and 1930 have been previously given. We have also the results of the Census of Production for 1924, and estimates for the value of dwelling-houses and domestic service have been made on similar lines for 1934. The net output of agriculture can be calculated by the method used in Table 29 above.

The figures so far published from the Import Duties Acts Inquiries make possible an estimate of the net output of industry up to 1934. Omitting building and contracting (whether done by the building and contracting industry or by other trades), about which we have other information, and including small firms, the net output of industry in 1930 was £1513 millions. The trades covered by the 1934 Inquiry had a net output of £701 millions in 1930 (the scope of the 1933 Inquiry was slightly less), or of £200 per worker. By 1934 this had risen to £724 millions, or £209·5 per worker, despite the fall in prices between the two years. The excluded trades (see p. 130 above) include a number of trades in which net output per worker was above the average. If we assume that in these trades output per worker showed a similar increase between 1930 and 1934, and calculate the net output of building from the gross output (Table 81), we can obtain a rough estimate of the net output of industry in the following manner:

TABLE 105

NET OUTPUT OF INDUSTRY, 1930–34

		1930	1933	1934
Numbers employed in industry as given by Unemployment Insurance statistics	000's	5924	5602	5880
Do. including workers over 65 and under 16	000's	6414	6028	6354
Do. with allowance for discrepancy in certain industries	000's	6690	6308	6644
Do. with allowance for sickness .	000's	6450	6090	6410
Including employers and higher salary-earners	000's	6950	6590	6910
Numbers covered by 1933 Inquiry	000's	3262	3015	3208
Net output per head . .	£	197·1	198·1	206·8
Estimated net output, all industry	£m.	1513	1445	1582
Do. on basis of 1934 Inquiry .	£m.	1513	..	1576
Net output including building .	£m.	1639	1576	1719

We may now give for the four Censal years the table showing the contribution to national income of the principal industries (p. 238).

The money value of the net per-capita output of industry shows a steady upward trend, except during the period of declining prices, 1924–30, when it was constant. But the productivity per head of the different forms of economic activity should be examined relative to the average productivity per head of the whole community at each date. In 1911, strange though it may seem, industry was one of the less productive forms of activity, having a productivity per head of only £80 as against a

TABLE 106

PRODUCTIVE SOURCES OF INCOME

	Nos. Occupied (000's)	Net Output, £ m.	Net Output per Head, £	Share of National Income (%)
1911:				
Agriculture . . .	2,320	139	60	8·0
Industry . . .	8,595	688	80	39·3
Railways . . .	620	90	145	5·2
Domestic service . .	2,310	90	39	5·2
Other transport distribution and services	6,155	740	120	42·3
Home-produced national income (excluding indirect taxation and rent of dwellings)	19,900	1747	88	100·0
1924:				
Agriculture . . .	1,100	105	95·5	3·4
Industry . . .	7,928	1527	192·5	49·2
Railways . . .	700	160	229·0	5·2
Domestic service . .	1,450	140	96·5	4·5
Other transport distribution and services	6,872	1169	170	37·7
Home-produced national income (excluding indirect taxation and rent of dwellings)	18,050	3101	171·8	100·0
1930:				
Agriculture . . .	1,020	126	123	3·8
Industry . . .	7,868	1496	190	45·4
Railways . . .	648	153	236	4·7
Domestic service . .	1,540	150	97·5	4·6
Other transport distribution and services	7,379	1364	185	41·5
Home-produced national income (excluding indirect taxation and rent of dwellings)	18,455	3289	178	100·0
1934:				
Agriculture . . .	964	130	135	4·1
Industry . . .	7,885	1570	199	49·3
Railways . . .	650	140	216	4·4
Domestic service . .	1,640	160	97·5	5·0
Other transport distribution and services	7,928	1185	150	37·2
Home-produced national income (excluding indirect taxation and rent of dwellings)	19,067	3185	167·1	100·0

general average of £88. Now it has a productivity much above the general average. In the earlier years transport and distribution appear to have been the most productive (most highly capitalised) forms of activity.

The productivity of agriculture, it will be noticed, is now not so far below the general average as previously, while the productivity of the service industries is apparently showing a tendency to fall. We may now examine the changes in the relative share of money income contributed by the various industries.

The remarkable decline in the relative share contributed by agriculture between 1911 and 1924 is only partly accounted for by the exclusion of Southern Ireland. In 1911, the whole of Ireland contributed almost exactly one-quarter of the agricultural output of the whole United Kingdom. Since 1924, the share of agriculture in the national income has been rising. Between 1924 and 1930 there was a considerable decline in the price of the principal purchased materials used in agriculture; since 1930 there has been an appreciable rise in the physical quantity of agricultural output, and a number of steps have been taken to raise the prices at which it sells.

Manufacturing industry is apparently contributing an increasing proportion of the money income of the community, while using a diminishing proportion of the labour force. 1924 was a year of high selling prices for industrial produce, and the high level of industrial output relative to national income can be understood. By 1930 the share of industry in the national income had fallen to 45·4 per cent, which was, however, a higher percentage than had prevailed in 1911. Between 1930 and 1934 the value of the net output of industry has risen considerably more rapidly than has income from other sources.

The rapid decline in the proportion of income contributed by railway transport is noticeable. It is unfortunate that no estimate is possible of the net income produced by road transport, but no doubt it is considerable.

"Other transport, distribution and services" is absorbing an increasing proportion of the labour force, but tends to contribute a declining share of the national income. The principal industries involved are retail distribution,[1] Government and municipal services, hotels, entertainments and such. These are all industries in which, so far, opportunities for economising labour or increasing output per head are few. As the demand for these services increases, they tend to absorb an increasing proportion of the labour force but contribute a declining proportion of the national income. It will be noticed that the average income per head in these industries was 29 per cent above the average income per head in all industries in 1911. During recent years the average productivity per worker in these trades has fallen considerably below the general average.

The varying levels of output per head in the different branches of economic activity may be partly due to the very different extent of capital equipment in the different industries. The statistical measurement of national capital is a treacherous and difficult proceeding. Estimates for 1914 and for 1928 have been made by Sir Josiah Stamp.[2] We may alter his definition so as to exclude movable property (i.e. furniture and motor-cars), the national debt and capital held overseas. We may then specify the capital held under various heads in which we are interested, and determine by difference the capital in the remaining industries.

Sir Josiah does not give the capital used in manufacturing industry in a form comparable with the scope of the Census of Production. For 1928 he gives a figure of £3480 millions for the capital of industrial concerns for comparison with their Schedule D assessments. This means we must make an addition for industrial buildings (not covered by Schedule D) of, say, £500 millions, and must

[1] The gross cost of distribution of consumable goods was given in Chapter VII as £707 millions in 1930, or about £650 millions excluding railway transport—nearly half of the whole category.

[2] *British Incomes and Property* and *Statistical Journal*, 1931.

deduct approximately £600 millions for industries operating overseas.[1]

For 1914, we have a careful estimate made by Sir Alfred Flux in the report on the First Census of Production of £1500 millions as the capital value of plant and buildings of industrial concerns. Allowing for the additions to capital during the seven years between 1907 and 1914, and for the rise in prices, we may put this figure at £2000 millions in 1914.

TABLE 107

CAPITALISATION OF INDUSTRY, 1914 AND 1930

	Capital, £s million		Capital, £s per Occupied Person	
	1914	1928	1911–14	1928–30
Agriculture (land and tenants' capital)	1500	1,400	650	1370
Industry . . .	2000	3,400	233	433
Railways . . .	1140	1,100	1840	1700
Dwelling-houses . .	1400	2,000	. .	. .
Shipping . . .	160	250	1330	2000
Other	2700	5,450	450	750
Total . .	8900	13,600	447	738

The valuation of capital is affected not only by changes in the price-level, but also by changes in the rate of interest, and by many institutional factors, particularly in the case of land and buildings. No serious comparison, therefore, can be made between the gross values of capital in the two years. But we can draw some approximate conclusions about the amount of capital per occupied worker in the different forms of industry, and about changes between 1911 and 1930.

A most striking feature is the very low amount of capital required in manufacturing industry per worker employed, although this has shown a tendency to rise more rapidly than the capital per worker in non-manu-

[1] This figure is based on figures of British holdings in industrial companies operating overseas given by Sir Robert Kindersley.

facturing industry. The biggest capital requirements per worker are of course in railways and shipping. The enormous figure of capital per occupied worker in agriculture is also noticeable. In this case, the rise since 1911 is largely explained by the exclusion of Ireland, where the value of land per occupied worker was much lower. Three-quarters of the total represents the actual value of land rather than tenant's capital, but a great deal of this must be explained by the sporting and amenity value of the land rather than its agricultural value.

Figures to correspond with those of Table 106 cannot be calculated for years before 1911, but there are a number of figures which throw some light on the relative importance in the national income of the different forms of production in the earlier years. Estimates of agricultural output by Gregory King and MacCulloch have already been quoted and can be re-expressed in terms of present-day prices, as also can the estimate made by Sir James Caird for 1867. For figures of industrial production we are chiefly indebted to a remarkable investigation by Dr. Walther Hoffmann,[1] who has calculated an index number of the quantity of industrial production in Britain right back to the early years of the eighteenth century. Though no great precision can be claimed for it in the earlier years, when the data are very few and the line between domestic and industrial production was not clearly marked, it appears to be valid at any rate for the nineteenth century. Another interesting investigation was published shortly afterwards by Dr. Drescher dealing with the volume of agricultural production in Great Britain and Ireland since 1867, the year in which official statistics first became available on this subject.[2] British statisticians should feel a sense of shame that no one in this country has had the time and interest to conduct such work, and Dr. Hoffmann and Dr. Drescher are to be congratulated on their results.

[1] *Weltwirtschaftlisches Archiv*, September 1934.
[2] *Ibid.*, March 1935.

MacCulloch's statement of the output of agriculture in England and Wales can be revalued at present prices. In the case of wheat and barley, he gives an estimate of the aggregate yield of crops. In the case of potatoes, he does not give the yield or acreage, but quotes a figure to show that in Scotland the acreage then was 80,000, or a little over half what it is at the present time. It is assumed that the same proportion prevailed in England. MacCulloch claims a higher average yield per acre than prevails at the present time. In the case of live-stock, he gives an estimate of the numbers of beasts slaughtered, with some evidence that the average weight of a carcase was about the same as that at the present time. In the case of dairy produce, MacCulloch quotes the following retail prices :

Butter . .	10d. per lb.
Cheese . .	6d. ,,
Milk . .	5d. per quart

On the basis of these prices, the sales of dairy produce can be revalued at present prices. Finally, the fodder consumed by approximately 800,000 non-agricultural horses in England and Wales can be revalued at the present estimated cost of a year's fodder for a horse (about £8).

TABLE 108

MacCulloch's Estimate of Agricultural Produce in England and Wales, 1837, revalued at Present Prices

	£s million
Wheat (12·35 mn. qtrs.)	12·85
Barley (3·6 mn. qtrs.)	5·56
Potatoes (280,000 acres) . . .	8·4
Cattle and calves	18·5
Sheep and lambs	11·3
Pigs	2·6
Dairy produce	9·0
Horses	4·0
Wool	2·4
Other products	2·0
Fodder for non-agricultural horses .	6·4
Total . .	83·0

In current values, the output of Great Britain exceeded that of England and Wales by 18·3 per cent. We may estimate £97·4 millions as the value at present-day prices of the output of Great Britain, or £67·2 per occupied person per annum.

The first firmly based estimate of the value of agricultural output could not be made until official statistics were collected of the acreage of crops and the number of livestock. This was in 1867. Sir James Caird [1] makes an estimate for the agricultural output of the United Kingdom in that year. He includes estimates of the values of meat and dairy produce, and of fodder crops, omitting the output of horses and pig-meat to balance the inclusion of fodder crops. For the whole United Kingdom the results are as follows :

TABLE 109

AGRICULTURAL OUTPUT IN 1867 (GREAT BRITAIN AND IRELAND)

	£s million at Current Prices	£s million at Present-day Prices	£s million at 1913 Prices
Wheat	31·5	16·6	21·6
Barley	20·4	16·8	16·4
Oats	25·7	18·0	17·1
Beans, peas, rye and potatoes	25·0	25·0	25·0
Beef and veal	28·4	32·5	35·7
Dairy produce	30·1	28·6	36·0
Mutton and lamb	18·9	23·5	21·2
Wool	8·0	3·0	6·2
Flax	2·0	2·0	1·5
Total	190·0	166·0	180·7

Of the output of £190 millions, Caird estimated that £140·3 millions was produced in Great Britain. At present prices this corresponds to £122·8 millions. The number of persons engaged in agriculture in Great Britain was 1,950,000 in 1861, and 1,700,000 in 1871. For 1867 we may put it at 1,800,000, and the average output per head at £68·2, measured at present-day prices. This is only

[1] *J.R.S.S.*, 1868, p. 139.

slightly higher than MacCulloch's figure, and causes one to suspect that the latter is too high.

Caird estimated the number of producers at over $2\frac{1}{4}$ millions in 1867. It appears that he must have included a number of children who were excluded by Booth. As Booth's estimates were prepared on a systematic basis over the whole period, we will use his rather than Caird's. The average output per producer in Ireland, on Booth's basis, was about £45 at current prices, as against £78 in Great Britain.

The figures quoted above for agricultural output require certain adjustments. They refer to gross output. No deduction is made for materials purchased by agriculture. Caird, as has already been mentioned, thought he had disposed of this problem by omitting horses and pigs from his output. His estimate for the net value of output in England and Wales (£117 millions) agrees exactly with an independent estimate made by Purdy for 1860 (*J.R.S.S.*, 1861, p. 328), by adding together the estimated incomes of farmers, farm-workers and landlords. It therefore follows that Caird's figures have probably already made full allowance for fodder crops and purchased materials. But in later years substantial deductions must be made from figures of gross output. The first year for which a real ascertainment was made of the net agricultural output of Great Britain and Ireland was 1908. Allowance must also be made for store cattle which were sold from Ireland to British fatteners. Excluding these, and including the produce of horticulture, the gross output of agriculture was £210 millions in that year. However, the materials used up in producing this output included £28·8 millions of home-produced industrial produce (fertilisers, feeding-stuffs, etc.) and £17 millions of imported produce. The net output in 1908 was therefore £164 millions. Allowing for a certain amount of expense in the earlier years under these heads, we can make the following estimates of the volume of agricultural output valued at 1913 prices:

TABLE 110

Agricultural Output, 1866–1913 (based on Dr. Drescher's figures)

(£s million)

	Produce sold off Farms at 1908 Prices		Net Output of U.K. at 1908 Prices	Net Output of U.K. at 1913 Prices
	Great Britain	Ireland		
1866–9	124·0	39·8	164	167·5
1870–76	133·0	41·8	166	170·0
1877–85	131·3	39·5	150	153·5
1886–93	144·6	42·3	158	161·5
1894–1903	144·1	45·2	154	157·5
1904–10	156·2	48·4	160	163·5
1908	159·5	50·5	164	168·0
1911–13	151·0	50·8	160	163·5
1913	148·7	51·8	152	155·5

The long-period growth of agricultural productivity can be traced in the following table :

TABLE 111

Net Output per Person occupied in Agriculture

(At 1913 prices)

Year	Source	Great Britain			Ireland			U.K.
		Net Output, £ million	Nos. Occupied, 000's	Output per head, £	Net Output, £ million	Nos. Occupied, 000's	Output per head, £	Output per head, £
1688	Gregory King (England and Wales)	60·4	1250	48·3	. .	. .	. .	. .
1837	MacCulloch	105·3	1450	72·7	28·7	1840	15·6	40·7
1867	Caird	133·5	1800	74·3	47·2	1160	40·7	61·1
1908	Census	127·5	1500	85·2	40·5	820	49·5	72·5

The features most worthy of note are the slow rate of improvement in Great Britain and the very rapid improvement of Ireland from her miserable level of productivity of the 1830's, as her population fell.

With Dr. Hoffmann's figures, we now have some indication of the contribution to real income of industry and of agriculture back to the 1830's. If we care to make the further assumption that the remainder of the real income of the community (largely domestic service in the earlier years) varied in proportion to the numbers engaged in employments other than industry and agriculture, we can make some sort of an estimate of movements of real income between 1830 and 1860.

From this we deduce that the real income per occupied person at 1913 prices, for use in continuation of the series given in the previous chapter, was as follows :

1830–39 . . .	£47·9
1840–49 . . .	50·9
1850–59 . . .	55·5

CHAPTER XII

CHANGES IN CONSUMPTION, INVESTMENT, PRICES AND COSTS IN THE TRADE CYCLE, 1929–36

In a previous chapter data were given showing changes in the proportion of the national income invested during various recent years. It is of course a universal rule that the proportion of the national income invested declines during a slump. Some much more interesting conclusions, however, can be obtained by comparing the *absolute* change in investment with the absolute change in national income during any period, rather than the relative changes.

It was suggested by Mr. R. F. Kahn [1] that a given change in the numbers employed in the production of investment goods or capital goods should be accompanied by a determinate change in employment as a whole, the ratio between which two changes he described as "the multiplier". This article assumed an unchanging level of output per worker, which is an assumption clearly not fulfilled over recent years. There is no need to make this assumption, if we make the argument refer to *value of output* rather than to numbers in employment. Mr. Kahn's other assumptions, namely, that:

(1) The majority of industries are working below the full level of productive capacity, and can raise their output without increasing average costs;

(2) That no considerable changes in wages would be caused by increasing or diminishing unemployment;

(3) That a reduction in the cost of unemployment benefit and relief will be mainly reflected in a reduction of net borrowing, or an increase of net saving, on the part of public authorities;

[1] *Economic Journal*, June 1931, "The Relation of Home Investment to Unemployment".

are approximately fulfilled under conditions of the present day.

On these assumptions, Mr. Kahn calculates that the multiplier should have a value of approximately two. The accompanying diagram shows the relation between investment and total value of output (i.e. national income). The scale of differences of investment is twice that of differences in national income.

DIAGRAM III

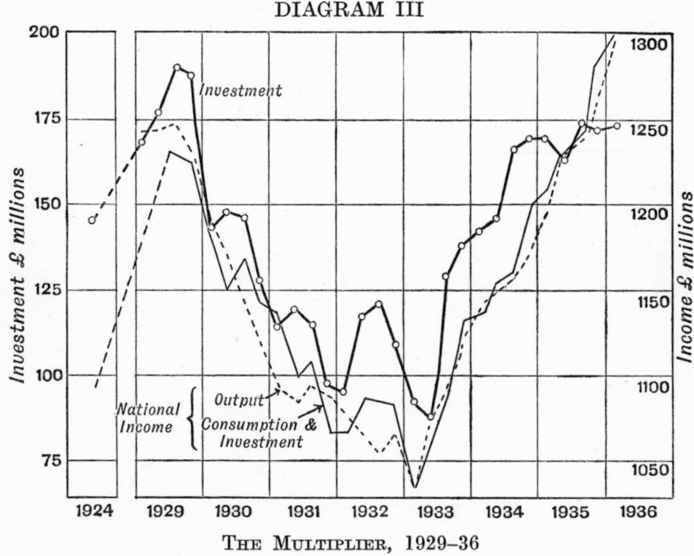

THE MULTIPLIER, 1929–36

For the period of 1929–35 the resemblance is most striking, and gives considerable support to the theory of the multiplier. The calculation may be stated in another way thus, that a sudden change, either upwards or downwards, in the output of capital-goods-producing industries is likely to cause a similar change of approximately equal magnitude in the value of the output in consumption-goods industries.

It is clear that this is only a phenomenon of the short period, indeed longer period validity is not claimed for it. During the period 1924–9, for instance, national income rose considerably at a time of stationary investment. In 1935, investment again stood at about the 1929 level, while the national income was considerably higher. Both these point to a secular upward tendency in national income in spite of the fact that the aggregate value of investment is on the whole tending downwards. On Mr. Kahn's enlarged definition and exposition of the multiplier, this must be taken as an indication of an increasing " propensity to consume " on the part of those in possession of large incomes, or else of a diminishing inequality of distribution of income. We have shown that the latter is not present to any great extent, but there is a certain amount of evidence to show that the former factor has been present.

We have already shown that during recent years impersonal saving through undistributed company profits and local-authority sinking funds accounted for the greater part of the observed total of investment. During the last few years, it appeared that private saving by the rich had altogether disappeared or even became negative.

We can examine this problem from another angle by making a direct comparison between the incomes of the well-to-do section of the community and their estimated consumption.

The incomes of wage- and salary-earners receiving less than £250 a year have already been calculated. Other incomes below £250 a year are those of small employers and independent workers, and certain incomes derived from capital. These are of the order of magnitude of £240 millions a year and we can assume that they change very little from year to year. Deducting these incomes, and the income of the State and local authorities, from the whole national income, we have a figure of the incomes accruing to persons with incomes over £250 a year. In order to convert these figures into spendable income in the ordinary sense we must make the following adjustments :

Deduct—

(1) Direct taxation.

(2) Sums needed for writing down inventories.

(3) Undistributed company profits.

Add—

Interest on National Debt.

This calculation will give us what might be called the spendable incomes of the rich (rich being defined as those with incomes over £250).

We may next determine the amount which they actually spend from the consumption statistics, making a deduction for the estimated consumption of the working classes. We may first of all omit the involuntary consumption of different services which are paid for through taxation and then reckon the total of working-class consumption. This will consist of working-class incomes as estimated above, transfer incomes received by the working classes in the form of unemployment benefit, old-age pensions, etc., less workers' contributions to State Insurance and working-class savings. In a previous table the principal items of working- and middle-class savings have already been shown. There are no data for dividing these figures between savers with incomes above and below £250, but it will be assumed that all the insurances, and half the repayments of principal to building societies, represent savings by people with incomes above £250 and the remainder by people with incomes below £250.

The incomes of the rich can only conveniently be calculated on an annual basis, but it is possible to calculate quarterly figures of their consumption. In the following table the annual figures are given, but the quarterly figures are plotted on the diagram.

The results are plotted on the following diagram. Too close a comparison cannot be made between the absolute levels of the curves, because some approximate assumptions have been made about what constitute working-class savings ; although the assumptions are probably biased in the direction of under-estimating the amount of working-class savings, and hence of under-estimating the amount

TABLE 112

INCOMES AND CONSUMPTION, 1924–36 (£s million)

	Net National Income excluding Government	Incomes under £250	Adjusted Spendable Incomes of Persons over £250	Consumption by Persons	
				Incomes under £250	Incomes over £250
1924	3600	1969	1319	2091	1229
1925	3902	2037	1367	2174	1212
1926	3686	2002	1376	2169	1274
1927	3854	2122	1369	2252	1263
1928	3811	2129	1397	2261	1286
1929 :	3868	2166	1372	..	..
iii	..	..	..	583	352
iv	..	..	..	584	352
1930 :	3817	2130	1178	..	..
i	..	..	..	579	358
ii	..	..	..	575	323
iii	..	..	..	574	348
iv	..	..	..	569	344
1931 :	3387	2069	1020	568	351
i	..	..	..	573	304
ii	..	..	..	565	325
iii	..	..	..	564	304
iv	..	..	..	..	..
1932 :	3313	2029	944	..	..
i	..	..	..	556	317
ii	..	..	..	550	321
iii	..	..	..	544	320
iv	..	..	..	548	326
1933 :	3430	2067	1083	..	..
i	..	..	..	546	302
ii	..	..	..	551	330
iii	..	..	..	562	301
iv	..	..	..	570	322
1934 :	3679	2174	1158	..	..
i	..	..	..	571	314
ii	..	..	..	580	325
iii	..	..	..	586	305
iv	..	..	..	593	327
1935 :	3915	2270	1256	..	..
i	..	..	..	596	334
ii	..	..	..	603	350
iii	..	..	..	612	336
iv	..	..	..	617	371
1936 :					
i	..	..	..	621	384

of consumption by the rich. But it seems to be clear that the amount of consumption by the rich was in 1929 about level with their private incomes, and now is considerably in excess. During the slump, it is noticeable that the standards of living of the rich should have been maintained at the expense of part of their capital, but it is more sur-

DIAGRAM IV

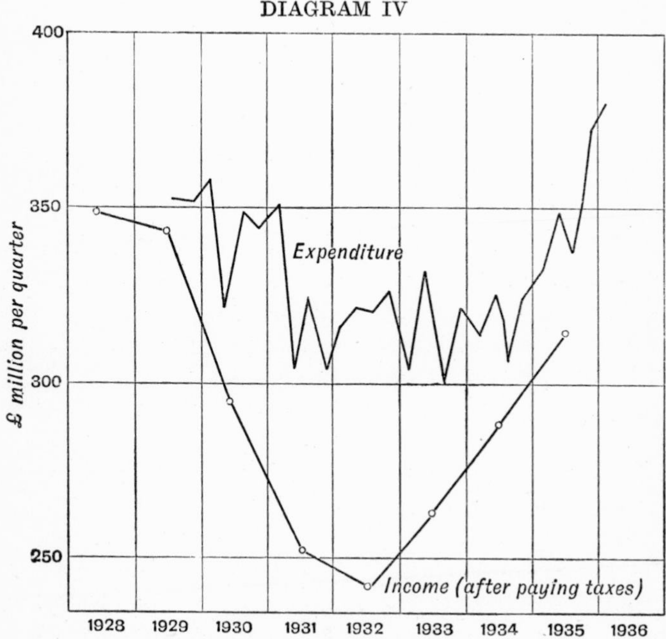

INCOME AND EXPENDITURE BY PERSONS WITH INCOMES OVER £250, 1928–36

prising to see that the recovery of incomes during recent years has been accompanied by a rapid rise in consumption leaving no margin for private saving.[1] From the ordinary man's point of view, this often represents nothing more imprudent than the spending of the proceeds of capital appreciation, but from the social point of view it means

[1] Or, in other words, that the net new total of private saving in each year is only just enough to balance the payment of Death Duties out of private capital (£80–90 millions a year in recent years).

that the private incomes of the rich have ceased to be a source of saving,[1] and indeed that an appreciable part of the institutional saving through companies, etc., is used up in meeting the capital consumption of the well-to-do.

Another interesting feature is the remarkable delay in the movements of the curve representing the expenditure of the well-to-do. Up to the beginning of 1931 they continued spending at practically the 1929 level, although their incomes had heavily diminished. There was then a fairly rapid fall in the level of consumption of about 10 per cent. This level of consumption persisted till the end of 1934, two years after the rise in incomes had begun. During 1935 and 1936 there has been a rapid increase in consumption. Working-class consumption, during the period of declining incomes, was perforce rapidly adjusted to incomes, and began to rise much sooner during the period of revival, though even here there was some evidence that the first increments of working-class income were used for paying debts, or were saved.

Many of the most puzzling phenomena of the timing of income and consumption movements in the trade cycle can be explained by the simple fact that the poor have no securities to sell when their incomes go down, but the rich have.

We may return now to the question of " the multiplier ". We have seen that an increase in the personal incomes of the well-to-do is more likely to be spent than saved, though possibly after some considerable delay. The key factor in the situation would therefore seem to be the propensity (if that word may be used) of company officials to distribute in dividends, or not to distribute in dividends, any given increment of income. The situation here may be examined by a simple graphical treatment. Reverting to the data of Table 85, of company profits and savings, we can make a scatter diagram showing the rela-

[1] If a man holds securities whose value appreciates, there has been no increase of the national income on our definition, i.e. no increase in the output of goods and services. If he spends the whole or part of the proceeds of this appreciation, he is, in effect, un-saving or using up the savings of others.

tionship between any given absolute figure of profits and the amount saved in the form of undistributed profits.

The analysis is delightfully simple. The data for the period 1924–35 lie almost exactly along a straight line, indicating a more or less constant propensity to save on the part of company authorities. Of each additional £1 of income, whether starting from a low level or a high level,

DIAGRAM V

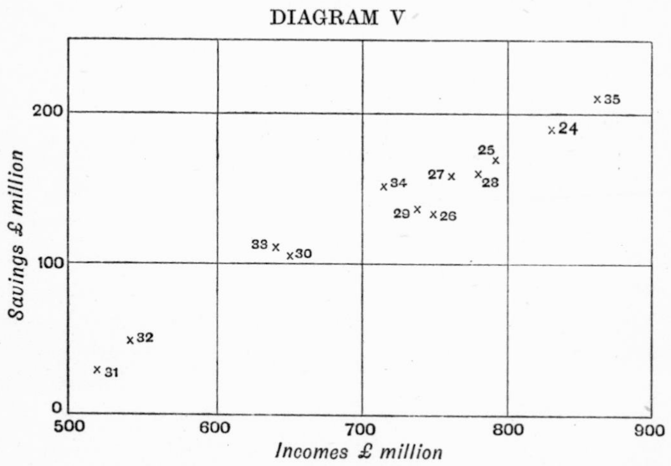

COMPANIES' "PROPENSITY TO SAVE", 1924–35

on the average £0·46 will be distributed in dividends and the remainder added to reserves.[1]

The remarkable constancy of this relation probably explains the closeness with which the multiplier 2 is adhered to in the relation between investment and national income.

Table 89 gives quarterly data for the analysis of changes in the prices of consumption and investment goods during the 1929–36 trade cycle in Great Britain. These data yield one result of interest which is in flat contradiction to the views generally held by economic theorists.[2] The view at present advocated is that during periods of

[1] In other words, as the proverb goes, "£1 for the company and £1 for the shareholders".

[2] See, for instance, Prof. Robbins' "Consumption and the Trade Cycle", *Economica*, 1931.

recovery, whether natural or artificial, an increasing proportion of income is spent upon investment goods, and their price must rise relative to that of consumption goods. During a period of depression, there is an increase in the relative price of consumption goods. In fact, however, during the period of depression and decline in investment from 1929 to 1932, investment goods were becoming relatively dearer, i.e. their price was falling more slowly than that of consumption goods. During the period of reviving investment from 1932 to 1936, investment goods were becoming relatively cheaper. This generalisation, though it may appear surprising, is exactly confirmed by the movement of the German price statistics, in which country official index numbers are calculated of the prices of investment goods and consumption goods. It probably means nothing more than that the most important investment goods are produced under conditions of short-period increasing returns. This is not very surprising, but it will mean that certain monetary theories have to be rewritten.

A more interesting analysis can be made of changes in costs of production. Our quarterly figures in Table 28 show the amount laid out each quarter in wages and in salaries under £250. In the last analysis these represent the principal element in all costs of production, apart from the question of possible changes in the terms of trade. If we re-express these wages and salaries at 1924 wage-rates, thus eliminating the effect of changes in the money rate of wages, we obtain a measure of the real labour cost incurred in producing the output of each period. By this method, it will be seen, we take into account the increasing proportion of the more expensive grades of labour which are now being used in production. Output may conveniently be analysed into the output of industries covered by the Census of Production, and all other. In the former category, it is found that the average wage and salary payment between 1924 and 1930 moved proportionately to the change in wage-rates, without any upward bias due to increases in the proportions of the more expensive grades of labour among the employees of industry. We can therefore measure labour costs in this field by comparing the volume of production as shown by the Board of Trade index with the numbers of insured workers in manufacturing and mining employments as shown by the Ministry of Labour.

It is found that industry shows a strong tendency towards short-period increasing returns, i.e. a decline in average labour cost as output is increased. Other forms of productive activity show no such tendency, and for the last seven years appear to have worked under a condition of constant returns.

The following are the figures for mining and manufacturing industry :

TABLE 113

Output and Cost of Production, 1928–36 *

	Volume of Production 1927–9=100	Average Real Labour Cost per Unit of Production		Volume of Production 1927–9=100	Average Real Labour Cost per Unit of Production
1928 :			1932 :		
i	98·1	102·6	i	87·5	100·3
ii	97·5	102·3	ii	86·1	98·4
iii	97·8	101·3	iii	84·8	99·1
iv	98·3	101·7	iv	84·8	102·5
1929 :			1933 :		
i	102·0	99·2	i	85·4	100·9
ii	104·2	97·5	ii	90·3	96·4
iii	106·0	96·3	iii	93·9	96·2
iv	103·5	98·3	iv	95·6	97·3
1930 :			1934 :		
i	101·0	97·6	i	101·9	91·2
ii	97·0	98·0	ii	103·3	90·1
iii	95·8	97·1	iii	102·0	91·9
iv	89·6	100·9	iv	102·0	93·2
1931 :			1935 :		
i	86·2	101·9	i	109·0	86·1
ii	86·5	99·5	ii	112·0	84·2
iii	86·5	98·5	iii	107·9	88·9
iv	87·4	101·0	iv	110·1	88·7
			1936 :		
			i	117·1	83·0

* Both the output and employment figures are corrected for seasonal variations.

When plotted on a diagram the figures give very interesting results. For the first two years, 1928 and 1929, the data lie along a straight line indicating a fairly steeply sloping rate of diminishing costs with increasing output. 1930 was clearly a year of transition, under the stimulus of

DIAGRAM VI

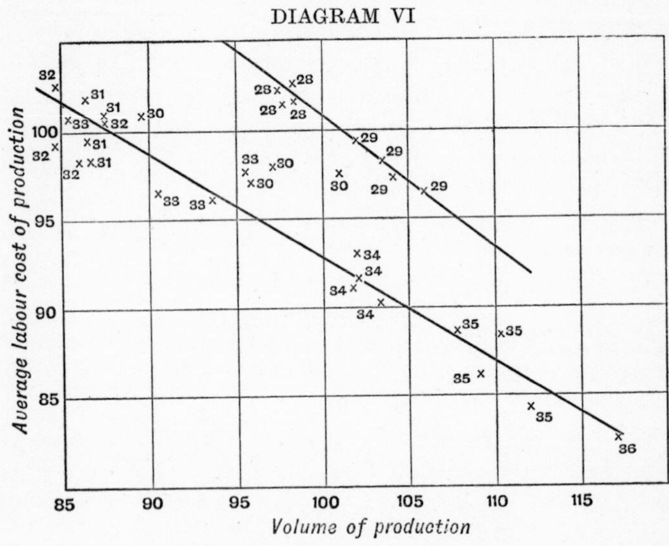

LABOUR COSTS PER UNIT OF OUTPUT

depression, to a new level of labour costs. Since that date we have moved first up and then down a new line, not sloping quite so steeply as the old one, indicative of the rate of diminishing costs under present conditions.

Taking the data as they stand, they indicate not only diminishing average but also diminishing marginal costs. The data are as follows:

[TABLE

TABLE 114

MARGINAL COST OF OUTPUT

Level of Output (as defined in above Table)	Marginal Cost (in Units of above Table)
87·5	44·9
92·5	43·2
97·5	37·4
102·5	40·0
107·5	28·4
112·5	27·4

If marginal costs continue to diminish we may expect an output of 125 (or 7 per cent above the output of the first quarter of 1936) to be produced by 6¼ million industrial workers, as compared with the 6,109,000 (seasonal variation eliminated) actually employed in the first quarter 1936. If this level of average productivity is not reached, it may be concluded that marginal costs have ceased to fall.[1]

The foregoing analysis gives some support to the view described by Mr. Keynes that changes in the amount of investment are the principal motive force in trade fluctuations. We have established his proposition that these changes are multiplied by a factor depending upon saving habits, taxation and other causes. We have also shown that an increase in the scale of output may have a considerable effect on costs of production and on profits.

It is clear that the next step for statistical analysis is an examination of the actual incentives to invest. It may be suggested that the following are the three principal factors in causing the amount of fixed investment to fluctuate :

(1) Changes in the rate of profit per unit of output.

It may be assumed that the industrialist, for want of

[1] This paragraph was written in June 1936, before the publication of the Board of Trade index of production for the second quarter of 1936. Correcting for seasonal variations, output in the second quarter rose to 124·0 (as defined above), with only a 1 per cent increase in employment as compared with the first quarter. It is clear that marginal costs are still falling.

better, takes account of current rates of profit per unit of output, and assumes that they will persist in the future.

(2) The price of capital equipment.

Other things being equal, it is clear that a high price of new capital equipment will act as a deterrent to investment.

(3) The rate of interest.

In the more short-lived types of capital instruments,

DIAGRAM VII

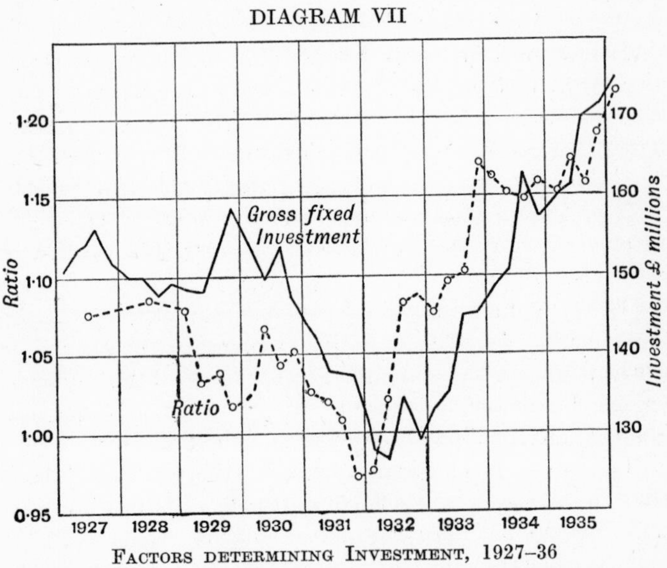

FACTORS DETERMINING INVESTMENT, 1927–36

considerations of the rate of interest are inappreciable in comparison with the maintenance and obsolescence charges. On the other hand, a substantial part of production of fixed investment goods is of buildings and other long-lived goods in which calculations of the rate of interest are of paramount importance. In the calculation which follows, the yield of industrial debentures has been taken as the most representative rate of interest for this problem, "diluted" by the addition of a constant 5 per cent to represent obsolescence charges.

The following ratio has therefore been calculated

$$\frac{\text{Present rate of profit per unit of output}}{\text{Price of capital equipment} \times \text{rate of interest}}$$

as a measure of the incentive to invest.

Annual figures for the years 1927 and 1928, and quarterly figures since the beginning of 1929, are plotted on the above diagram, together with movements in the gross total of fixed investment. The scales are chosen proportionately to the standard deviations of the two series. There is a very remarkable correspondence. But what is perhaps much more remarkable is that the movements of this ratio anticipate, by twelve months on the average, movements in the total of investment and hence of national income in general, and hence may perhaps be used for forecasting. This ratio was at a maximum in 1928 and fell heavily in the second quarter of 1929, while general business was still expanding. It reached its minimum in the fourth quarter of 1931 and then rose sharply, anticipating the movement of investment a year later. During 1935, however, the rise in investment has been considerably more rapid than was anticipated by the ratio.

CHAPTER XIII

THE RATE OF ECONOMIC PROGRESS

If it is permissible to leave figures for one occasion, and to express facts in more homely terms, I cannot do better than quote the following extract to show the extent of economic progress in this country within a single lifetime. It is from the autobiography [1] of my friend George Edwards, the founder of the National Union of Agricultural Workers, who was born in 1850 and died in 1934.

"In the middle of the nineteenth century there lived in the parish of Marsham, Norfolk, a couple of poor people by the name of Thomas and Mary Edwards. It was on October 5th, 1850, that Mary Edwards bore her last baby boy. At the time of my birth my father was a bullock feeder, working seven days a week, leaving home in the morning before it was light, and not returning in the evening until it was dark. He never saw his children, at this time, except for a little while on the Sunday, as they were always put to bed during the winter months before his return from work. At this time my father's wage had been reduced to 7s. per week, and had it not been that my mother was able to add a little to her husband's wages by hand-loom weaving the family would have absolutely starved. I have known my mother to be at the loom sixteen hours out of the twenty-four, and for those long hours she would not average more than 4s. a week, and very often less than that.

"The cottage in which the child was born was a miserable one of but two bedrooms, in which had to sleep father, mother, and six children. The family at this time was in abject poverty. When lying in bed with the infant

[1] *From Crow-Scaring to Westminster*, by George Edwards, M.P., Labour Publishing Company, 1922.

the mother's only food was onion gruel. As a result of the bad food, or, properly speaking, the want of food, she was only able to feed the child at her breast for a week. After the first week he had to be fed on bread soaked in very poor skimmed milk. As soon as my mother was able to get about again she had to take herself again to the loom.

"Before the repeal of the Corn Laws had the effect of reducing the cost of living to any great extent, the great Crimean War broke out. This, it will be remembered, was in 1854. Food rose to famine prices. The price of bread went up to 1s. per 4 lb. loaf, sugar to 8d. per lb., tea to 6d. per oz., cheese rose from 7d. to 1s. 6d. per lb.—in fact every article of food rose to almost prohibitive figures. The only article which did not rise to such a proportionately high figure was meat, but that was an article of food which rarely entered a poor man's home, except a little piece of pork occasionally which would weigh about 1½ lb., and would have to last a family of nine for a week! At the time of the Crimean War meat never entered my father's house more than once or twice a year!

"I was then four years of age, and the hardships of those days will never be erased from my memory. My father at this time was making 8s. per week of seven days. His wages were not sufficient to buy bread alone for the family by more than 4s. per week. My eldest brother Joseph, who was twelve years old, was at work for 1s. 6d. per week, my second brother John, ten years old, was working for 1s. 2d. per week.

"In order to save the family from actual starvation, my father, night by night, took a few turnips from his master's field. My father used to keep our little boots in the best state of repair he could. My sister and I went to bed early on Saturday nights so that my mother might be able to wash and mend our clothes, and we have them clean and tidy for the Sunday. We had no change of clothes in those days. This work kept my mother up nearly all the Saturday night, but she would be up early on the Sunday morning to get our scanty breakfast ready in time for us to go to Sunday school.

" This was the only schooling I ever had ! "

Conditions such as these were then the lot of about one-third of the population. In previous decades, particularly in the Hungry Forties, the evidence goes to show that still worse conditions prevailed. In the early years of the nineteenth century, the average real income of the mass of the people was probably not much above what it had been at the time when Gregory King wrote, and that, according to Thorold Rogers, was inferior to what it had been in the fifteenth and sixteenth centuries. At any rate, there was no evidence of progress. At the time of which George Edwards wrote, the rapid upward movement in real incomes had begun, but it had not yet touched the agricultural and rural workers. During the last eighty years covered by his lifetime there has been greater economic advance than there was in the previous four centuries. From the conditions which George Edwards has described, we have advanced to the " frugal comfort " (to borrow the words of the Papal Encyclical) of a large section of the present-day working classes, the qualified poverty of miners and agricultural workers at 30–40s. a week, and the promotion of an increasing proportion of the population to the ranks of the well-paid salariat.

In return for this degree of economic progress, at least half of the working population is now living in a condition of economic insecurity, and fear of unemployment, which in the past was the lot of only a minority.

A close numerical measure of the rate of economic progress is given by the statistics and diagram in Chapter IX, relating to the rate of growth of real income per head of the population, or per occupied person.

We may now turn our attention back to the diagram showing the rate of growth of real income per head. With one remarkable setback in the period 1870–76—it was repaired in the subsequent decade—the general course of the curve has been a slow rise in the first three decades, then a period of accelerated growth, then a period of declining rate of growth from 1900 to 1913. After 1924 the rate of growth appears to have been resumed at an increased speed, as compared at any rate with the period 1900–1913.

Over four cycles, from 1877 to 1910, the figure of unemployment averaged in each cycle something very close to 5 per cent of the working population. It was at its lowest at 4·0 per cent in 1884–1903, and at its highest at 5·7 per cent in 1904–10. The stability, subject to cyclical variations, of the general level of unemployment over a period of thirty years, is one of the most important features of pre-War economic development.

The data given for the remaining three years 1911–13, and for the year 1913 itself, cannot be properly compared with the averages of previous cycles. They were years of rapid economic expansion, and 1913 itself was a peak year. The data for a completed cycle including the subsequent period of recession would almost certainly have shown a lower output per head. Taking this consideration into account, it appears that in the years prior to 1913 a further increased falling-off in the rate of economic progress was noticeable. There are two pieces of supporting evidence for this. The present writer has made a comparison [1] between the index of the volume of industrial production for the years 1907–13 calculated by Mr. J. W. F. Rowe, and the occupied population, and found that there was no evidence of any increase in average output per head during this period. Mr. G. T. Jones [2] made a detailed investigation of three industries—cotton, iron and steel, and building—and found that in each of them the tendency to increasing average output per head had practically come to an end by 1900.

In 1914 began four years of war. Financially the cost of the War was met by borrowing, but economically the

[1] *Economic Journal*, September 1931.

[2] *Increasing Returns*, Cambridge University Press, 1932.

cost of war had to be met in other ways. Part of it was met by excess of imports, corresponding to the sale of overseas capital holdings. The Sumner Committee in 1918 reported that the average standard of consumption of the urban working classes in that year was quite as high as in 1913. But the consumption of other sections of the community was probably below the 1913 level, as was working-class consumption in the earlier years of the War. Many persons, normally leisured or engaged in domestic duties, entered into occupations, and those in work worked a great deal of overtime. But the provision for war expenditure, plus the maintenance of standards of consumption for the civil population, was largely provided at the expense of the cessation of capital accumulation (£300 millions, or nearly 15 per cent of the national income, in 1913) and the postponement of much depreciation, renewal and maintenance work (over £150 millions in 1913). It is not the case, as is sometimes said, that the average productivity of industry is high under war conditions.

These arrears of maintenance and renewal work were made good, and even net additions to capital were made, in a burst of feverish activity in the two years 1919 and 1920. For the first time for half a century there was an acute general shortage of labour, and the community was working up to its then full level of productive capacity. The Treasury and the banks pursued an inflationary policy, and the effect of rapidly rising prices was to cut down the real volume of working-class consumption, and to release further resources for the restoration and extension of capital equipment.[1]

In 1921 came a slump in prices and in production which was sudden, devastating, immediate and short-lived. The years 1922 and 1923 were years of rapid recovery in this as in other countries, and 1924, the first year of stabil-

[1] Students of Mr. D. H. Robertson's *Banking Policy and the Price Level* and of Prof. Hayek's *Prices and Production* would, I think, be well repaid by a detailed factual study of this period. It is the only recent period for which their assumption of full employment of productive resources is justified.

ised conditions, is made the subject of the first post-War studies of national income.

The figures given in previous chapters show that the real income produced per occupied person in work was slightly higher in 1913 than in 1924. This conclusion is not in conflict with that reached by Professor Bowley and Sir Josiah Stamp, who estimated that the real income per head of the population was about 5 per cent less. As unemployment had risen from 2 to 10 per cent, their estimate is consistent with a rise in the average real income per person in work.

Even when we allow for the rapid renewal and restoration of capital equipment in 1919–20 and 1922–3, it is surprising to find that the 1913 average productivity had been restored by 1924. It is still more surprising when we consider that there had been a general reduction in working hours in 1919. For industrial, transport and agricultural workers this reduction averaged 6 hours, or about 11 per cent of the working week. No data are available about changes in working hours in the distributive and service industries, where the reduction was probably less, but the average productivity of the whole working community, per hour worked, must have been substantially greater in 1924 than in 1913.

There were, of course, changes in working hours between 1860 and 1913, though we have no adequate information on the subject. In 1913 the 54-hour week was the rule for factory and building workers, and something between 60 and 70 hours for other workers. In the 'sixties a working week of about 60 hours was becoming the rule for factory workers. A 70-hour week represents about the utmost limit of human capacity, and we may reckon that this was probably the average working week of the less organised non-factory workers at the beginning of our period. The average length of the working week probably only fell by a little over 10 per cent in the fifty years preceding 1913. The average productivity per head *per hour* was rising at a more rapid rate than the figures given above as the rate of increase of productivity per week or per year, but not much more rapidly.

Since 1924 hours have been virtually unchanged. The average productivity per hour worked, as stated above, was in 1924 well above the pre-War level. But the figure for the year 1924 was merely the starting point for further considerable increases in the years which followed. Productivity rose to a maximum in the years 1929 and 1930, and then fell in 1931 and 1932, under slump conditions, when industry was in general working much below capacity. In 1933 began another rise in productivity per head, which has continued to increase at a rapid pace up to 1936. If the experience of the past is any guide, we are now approaching another peak which will be followed by a period of recession. At any rate, we cannot draw a line through the figures of 1924 and 1936 to estimate the present secular rate of economic progress.

Probably, however, we shall be not far wrong in estimating the general trend if we examine the figures for the two periods 1924–30 and 1931–6. Both are cycles starting at a low point and terminating in a peak year. The average output per occupied person, measured at 1930 prices, was £217·7 in the first cycle and £228·3 in the second, a rate of increase of 0·73 per cent per year, as compared with slightly under 1·0 per cent per year between 1880 and 1910.

The absolute increment of productivity per worker has remained about the same, namely, £0·8 per year, in currency of 1913 purchasing power. So far there have been no adequate theoretical investigations leading us either to expect, or not to expect, this decline in the relative, and maintenance of the absolute, rate of increase of productivity.

The figures of productivity throughout have been given per person in work, i.e. after deducting the unemployed from the occupied population. Data are also shown on the diagram of production per head of the whole "occupied" (employed and unemployed) population. The increasing divergence between the two curves shows the extent to which the gains from increased productivity are being thrown away in the form of unemployment. Of the remarkable gains in productivity which have been made since 1913, nearly the whole has been lost in this form.

In the earlier years the two curves are nearly parallel; in other words, the rate of unemployment remains nearly constant. It is at its lowest in the cycle 1870–76. It is interesting to notice that a considerable part of the increase in productivity between that cycle and the cycle 1877–85 is also lost in the form of increased unemployment.

The measurements of productivity have been made by use of a price index which eliminates the effect of changes in prices of imports and exports, and productivity is expressed in the form of the quantity of goods and services produced. The quantity available for consumption and investment in this country depends on the terms of international interchange. The terms of trade moved in favour of this country from 1870 to 1900, then became constant, and started to move against us in the years from 1900 to 1913. In 1924–9 the terms of trade [1] were constant at a level much more favourable to Britain than that of 1913. In 1930–33 there was a further violent movement in favour of this country, since when there has been a small recession.

In a country in which international trade represents so substantial a proportion of the national income as it does in Britain, these changes in the terms of trade have a considerable effect on economic welfare. Their effect on the level of real income per head during recent years has been commented on above in Chapter IX. Employed and unemployed taken together, we have during the last few years been producing per head only a little more than in 1913, the increase of 15 to 20 per cent in productivity per worker being almost exactly balanced by the increase in unemployment. But during the same period there has

[1] See diagram in *Economic Journal*, September 1931, p. 354, and data in Royal Economic Society Memo. No. 60, p. 27.

been an improvement in the terms of trade, in the quantity of imports obtainable in return for a given volume of visible and invisible exports, so great that, whereas in 1913 we produced 100 and consumed 100 units, we can now consume nearly 107 units for each 100 units of production. (The terms of trade have improved by 41 per cent, and international trade represents about 17 per cent of the national income.) Further, in 1913, 13 per cent of the national income was saved; during the period 1931–6 only 4 per cent. There has therefore been a very considerable rise in general standards of consumption, among the rich through the cessation of saving, among the poor through the cheapness of imported food. During recent years of low food prices it has been about true to say that an unemployed man with a wife and two children drawing benefit has been better off than an unskilled labourer in full work in 1913.

It is interesting to notice that the periods 1870–76 and 1911–13 were both periods of retail rising prices, diminishing unemployment and apparent prosperity, although these movements were all much more violent in 1870–76 than 1911–13; but it is interesting to notice that in both cases these phenomena were associated with a cessation of the normal increase of real productivity per head. It is still more interesting to notice that these were the periods during which the terms of trade were, so far as is known, moving adversely to this country. About 1877 the terms of trade began to move rapidly in our favour, and there was considerable increase in productivity at home. Yet the next cycle was marked by a heavy downward trend in prices, increased unemployment and a general atmosphere of trade depression. These two pre-War cycles seem to lend some support to what might be called the doctrine of Economic Indigestion. During the period when potentialities of real income production are rapidly increasing, either through a genuine increase in productivity or through an improvement in the terms of trade, it seems inevitable that a large part of this improvement should be wasted in the form of unemployment. Something akin to this doctrine, as I understand it, was urged by Mr. D. H. Robertson in his evidence to the Macmillan Committee. The corollary follows, that under our present organisation of industry a period of rising prices, low unemployment and "prosperity" is in fact a sign that fundamental conditions of production are adverse. It is a generally accepted doctrine that an improvement in the terms of trade is likely to cause unemployment in the export trades, and an adverse movement in the terms of trade to diminish it; but it is doubtful if general acceptance would be given to the doctrine that a period, not of increasing productivity, which is the normal state of affairs, but of an increase in the rate at which productivity is rising, is likely to cause secular unemployment.

Income studies over a long period may also be expected to throw some light on some of the economic problems connected with the accumulation and productivity of capital. Omitting the peculiar movements of the period 1870–76, the growth of real income per head of the occupied population between 1830 and 1913 tended to conform to a curve of the type known as "logistic". There can be no doubt about the trend in the years before 1913, supported as this evidence is by auxiliary data, namely, a strong slowing-down of the rate of increase. The curve was approaching a very definite ceiling. But during the years since then, something has happened to break that ceiling, and that fraction of our resources which we care to employ again gives us a rapidly increasing yield. At the present time we have only ourselves to blame for a large part of our troubles. With a reserve of labour of 2 million workers and a large part of our productive equipment unused, we must not complain if our real income per head is not higher than it is. But in 1913, apparently, this was not the case. Although people then were working their labour force and most of their industrial equipment nearly to the practical limit of capacity, their real income was increasing at a diminishing rate and showing every sign of becoming stabilised at a level much lower than seems now possible. If technical knowledge had then been better, or the quality of the population ; or if British industries had been able to work for a larger market at home or abroad, and to enjoy further economies of increasing returns, without suffering diminishing returns in their supply of foodstuffs and raw materials, the general level of productivity might have been greater. But these three factors between them seem to have been the consideration, setting an upper limit to which the curve of productivity was tending. We have now broken through that particular limit, largely, I think, through improvement in our technical knowledge, and, what is equally important from the point of view of the national productivity, the growing up of a generation of trained and experienced workers and technicians who can apply this knowledge.

I have stated above a positive view of the conditions dominating the long-term possibilities of an increase in productivity, because I believe the facts have destroyed the view up till now generally prevalent, i.e. that the rate of economic growth was primarily dependent upon the rate at which capital could be accumulated. The very rapid expansion in productivity at the present time is taking place at a time of heavily diminishing capital accumulation. What is more remarkable, practically none of the capital which is being saved is being put into productive industry proper. Without new investment the replacement of obsolete capital, for which a high obsolescence allowance is properly now claimed, appears to give all the necessary scope for the introduction of technical and organisational improvements, and to bring about the rapid increase in productivity under which we are now living. But this is no more than the continuation of an historical process which has been going on for generations. Professor Paul Douglas[1] collected and put on a comparable basis the various estimates of capital in this country for the years between 1865 and 1914. He omitted the value of agri-

[1] *American Journal of Economic and Business History*, August 1930.

cultural land, dwelling-houses, furniture and similar movable capital, and expressed the results in terms of the 1865 price-level, which was about 15 per cent below that of 1913. The data when smoothed give the following results :

TABLE 115

INDEX OF REAL CAPITAL PER HEAD OF POPULATION (EXCLUDING CAPITAL OVERSEAS)

Year	Index	Year	Index
1865	100	1895	163
1875	135	1905	174
1885	154	1909	178

It was during the 1860's that capital per head of population was being most rapidly accumulated, and during that period the real income per head had risen and was rising most rapidly. The absolute additions to home capital, expressed in terms of the price-level of 1865, were at a maximum of £110 millions a year in 1875 and have declined since. The absolute rate at which home capital was being accumulated was as follows :

	£s million per year
1865–75	83
1875–85	66
1885–95	49
1895–1905	62
1905–9	66

But, as is well known, the available savings of Britain have been far in excess of the amounts invested in home industry. Between 1905 and 1913 the major part was invested abroad, and before 1905 very large sums were being invested in dwelling-houses. Shortage of capital cannot have been the cause of the slowing-down of the rate of increase. There remain yet to be discovered the laws determining the rate of economic growth of particular communities, and the amount of capital invested seems to be an effect rather than a cause.

APPENDIX I

THE NUMBER OF INCOMES

Our principal sources of information on this question are the Census and Social Insurance statistics. Unfortunately there is a serious lack of co-ordination between these two sources.

In the Census returns for England and Wales no question was asked on the Census form as to whether individuals were within the scope of Health Insurance or not. No direct comparison is therefore possible between the Census statistics of occupied persons and Health Insurance statistics. In the Census for Scotland, however, this question was included in the Census form, and the results tabulated so as to show the numbers of insured males and females in different occupations. This enables us to derive some useful information as to the proportion of insured persons who are not " occupied " by the Census definition, and also the proportion of insured workers in certain of the better-paid occupations where a substantial proportion of employees earn over £250 per annum. For this latter comparison we do not have to assume that the occupational distribution in Scotland is the same as in England. Our only assumption is that the frequency distribution of salaries in any given occupation is much the same in the two countries, an assumption which cannot be seriously wrong.

The returns of the Scottish Department of Health show 1,281,000 males insured in December 1930, including men over 65, voluntary contributors and members of the Forces, and 1,291,000 in December 1931. Interpolating to April 1931, we obtain an insured population of 1,284,000, including 24,000 voluntary contributors, 13,000 members of the Forces and 83,000 men of 65 and over. Of these men over 65, 31,000 were returned as paying contributions. The number of insured men over 65 " occupied ", which will also include those looking for work but at present unemployed, will be higher.

Table 12 of Volume III of the Census of Scotland gives the number of insured males as 1,202,100. It is clear that there is a certain deficiency in the Census returns of the insured population. One can only suppose that many people who are entitled to medical benefit under the Health Insurance Acts were not aware of that fact. The deficiency seems to be more serious among older people. Of persons returned in the Census as insured, 64,300 were returned as over 65, 37,100 of them being occupied. The number of insured men under 65 years of age returned as unoccupied or retired was 8300.

Including only the occupied persons (whether unemployed or not) above the age of 65, the Census return gives us 1,175,000 insured males, which includes 8300 unoccupied persons under 65, and presumably the 24,000 voluntary contributors.[1] A further 20,000 should be omitted from this figure to allow for sailors and fishermen absent from Scotland on the day of the Census. The Department of Health figures, omitting members of the Forces, who are not reckoned as insured in the Census, and omitting permanently retired persons over 65, give 1,228,000. It thus appears that, comparing like with like, there was a deficiency of 2·7 per cent in the returns of insurability made to the Scottish Census by occupied males.

It is rather interesting to examine the size of this deficiency among various classes of manual workers, all of whom will be in fact insurable. The Census returns show a deficiency of 2·5 per cent among miners, 3 per cent among enginemen, 9 per cent among general labourers and 15 per cent among farm workers. This is consistent with the idea that certain classes of insured persons are only vaguely aware of their rights to medical benefit.

Insurance is in general compulsory for all manual workers, and for non-manual workers earning less than £250 per annum. About 11,000 men were excepted from Health Insurance but paid contributions for Contributory Pensions. There were a number of others (e.g. teachers) statutorily excepted from all compulsory insurance. Insurance only applies to employed persons and not to employers or to independent workers. We may assume that all those returned in the Census as following manual-working occupations will be insured, with the exception of a few excepted workers, those working on their own account, and boys under 16. If we apply a similar calculation to the non-manual occupations, we shall be able to determine what proportion of those following these occupations will be salaried men in receipt of over £250 a year, or excepted.

In order to determine from the Scottish Census data the proportion of employed persons earning less than £250, which

[1] Many of these are not in fact entitled to medical benefit, but they think they are.

we shall require if we are to make use of this information in working out the English figures, we must omit from the figures of the Scottish insured population the unoccupied insured persons and also the voluntary contributors. Of the voluntary contributors, we may assume that one-third are workers on their own account, and the remaining two-thirds, or 16,000, belong to the various types of salaried occupation given in the table below. About 10 per cent of the numbers insured in the trades specified below will thus be voluntary contributors. We may also assume a 2·7 per cent deficiency in the Census returns due to men's ignorance of their insurability, or misunderstanding of the Census form, as indicated above. This means that the Census returns of the number of insured men in different occupations should be lowered by 7·3 per cent for comparison with the total numbers employed. Unoccupied insured men have not been included in the figures of the numbers of insured men in particular occupations.

The non-manual occupations are classified into the following more or less homogeneous social groups :

(1) Salesmen and shop-assistants (including also canvassers, roundsmen and insurance agents).
(2) Clerks and typists (including also telegraph and telephone operators).
(3) Office staffs (including also railway and dock officials, buyers, commercial travellers, advertising agents, company secretaries, office managers, draughtsmen, etc.).
(4) Shopkeepers (proprietors and managers, including also moneylenders, bookmakers, restaurant, boarding-house and innkeepers).
(5) Professions (including also ships' officers, national and local Civil Service, men professionally engaged in entertainment and sport).
(6) Farmers and crofters.
(7) Sons, etc., of above, working on the farm.
(8) Proprietors and managers of industrial, wholesaling and transport businesses.

The following table shows for Scotland the number of males over 16 occupied (inclusive of unemployed) in these categories, excluding workers on their own account, and the numbers recorded as occupied and insured. Deducting 7·3 per cent from the numbers insured, we can then calculate the percentages of occupied persons who are employed at salaries above

£250 or excepted. These percentages can then reasonably be applied to the English data.

TABLE 116

NUMBERS INSURED IN VARIOUS OCCUPATIONS IN SCOTLAND, 1931

	Numbers Occupied (excluding Boys and Workers on own Account)	Numbers Insured	% Excepted or Employed at Salaries above £250
Salesmen and shop-assistants	66,521	58,675	18
Clerks	60,373	43,569	33
Office staffs	28,593	16,703	46
Shopkeepers	28,331	8,436	72
Professions	58,538	23,532	63
Farmers	25,337	3,425	87
Farmers' sons, etc.	11,344	770	94
Proprietors and managers	40,176	6,386	85
Total	319,000	161,000	..
Other occupations (manual workers)	1,090,000	1,006,000 *	..

* Excluding unoccupied insured.

To this residue of 1,006,000 we must add 13,000 members of the Forces, a portion of the 11,000 excepted workers, and deduct another 8000 voluntary contributors, giving about 1,020,000. To this must now be added 33,000 for persons who are in fact insured but have not so returned themselves at the Census, giving 1,053,000 as against the 1,090,000 anticipated. We may thus estimate that the number of occupied male manual workers recorded by the Census who are for various reasons not insured will probably be about 37,000, or $3\frac{1}{2}$ per cent of the whole ; but this result must not be pressed too hard, as the data are just about " within the limits of experimental error ".

The figures of the Scottish Department of Health, interpolated to April 1931, show an insured population of 627,300 women under 65, of whom 4700 were voluntary contributors. In addition to these there were 19,000 insured women over 65. The total includes 18,000 married women of the category not occupied in industry, but still eligible for medical benefit under the special provision made for women during the first two years after their retirement from industry.

Table 13 of the Census Report gives only 564,600 insured

women, of whom 551,700 were under 65, and 7200 were unoccupied women over the age of 65. The number under the age of 65 returned as unoccupied or retired was 38,700, a considerably larger number than can be accounted for by the special category of married women described above. As Sir Alfred Watson has pointed out (*J.R.S.S.*, 1927), there are certain delays in the notification of retirement of women from industry, retirements for causes other than marriage, and other factors to be taken into account.

It is probable, however, that there were many other women (mostly unoccupied) who were in fact eligible for benefits but did not enter themselves as such in the Census. The deficiency as compared with the Department of Health returns was over 80,000 or 12 per cent, and unfortunately we have no means of telling exactly how many of these were occupied and how many unoccupied. The total of occupied employed females over 16 in Scotland, excluding employers, managers and workers on own account, is given by the Census as 575,400. The number of insured women and excepted women, less voluntary contributors and 46,000 *known* to be unoccupied, is 600,000. But also there may be anything up to 80,000 further insured women who were unoccupied. All we can say is that well over 90 per cent of the 575,400 female operatives are insured or excepted, and probably therefore the great majority of the 200,000 female operatives in non-manual occupations.

In the case of females, it is more convenient to determine the proportion insured in the managerial class alone, rather than in particular groups of occupations. It is clear from the above that nearly all female operatives will earn salaries below £250.

The Census returns of insured females are subdivided only by occupation, and not by industrial status. We must proceed, therefore, by selecting the occupations containing appreciable numbers of females of managerial status, and none of operative status, and finding the proportion insured in these occupations (between the ages 16–64).[1] We have results as given in Table 117 (p. 280).

Out of 38,000 females 16–64 of managerial status in Scotland, it may thus be estimated that 14,100 were insured. Of these 2600 are estimated to have been voluntary contributors, leaving 11,500 or 30 per cent.

[1] Where the occupation covers independent as well as managerial workers, the allocation of numbers aged over 65 to these two classes has to be done by estimate.

TABLE 117

NUMBER OF MANAGERIAL WORKERS INSURED IN SCOTLAND, 1931

Occupation No.	Managerial Workers, 16–64	Insured
011	1200	31
300	94	58
340	690	110
370	324	112
410	32	8
460	47	11
612–13	50	11
670–689	4700	2475
830	40	19
864	975	200
Total .	8152	3035

We can apply the proportions above calculated to the occupied male population of England and Wales, and thus obtain a check on the composition of the Health Insurance statistics. Interpolating the figures for December 1930 and December 1931, we find 10,114,000 males under 65 eligible for Health benefits in April 1931, of whom 333,000 were voluntary contributors and 303,000 members of the Forces, including discharged and disabled ex-Service men, and men serving overseas. There were also 264,000 excepted men. The number of persons in work over the age of 65 was not subdivided by sex before 1932, but the number of insured males above this age in work may be estimated at 261,000 in April 1931.

The comparison which we are about to make will give us, if we look back at the way in which the Scottish figures were compiled, an estimate of the proportion of non-manual workers who are compulsorily (i.e. our figures exclude voluntary contributors) insured : our results will not therefore include retired persons, or excepted workers. In April 1931, in addition to men over 65 who were in work, it may be estimated that there were in England and Wales 456,000 retired insured persons above that age. There were 120,000 unemployed men over 65 in 1931 who described themselves as occupied and not as retired.

By applying the Scottish ratios obtained above to the English data of the numbers occupied in the various non-manual occupations, we shall obtain estimates of the number of insured workers, exclusive of voluntary contributors, excepted and retired persons. The total numbers insured, omitting these three categories and members of the Forces, but including unemployed over 65, is 9,859,000. (10,114,000 + 261,000 + 120,000 − 333,000 − 303,000.)

On the basis of the Scottish figures we may estimate that 70,000 of the insured males will be men who in fact are unoccupied at the time. Deducting these also we obtain a total of 9,789,000. In the following table estimates are made of the numbers of insured male workers in non-manual occupations, on the basis of the Scottish figures :

TABLE 118

NUMBERS INSURED IN CERTAIN OCCUPATIONS, ENGLAND AND WALES

	Numbers Occupied over 16 excluding Own Account (000's)	Estimated Numbers Insured (000's)
Proprietors and managers of businesses	436·7	66
Farmers	140·7	18
Farmers' sons . . .	66·1	4
Shopkeepers . . .	270·5	76
Office staffs . . .	297·6	161
Clerks	680·6	456
Professions . . .	460·5	170
Salesmen	563·0	461
Total of above .	2,915·7	1412
Forces * (in England at time of Census)	181·0	. .
All other occupations .	8,911·0	8377
Total for England and Wales	12,008·0	9789 (Excluding Forces, voluntarily insured and unoccupied)

* The General Volumes of the Census record 125,000 men in the Forces absent from Britain on the day of the Census.

The Census figure should be raised by 62,000 to allow for seamen away from England on the Census day. The insurance figure should be raised by 110,000 [1] to allow for excepted

[1] In the Industry Volumes of the Census of England and Wales, and of Scotland, data are assembled showing the numbers employed in any capacity by the Government, local authorities and the railway companies, subdivided under various industry headings. Examination of the tables for the individual industries then enables us to discover the

workers in manual occupations. We are left with a difference of some 486,000 to be accounted for by various causes, amounting to 5½ per cent as against the corresponding figure of 3½ per cent in Scotland.

In the whole of Great Britain, rather under 60,000 of this discrepancy can be accounted for by men over 65. The calculation is as follows :

TABLE 119

NUMBERS INSURED AGED OVER 65

	Occupied Men over 65 in Great Britain as shown by Census	Numbers insurable
Proprietors and managers of businesses	204,000	31,000
Clerical, commercial and professional workers	54,000	33,000
Manual workers . .	286,000	286,000
Unemployed . . .	136,000	..
Total . .	680,000	350,000

---

numbers of males and females in important clerical and professional occupations, some estimation being necessary in the case of the smaller industries. The results may be given as follows :

Great Britain, 1931	Males	Females
Teachers and civil servants (whose occupations are statutorily excepted from Insurance)	95,000	165,000
Others	285,000	155,000
Total . .	380,000	320,000

Judging from the proportion of men earning over £250 in all clerical and professional occupations taken together, it may be estimated that 150,000 of the above men, largely teachers and Civil servants, will be earning above £250, and about 30,000 of the women, all in this first category.

It follows that 195,000 men and 155,000 women in non-manual occupations will be on the staffs of the State, local authorities, etc., and railway companies, and a considerable proportion of them, though not necessarily all, are likely to be covered by certificates of exception from Health Insurance. The total numbers thus covered were 275,000 men and 80,000 women. It may be estimated that the former represented 110,000 manual workers and 165,000 non-manual workers.

The proportions insurable are calculated from data previously given. No contributions are payable in respect of unemployed persons of this age. The number of contributors over 65, reported from the insurance statistics, is 293,000, a margin of 57,000.

For Scotland, where the numbers insurable were specially counted in the Census, the following results are of interest :

31,000 men over 65 were recorded by the Department of Health as in work and paying contributions.

37,100 men in work over 65 stated on their Census forms that they were entitled to medical benefit.

41,000 men in work over 65 were insurable, as calculated from a table similar to the above.

For insured females, excluding married women entitled to special benefit, the total below 65 for England and Wales in April 1931 was 5,025,000, including 50,000 voluntarily insured. It may be estimated on the basis of the Scottish figures that this included 300,000 unoccupied women and perhaps more, in addition to the 226,000 married women entitled to special benefits. Omitting these and also the voluntary contributors, we obtain a figure of 4,675,000. The insured women workers and unemployed over 65 amounted to 63,000, giving a total of 4,738,000 insurably occupied. To these may be added 76,000 excepted workers, making 4,814,000, or less if the number of unoccupied insured women is greater than estimated above.

The number of occupied females aged 16 and over was 5,290,000, and excluding workers on own account these reduced to 4,969,000, of whom 100,000 are over 65. There will be some 120,000 teachers under local authorities enjoying statutory exception from insurance, and 138,000 women in managerial positions, some of whom will not be liable for insurance. We are thus not far off from the figure given above of 4,814,000 or less.

Excluding voluntarily insured, unoccupied, members of the Forces, and workers over 65, and including excepted workers, we have, for April 1931, 10,865,000 males in Great Britain under the Health Insurance Scheme.

A similar calculation for females gives 5,307,000, excluding all unoccupied females and including excepted workers. This exclusion of unoccupied persons is necessary for comparison between the numbers insured for Health Insurance and the numbers insured for Unemployment Insurance, because there is no prolongation of rights for unoccupied persons under the

TABLE 120

NUMBERS ELIGIBLE FOR HEALTH INSURANCE BENEFITS, GREAT BRITAIN

(Figures in 000's)

	Dec. 1930		April 1931		Dec. 1931		Dec. 1932		Dec. 1933		Dec. 1934	
	M.	F.	M.	F.	M.	F.	M.	F.	M.	F.	M.	F.
Ages, 16–65 :												
Eligible for Health Benefits	11,293	5613	11,325	5621	11,388	5636	11,446	5588	11,344	5526	11,308	5538
Inc. voluntary	339	52	357	55	393	61	412	67	447	69	491	88
Serving soldiers	301	..	300	..	298	..	297	..	294	..	294	..
Discharged and disabled soldiers	17	..	16	..	16	..	15	..	15	..	14	..
Excepted (including some not contributing to pensions insurance)	273	80	275	80	286	80	296	85	300	93	295	93
Women, special beneficiaries (not included in above)	..	244	..	244	..	244	..	297	..	318	..	335
Over 65 :												
Working insurably	356		354		343		265	55	265	55	268	57
Not working insurably	625		639		677		616	150	644	164	679	175
Unemployed still eligible for pensions	..		..		..		..	..	95	10	Not known	

Unemployment Insurance Scheme as there is under the Health Insurance Scheme. It is rather difficult to tell where the " unemployed " end and the " unoccupied " begin, particularly in the case of women. It is left to the individual to decide into which category to place himself or herself when filling up the Census form. It is probable that more unoccupied people will describe themselves as unemployed than *vice versa*, and therefore for any given categories of persons the number of " occupied " shown by the Census will be somewhat larger than the numbers insured under the Unemployment Insurance Scheme.

The numbers of males and females insured in Great Britain under the Unemployment Insurance Scheme were :

TABLE 121

NUMBERS INSURED FOR UNEMPLOYMENT, 1930–31

	Males	Females
July 1930	8,769,000	3,369,000
July 1931	9,021,000	3,479,000
Estimate for April 1931 . .	8,969,000	3,456,000

This leaves 1,896,000 males and 1,851,000 females still to be accounted for. These will be made up of workers in agriculture and domestic service, who are liable for Health Insurance but not for Unemployment Insurance, and persons exempt from Unemployment Insurance either from certificates of exception or by the operation of statutory provisions applicable to Unemployment Insurance but not to Health Insurance, the majority of whom will either be contributing to Health Insurance or will be excepted from it by certificate.

The following figures are obtained from the Industry Volumes for England and Wales and for Scotland of the 1931 Census. They are exclusive of employers, managers and workers on own account, and of workers under 16 or over 65.

TABLE 122

Agricultural and Domestic Workers, 1931

	Numbers Employed	
	Males	Females
Agriculture	686,000	46,000
Domestic service . . .	262,000	1,207,000

We must also take into account at this stage some 22,000 farmers who are estimated to be included under Health Insurance.

The Ministry of Labour Report for the year 1931 shows 529,000 workers covered by certificates of exception from Unemployment Insurance. They are not subdivided by sex ; an estimate on the basis of the numbers of workers of different sexes excepted from Health Insurance divides this total into 410,000 males and 119,000 females.

The Industry Volumes for England and Wales and for Scotland also show the numbers employed by the State and by local authorities in all departments of their activity. Excluding men in the Forces, the numbers in State employment were 330,000 males and 94,000 females. These figures exclude all persons in managerial positions and also those below 16 or over 65. The largest department included was of course the Post Office.

The number of contributors to Unemployment Insurance in the employment of the Central Government in Great Britain in July 1931 was 96,000 males and 22,000 females. The numbers in Government employ covered by specific certificates of exception from Unemployment Insurance were only 12,000. We conclude, therefore, that approximately 225,000 males and 70,000 females in Government service enjoyed statutory exception (including a number with salaries above £250).

From the Census figures for the numbers in local government service, we may omit the industrial departments, namely, gas, water and electricity supply, and tram and bus service. We will include teachers, police and all other local government servants. The numbers shown by the Census, calculated in the same way as before, are 702,000 males and 315,000 females. The numbers insured were 304,000 males and 21,000 females, and 77,000 were covered by specific certificates of exception. We thus conclude that approximately 335,000 males and 280,000 females enjoyed statutory exception, making a total of 560,000 males and 360,000 females in national and local government service statutorily excepted from Unemployment Insurance.

These will include the following who are also statutorily excepted from Health Insurance :

TABLE 123

Statutory Exceptions from Health Insurance

	Males	Females
Teachers	66,000	163,000
Civil servants (not clerical) .	29,000	2,000
Men earning over £250 (not included in categories above)	40,000	..

In comparing Health Insurance and Unemployment Insurance figures we must therefore reckon that 425,000 males and 195,000 females who are statutorily excepted from Unemployment Insurance are not statutorily excepted from Health Insurance, and either contribute to the latter or are specifically excepted from it.

We may now add together the numbers in these different categories, which account for the bulk of the difference between the numbers insured under the Health and Unemployment Insurance Schemes (Table 124).

Although there still remains a considerable gap in the case of females, it is probably no greater than the ambiguity which enters into the calculation as a result of the uncertainty of the boundary line between " unemployed " and " unoccupied ", or the inclusion within the totals of Health Insurance of a

TABLE 124

NUMBERS EXCEPTED FROM UNEMPLOYMENT INSURANCE

	Males	Females
Specifically excepted from Unemployment Insurance	410,000	119,000
Domestic work . . .	262,000	1,207,000
Agriculture	708,000	46,000
Statutory exception . .	425,000	195,000
Total of above . .	1,805,000	1,567,000
Number to be accounted for .	1,896,000	1,851,000

number of workers who will not be insured under the more precise conditions laid down for the Unemployment Insurance Scheme.

APPENDIX II

NUMBER OF INCOMES ABOVE TAX EXEMPTION LIMIT

THIS appendix is an analysis of the statistics compiled by the Board of Inland Revenue of the number of individuals with total incomes above the exemption limit. A number of data are drawn from an article by the writer in the *Economic Journal*, September 1934.

The phrase " total incomes " draws attention to the fact that many people have mixed incomes partly derived from earnings and partly from property, and that these two types of income have different exemption limits. Since 1931 the exemption limit for earned income has been £125 per year, for unearned £100. All earned incomes are allowed in fact a deduction of one-fifth. As a result, the two following examples of mixed incomes are just on the exemption limit :

TABLE 125

INCOME-TAX EXEMPTION LIMIT

	Income, £ per annum	
	Type I	Type II
Earned income .	50	120
Property income .	60	4
Total .	110	124

The second type is of course far commoner than the first, while incomes derived solely from property at this level are very rare indeed. It may be estimated that the *average* limit of exemption works out at £123. Professor Bowley and Sir Josiah Stamp made a detailed study of this problem for 1924, at which date the exemption limit for earned income was £150. They concluded that the average limit of exemption was £147, and that in the aggregate £35 millions of incomes below £150 were brought into assessment. These will consist of *earned* incomes averaging appreciably below £150, but of *total* incomes very close to the £150 level. The number of incomes involved is about 235,000.

No adequate data are available which will enable us to transfer these results to the lower exemption limit now current. A frequency - distribution curve for wage-earners' incomes shows that the " density " of earned incomes at the points £125 and £150 is much the same, but additional incomes from property may be slightly less frequent at the lower level. We may estimate that 200,000 incomes will now be concerned.

Our reason for calculating the numbers of assessed incomes below the maximum exemption limit is that we shall wish to collate the Inland Revenue statistics with independent data showing the frequency distribution of certain types of incomes. There is another source of discrepancy which is more serious than the above, which has apparently not been resolved in previous investigations. A man earning below £125 is occasionally brought into assessment by his ownership of property, but is much more often brought into assessment by the earnings of his wife. Incomes of husband and wife are regarded as single taxable entity. There are approximately 250,000 married women engaged in salaried and business occupations, and 530,000 (excluding unemployed) in wage-earning occupations. In all but a small fraction of cases the combined earnings of husband and wife will be above £125. In the wage-earning class about a third of adult males earn less than £125, and assuming married men have the same income-distribution as unmarried, it may be estimated that 180,000 of them are brought above the limit of assessment by the earnings of their wives. Before 1931, when the exemption limit was £162, the number was probably about 275,000.

In the salaried [1] and business classes about 18 per cent of adult male workers earn less than £125, and 30 per cent less than £162. The numbers brought above the two exemption limits by the earnings of their wives may therefore be put at 45,000 and 75,000 respectively.

Returning to the question of persons brought into assessment by ownership of property, we saw that 200,000 persons earning incomes below £125 owned enough property to bring them into the scope of assessment, though not to bring their

[1] This term, as used by the Inland Revenue and the Census of Production, covers a wider range than the word commonly applies to. It covers all shop-assistants, clerks, etc.—in fact the whole range of occupations which Americans so precisely designate as " white-collar work ".

total incomes above £125. We may assume that a somewhat larger number of persons earning incomes below £125 owned property which *did* bring their total incomes above £125. Altogether we may estimate that this category covers 500,000 persons, of whom 350,000 were wage-earners, since 1931, and 700,000 and 500,000 respectively before 1931.

Our information about the incomes of wage-earners is derived from sources other than Inland Revenue statistics, and we only require to know their numbers in order to exclude them. The Inland Revenue reports give the aggregate income from wage-earnings assessed to tax, but not the numbers assessed, and hence some knowledge of their average income is required. In *The New Survey of London Life and Labour* the frequency distribution of earnings of adult male wage-earners are given for London in 1929–30. The table does not include the earnings of women and juveniles, nor can London wages be taken as representative of wages throughout the country. But for our present requirement, namely, frequency distributions within the group from £125 upwards, these data should be adequate.

In the case of wage-earners who have been brought into assessment by the ownership of property, we may assume that their average income is slightly above the exemption limit, while in the case of wage-earners brought into assessment through their wives' earnings, an average earning of 30s. a week for the wife is assumed and a new frequency distribution constructed for the earnings of the two taken together.

TABLE 126

NUMBERS AND AVERAGE INCOME OF WAGE-EARNERS ABOVE EXEMPTION LIMIT

	WAGE-EARNERS					
	Exemption Limit (£ per annum)	Numbers above exemption limit due to:				
		Income from Property		Earnings of Wives		Own Earnings
		Nos. (000's)	Average Income	Nos. (000's)	Average Income	Average Income
			£		£	£
1924–5	147	450	155	240	225	181
1925–6 to 1930–31	159	500	167	275	225	191
1931–2 to 1935–6	123	350	130	180	225	169

The first two categories account for 690,000 assessments and £124 millions in 1924–5, for 775,000 assessments and £145 millions in 1925–31, and for 530,000 assessments and £86 millions since 1931. The estimates on which these figures are based are rough, but it does not in this case seriously matter, as the average incomes attributed to wage-earners in these categories are not seriously different from the incomes of wage-earners not in these categories.

We can now make a calculation of the number of wage-earners included in assessments to tax in each year since 1924.

TABLE 127

WAGE-EARNERS AND OTHERS ASSESSED TO TAX, 1924–34

	Wages Assessed to Tax (£ m.)	Less Amount due to Earnings of Wives and Income from Property	Numbers of Wage-earners Assessed on Own Earnings (000's)	Total Number of Wage-earners Assessed (000's)	Other Assessments (000's)
1924–5	343·5	220	1215	1905	3295
1925–6	243·1	198	1038	1813	2787
1926–7	196·3	51	267	1042	3458
1927–8	285·4	140	734	1509	3441
1928–9	284·5	139	728	1503	3497
1929–30	289·7	145	759	1534	3616
1930–31	269·1	124	649	1424	3696
1931–2	519·2	433	2560	3090	5010
1932–3	486·5	400	2365	2895	5005
1933–4	504·1	418	2470	3000	4850
1934–5	520·0	434	2565	3095	4905

The figures in this last column will include, since 1931, 45,000, and prior to that date 75,000, non-wage-earners with incomes below current exemption limits, who are brought into assessment through the earnings of their wives. The average incomes involved (husband and wife taken together) can be estimated at £200 and £180 respectively. Also 150,000 since 1931, and 200,000 before 1931, brought into assessment through ownership of property, with average incomes a little above exemption limit.

Of the 250,000 married women engaged in salaried and business occupations, apart from those included already, 50 per cent will probably be earning below £125, with an average income of £85, and 80 per cent below £162, with an average income of £100.

We have therefore :

TABLE 128

NUMBER AND AGGREGATE INCOME OF NON-WAGE-EARNERS ASSESSED BUT EARNING BELOW EXEMPTION LIMIT (INCLUDING MARRIED WOMEN)

	Numbers (000's)	Aggregate Income (£s million)
1925–6 to 1930–31 .	475	69
1931–2 to 1935–6 .	320	39

APPENDIX III

STOCKS

IN Chapter I we have defined the contribution to the national income of any concern or industry as its net output, i.e. its surplus of proceeds over purchases, plus any net increment or minus any net decrement of the quantity of stock in trade and/or work in progress, valued at the average current price over the period. On the other hand, the accounts of industrial and commercial concerns reckon all stocks at cost or current value whichever is lower, and this method of accounting is recognised by the Inland Revenue in the preparation of tax assessments. It will be seen that there is no difference between the two methods of defining income during a time of rising prices ; but during a year of rapidly falling prices, such as 1930, a large amount (from the point of view of the national income) is taken out of income to write down stock in trade. The following calculation gives us the formula for correction :

Let the gross surplus of sales over purchases for any industry (or concern) be Q.

Let the quantity of stock (assumed to be measured at an unchanging price-level) be q_0 at the beginning of the trading year and q_1 at the end.

Let the respective relevant price-levels be p_0 and p_1, and let the average price-level over the trading year be p.

Then for calculations of the national income we require

$$Q + p(q_1 - q_0).$$

But at a time of falling prices the accounts and assessments will show

$$Q + q_1 p_1 - q_0 p_0.$$

Therefore we must add

$$q_1(p - p_1) + q_0(p_0 - p)$$

to the figures as obtained from assessments.

The amount of the addition, it will be seen, depends on the *rate* of price change. Stocks are in fact turned over more frequently than once a year. But a simple calculation will show that if the addition is worked out for shorter intervals the result will be practically the same.

In many branches of industry and trade the amount of

stocks held is quite considerable relative to the year's profits, and during years when there has been heavy fall in prices, estimates of national income built up from statistics of wages and assessable profits will for this reason differ by an appreciable amount from the aggregate selling value of goods and services produced. The extent of this difference can be estimated from a study of a representative sample of company balance-sheets.[1] We require to estimate the absolute amount of such differences and not only their changes from year to year. For this purpose we must have some measure to relate the size of our sample to the size of the whole aggregate of assessable incomes. For this purpose the paid-up capital is taken. For the companies shown below, therefore, the value of the paid-up capital in 1931, and the valuation of stocks at the end of 1931, 1932, 1933 and 1934, is given.[2] The phrase "end of 1931" covers a balance-sheet drawn up to any date between 30th June 1931 and 31st March 1932, thus making the data correspond fairly closely both with the "Inland Revenue Year" and the "Census of Production Year". The mean terminal date is not far off 31st December.[3]

In "The National Capital"[4] Sir Josiah Stamp estimates the aggregate capital used in industry and commerce by capitalising tax assessments. In 1928 he found the average profit on paid-up capital of companies (excluding Home Railways) quoted on the Stock Exchange to be 9·67 per cent taking debenture, preference and ordinary capital together. His object was to determine *market* rather than *nominal paid-up* capital values. Retracing the steps of his calculation, however, we find that the amount of assessable profits in 1928 can be put at £336 millions for manufacture and mining, £37 millions for home railways and £394 millions for other transport and distribution. (These figures are after deducting for depreciation and overcharges, but not deducting for small businesses; we wish to cover these.) These correspond to a capital of £1110 millions in the case of the railways, and about £3480 millions and £4080 millions respectively under the other two heads.

These are the only forms of capital containing appreciable

[1] The sample referred to in this section, and also the sample referred to on p. 58, were both drawn from a tabulation of company balance-sheets which is in preparation for another purpose.

[2] In certain trades figures were only available for 1931 and 1932.

[3] Cf. Stamp, *J.R.S.S.*, 1932, Part IV.

[4] *J.R.S.S.*, 1931, Part I.

amounts of stock in trade. We may neglect the stocks carried by financial and professional firms and individuals, or by traders with incomes below assessment limits. The stocks carried by the railways are given in their annual returns. For the manufacturing and distributive trades, weighted averages showing the relative importance of stocks in total capital are compiled from the data for individual trades given in the table. The weights are estimated from such data as are available as to the aggregate profits of the different industries.

TABLE 129

STOCKS

A.—MANUFACTURE AND MINING

	No. of Companies in Sample	Nominal Paid-up Capital (£000's)	Proportion of Stocks to Capital (%) at end of:				Weight
			1931	1932	1933	1934	
Coal mining	9	7535	4·4	4·6	..	..	5
Iron, steel and engineering	15	7259	20·4	17·4	..	..	23
Boot and shoe	9	3910	55·3	51·9	53·7	52·3	3
Chemicals	5	878	19·8	15·6	16·7	15·1	8
Clothing	6	2564	28·6	26·4	28·9	29·7	7
Leather	7	1552	24·1	28·2	29·8	26·2	3
Food and tobacco	22	6424	19·5	16·9	17·3	19·7	16
Paper	10	2921	22·5	21·7	21·5	22·4	5
Printing	11	4942	16·4	16·0	15·7	16·1	7
Distilling	14	5319	91·0	84·4	78·9	78·4	5
Brewing	14	9497	6·0	6·0	6·3	6·1	9
Miscellaneous	14	4578	31·2	30·9	31·9	33·8	9
Weighted average	..	..	24·16	22·17	22·62	23·14	100

B.—TRANSPORT DISTRIBUTION AND SERVICES

	No. of Companies in Sample	Nominal Paid-up Capital (£000's)	Proportion of Stocks to Capital (%) at end of:				Weight
			1931	1932	1933	1934	
Retail trade	34	20,188	22·1	21·3	20·9	21·1	33
Retail trade from Bank of England returns	..	..	22·5	21·2	21·1	20·8	..
Wholesale trade	40	16,013	38·7	37·0	33·9	31·2	29
Hotels and catering	20	8,238	6·6	6·3	5·7	5·5	9
Entertainment	23	4,253	1·5	1·3	1·3	1·3	3
Other services	6	1,004	2·6	2·9	2·9	3·1	1
Shipping, Other transport, Foreign rails, etc.	Very small		..	..	..	..	25

Alternative figures for retailers' stocks can be obtained from the monthly returns of the Bank of England, which of course are on a more comprehensive basis than our sample. These, however, only relate stocks at any given date to the value of stocks twelve months previously, and therefore the original sample must be used to estimate the relation of stocks to paid-up capital, the Bank of England returns being used to calculate year-to-year variations. The end of the trading year in this case is taken as 31st January. The corrected figures are used in the calculation of the general weighted average.

The price index used in the following calculation is the Board of Trade index for industrial materials (i.e. all goods other than food) averaged over the six months October–March round the end of each year.

TABLE 130

CHANGES IN STOCKS, 1931–4

Stocks at Current Value at End of Year (£ m.)	1931	1932	1933	1934
Manufacture . .	841	771	787	805
Distribution, etc. . .	789	750	707	673
Home railways . .	18	17	15	16
Total .	1648	1538	1509	1494
Price index (1930=100) at end of year	87·4	84·7	90·6	88·5
Value of stocks at 1930 prices (£ m.)	1885	1813	1690 *	1688
Price index (average of year)	87·4	84·6	87·2	89·7

* As this was a year of rising prices, stocks at the end of the year were revalued by use of the index number of average price-level during the previous six months.

Using the formula given above, the additions to be made to the published assessments are as follows :

For 1932 : 1885 (0·874 – 0·846) + 1813 (0·846 – 0·847) = 51.
For 1933 : No addition.
For 1934 : 1690 (0·906 – 0·897) + 1688 (0·897 – 0·885) = 32.

The net investment or disinvestment in working capital, at current price-levels, for each of the three years, can be obtained as follows :

1932 : 0·846 (1813–1885) = – £61 m.
1933 : 0·872 (1690–1813) = – £107 m.
1934 : 0·897 (1688–1690) = – £2 m.

These figures of steady disinvestment of working capital are remarkable, but accord with other evidence of economies in stockholding.

For previous years the data given in *The National Income, 1924–1931*, though not based on so wide a sample, may be accepted as approximations.

STATISTICAL INDEX

(Numbers refer to numbers of Tables and Diagrams)

G.B.—Great Britain. E.W.—England and Wales

STATISTICAL INDEX

THE END

Printed in Great Britain by R. & R. CLARK, LIMITED, *Edinburgh.*